FEB 1 1 1997

U.S. PRESIDENTS ON THE AMERICAN CLASS SYSTEM:

John Adams.   The great functions of state should be reserved to the rich, the well born and the able.

Thomas Jefferson.   Money, not morality, is the principle of commercial nations.

James Madison.   The most common and durable sources of faction, has been the various and unequal distribution of property. Those who hold, and those who are without property, have ever formed distinct interests in society.

Theodore Roosevelt.   We keep countless men from being good citizens by the conditions of life with which we surround them.

Franklin Roosevelt.   We have always known that heedless self-interest was bad morals; we know now that it is bad economics.

John F. Kennedy.   If a free society cannot save the many who are poor, it cannot save the few who are rich.

Lyndon Johnson.   Even the greatest of all past civilizations existed on the exploitation of the misery of the many.

Ronald Reagan.   What I want to see above all is that this remains a country where someone can always get rich.

George Bush.   Class is for European democracies or something else—it isn't for the United States of America. We are not going to be divided by class.

Bill Clinton.   We need a national strategy to create a high-wage, high-growth, high-opportunity economy.

The American Class System

Divide and Rule
by Paul Kalra

Antenna Publishing Co.
Pleasant Hill, California.

Published by: **Antenna Publishing Co.**
Post Office Box 23826E
Pleasant Hill, CA 94523–826E, USA.

Printed in the United States of America

Copyright ©1995 by Harryjan Enterprises Inc.

1 3 5 7 9 10 8 6 4 2

Publisher's Cataloging in Publication Data
Kalra, Paul S.
The American Class System : Divide and Rule / by Paul Kalra
348p.: ill.; 23 cm.
Includes bibliographical references and index
1. Social classes—United States
2. Equality—United States
3. Social conflict—United States
4. United States—Economic policy
I. Title
305.50973   LCCN: 95-77766
ISBN 0-9647173-5-2 : $23.45 Hardcover

To my illiterate mother
who had the energy,
common sense and family values
to guide her children in
achieving the best.

CONTENTS

ACKNOWLEDGMENTS

This book could not have been written without the assistance of many people. I benefited greatly from the following in terms of research and administrative support, ideas, information, suggestions, or criticisms they gave me: Kenneth Arrow, Gary Blouse, Barbara Branton, Daniel Casey, Jim Doyle, Patricia Edwards, Stephen Ellis, Thomas Emerick, William Espey, Theodore Fuller, Lorri Fein, Julie Fogo, Stanley Garvey, Peter Goodman, Edward Gorzynski, Irene Haggerty, Marcie Haley, Joan Hannon, Laurie Harper, Valerie Hendrix, Katherine Husen, Marilia Ingles, Marcia Jacobs, Win Kapur, Beverly Lauderdale, Roger Laurel, Kenneth Lawson, Suzanne McPherson, Sherry Nolan, Neil O'Brien, Marta Pachione, Shirley Peters, Carol Philips, Linda Queenie, Michael Reich, Danielle Russell, Michele Saadi Richard Simpson, Richard Tancredy, Ralph Victory, Stefanie Wayson, George White, Michelle White, Sharon Wilkerson, Adam Ukarine, Malcolm X, Julie Yesmann and Eugene Zolnay.

My special thanks to Judith Moretz and Valerie Johnstone for editorial assistance beyond the call of duty. Elizabeth Fuller of the Contra Costa Central Library made available research materials with inter-library loans from all over the country.

At an early stage Joan Brookbank and Richard Krause provided encouragement by confirming the basic soundness of the hypothesis.

AUTHOR'S FOREWORD

The American class system does not officially exist. Most Americans can, however, feel the impact of the class system and are aware of it but are unable to define it.

It was this reality of American life which set me off on a trail of inquiry. Obviously, if society is divided into classes, the basis of the division should be their respective shares of the national wealth. However, when one looks for data on the subject, one finds it is just not there. In a country which is so statistically minded this cannot just be an oversight. During the course of my study of the subject I was forced into the conclusion that the absence of data is deliberate. It is part of the strategy to keep the reality of the class system out of the public eye that such data on the distribution of wealth is not collected.

My research revealed two wealth surveys conducted by the Federal Reserve Board in 1962 and 1983. Combining the pieces of the jigsaw puzzle, the overall picture confirmed the outline of the class system. This book represents the fruit of my endeavors over a period of five years to collect data on the subject and dig deep beneath the surface to understand the reality of the American class system.

I found that there is indeed a well defined class system in America and that its roots go back to the period of slavery. The subsequent abolition of slavery changed the pattern of class system but did not put an end to it.

At the upper end there is the class of the rich, which I have called the upper class, which constitutes the top ten percent of households. Then come the next forty percent, constituting the middle class. The working class makes up the next forty percent of the population and the underclass covers the bottom ten percent of the households. It may be noted that the terms Upper, Middle, Working and Underclass as categorized by me bear no relationship to conventional meanings and usages.

After studying the status and the pattern of functioning of each of these classes, I went on to examine the impact of the class system on some of the important institutions of American society.

Free enterprise and competition are widely believed to be the cornerstones of the American economy. Is this really so? A closer look reveals that the upper class has violated these principles and substituted for them a system of institutional monopoly whereby a group of the leading companies in an industry constitute themselves into an oligopoly and with the help of well established conventions reap the benefits of monopoly.

An examination of the pattern of taxation similarly brings out how—though the appearance is one of a progressive income tax—the existence of loopholes and exemptions on the one hand and the regressive nature of the sales taxes enables the upper class to appropriate the savings of the nation, and perpetuate its dominance over the other classes. In achieving this goal, the American class system does not bother about waste or economic efficiency.

Similarly the underlying reality of American democracy is that government of the people, by the people, for the people is just so much rhetoric, while the electoral system ensures that no matter who wins, the upper class control of the government remains unaffected.

By making the Press dependent on advertising the American class system forces it to reflect the concerns and goals of the upper class and thus instead of informing the public and providing checks on the government, the Press and the media become an instrument in the hands of the upper class.

Defense spending is another area where the upper class is able to reap monopoly profits, because this expenditure is shrouded in secrecy and is not subject to public scrutiny. Ever since expenditure on defense started being funded through budgetary deficits this has become a means by which the upper class lends to the government huge amounts and takes back by way of interest a large share of the revenues of the government.

Equal opportunity and education for all turn out to be slogans which have little basis in reality. Moreover, the American class system effectively solves the problem of equal opportunity by tokenism. By deliberately including black tokens of high visibility in all institutions an impression is created that equal opportunities for all are guaranteed by the American system.

Despite my sharp criticism of the inequities of the American class system I felt that I had to make certain constructive proposals and suggest solutions to the problems that I had posed. It seems to me that there is a definite relationship between inequality, decline of the United States economy and the present class system in America. I have therefore in my concluding chapter explored this cause and effect relationship and have tried to provide a road map for a classless society. Let me make it clear that a classless society of my conception does not mean equality of capacity or equality of condition for all the people. It does mean, however, the absence of an artificially created underclass and the opportunity to save for the working class. Access to a free education, universal health care and a minimum wage job are the cornerstones of a classless society. A floor for the basic necessities is required if investment in education, training and human capital is to be made effectively.

The world is moving towards a global economy. America has to become part of the global class system to survive and flourish in an age of instant communication and rapid flow of capital and resources across borders. The focus has to shift from the interests of the upper class in America to ensuring that the United States remains an upper class economy in a

global class system. It is with this in view that I have presented a ten-point plan to restore America's position in the
world before it is too late.

Concord, California
July 4, 1995.

CHAPTER 1

IS THERE A CLASS SYSTEM?

An elephant has two sets of teeth—one set for eating and another for the photo opportunity.–**Anonymous**

All for ourselves and nothing for other people seems, in every age of the world, to have been the vile maxim of the masters of mankind.–**Adam Smith**[1]

In every economy there are dinners without appetites at one end of the table, and appetites without dinners at the other.–**William Sumner**[2]

For whosoever hath, to him shall be given and he shall have more abundance . . . but whosoever hath not, from him shall be taken away even that he hath.–**Matthew 13:12**

Class in the U.S. is like the wind in its effects: "The wind bloweth where it listeth, and though thou hearest the sound thereof, but canst not tell whence it cometh and whither it goeth".–**John 3:8**[3]

President George Bush claims class is "for European democracies or something else—it isn't for the United States of America. We are not going to be divided by class". Coming

1

from the lips of a seasoned politician keenly aware of his upper class origins and consistently trying to mold appearances this, some might say, is proof that an American class system does exist, banking on the strategy of divide and rule. Most people will not be so easily persuaded: the existence and operation of the American class system needs explanation.[4]

George Bush, the tennis playing, fly-fishing, quail-hunting, Skull and Bones Yalie, is by all accounts a wealthy man. Not only is he a millionaire many times over on his own but also the son of a U.S. Senator and married into money. The family owns a five million dollar summer estate, controls substantial trust funds and is accustomed to spending hundreds and thousands a year.[5]

Yet George Bush goes great lengths to claim he is an average middle class American. He enjoys pork rinds and Tabasco, likes to eat popcorn at the movies and lets Crystal Gayle and Loretta Lynn tapes at bedside put him to sleep. His favorite country music show is *Hee-Haw*. On television he draws attention to the hispanic babies in a flock of his largely WASP (White Anglo Saxon Protestant) grandchildren.[6]

What is the basis for class? Does it depend on the wealth or the income of the family? Or is it determined by the occupation of the family head, that is, blue blood or blue collar? Is the level of education, and its status, whether Ivy league or a state university, what finally counts? Does it have anything to do with whether one plays tennis or baseball? Ultimately do real activities matter or is it appearances and externalities that cast the die? White, black, hispanic, Christian or Jew?

The debate on class goes back to the founding of the United States. A few months after the Declaration of Independence Adam Smith produced *The Wealth of Nations*. There were extensive debates on economic classes and workable, stable democratic systems of government at the time of writing the Constitution. Although James Madison and Alexander Hamilton were not economists they understood the political dimensions of class and wrote it into the Constitution. If anything, the United States Constitution is primarily an economic document.

The American economy and way of life have constantly changed in the last two centuries. The future is a global economy. Classical economists could not have foreseen the changes in this century, so it becomes necessary to examine what contemporary Nobel prize winners in Economics have to say about the class system.

A tricky subject like this demands that the questions be framed, even if all the answers are not immediately obvious. That would lead to a consistent theory drawing upon economics, sociology and politics to define the contours of the American class system. The theory can then be tested on the bedrock of American reality to validate it. Such a theory could not only explain the existing reality but also help predict the future in changed economic scenarios. This would make it possible to outline national economic goals based upon agreed objectives and reacting to global forces and changes. However, the place to start is scrutinizing the truths of classical economists, sociologists and politicians.

Classical Economic Thinking

Savings are the storehouses of transformation. The transition from a nomadic to an agricultural civilization was only possible through savings. A viable agricultural economy, to grow food, needs to store the seed for the next crop. It also needs to have enough food stocks till the next harvest. This apart, it requires control over land. Accumulated savings over time become wealth. The disparity of savings among different groups results in classes. The concept of savings and working for a product which can be enjoyed later applies even to an industrial economy. Only this time the final product is something other than food.

The division of savings is the fundamental problem of economics. There are no lack of theories for the control and division of savings. The process is not simple because the division of savings itself affects the level of savings. Industrialization, computerization and push button communication have added more complex dimensions to it. But the principles fundamentally remain the same. The saving levels are determined by the productivity of the population, the levels of consumption and the degree of wastage. The problem is compounded by lack of information and outright deception in respect of certain groups.

Initially the area of application for the theory was confined to national boundaries. It has since expanded to cover continents and in future its application will have to occur at the global level. With the target changing constantly, it is unrealistic to expect the classical economists to have foreseen the future. Though tomes have been written on the shortcomings of the classical economists, they have concepts to offer which help in understanding the control and division of savings in the American context.

Among the classical economists, the ideas of Adam Smith (1723–1790) are significant. His major contribution was the concept of the invisible hand in competitive markets determining prices and allocation of resources to different activities. He showed that free markets were efficient with little wastage while monopoly resulted in reduced volume of goods and services for the economy at a macro level. What he did not say was that for individuals and groups, the preferred rule is competition for the other guy but monopoly for oneself. The free market system, as will become clear later, is a myth in America; protective barriers are created and enforced for different sectors of the class system.

Thomas Malthus (1766–1834), Adam Smith's contemporary, formulated the natural law of wages as a result of the uncontrollable breeding habits of humans. As the population grew, increased competition for the available jobs resulted in wages being reduced to the subsistence level. This would be the guiding principle for wage slavery. Birth control has allowed some control over procreation but the American class system attains, by design, the same result for particular segments of the population.

At the time Adam Smith and Thomas Malthus were outlining factors involved in the enrichment of nations at a macro level, David Ricardo (1772–1823) was working on laws which governed the distribution of income or product between the landlords, merchants and workers involved in production, marketing and savings. "Political Economy you think is an enquiry into the nature and classes of wealth—I think it should rather be called an enquiry into the laws which determine the division of the produce of industry amongst the classes who concur in its formation". Thus the search for the rules governing the American class system is an old one, which assumes that there is a class system in the first place.[7]

In the Declaration of Independence, Thomas Jefferson (1743–1826) listed among "self evident truths" the "inalienable rights" of "life, liberty and the pursuit of happiness". It had important implications for the American class system. From the beginning it was clearly understood to be a declaration and nothing more. The equality of all men could not be taken literally since the humanity of blacks was denied in the State laws and even in the U.S. Constitution. Jefferson understood that liberty could not exist without property because you were then at the mercy of your employer. As property was distributed unequally, liberty was not to be taken seriously. Happiness is an ambiguous term anyway, and it remains unclear whether it refers to the happiness of the majority, that of the ruling minority or if the country in the aggregate gets priority.[8]

James Madison (1751–1836) quite early identified the parts of the American class system. In the tenth issue of *Federalist*, he noted that classes are determined by unequal distribution of property and represent distinct interests in society. Madison did more than perceive an outline of the class system; he also wrote it into the U.S. Constitution.[9]

Any discussion about class is sure to bring up the theory of Karl Marx. Karl Marx (1818–1883) is the "straw devil" of the American class system. If Madison wrote the American class system into the Constitution, Marx could have little influence over it because he was not even born at that time. It appears Karl Marx is not necessary to understand the laws, operation or the existence of the American class system.

Sociological Thinking

Sociological thinkers have categorized classes into the rich, the poor and those in between. This is of little help. There is no way to determine the boundary between the rich and the middle class or between the middle class and the poor. It has been said that "the ambiguity of the term 'class' makes it difficult to find one's bearings among the divergences between the different viewpoints involved". Joseph Schumpeter notes that, in view of its dependence on the subjective predilections of the individual who does the classifying, "class is a creation of the researchers".[10]

Sociologists feel that if wealth and income alone cannot explain the class system, other intangibles such as status, prestige, power, occupation, education and religious belief might help. However, most of these variables are mutually interdependent with almost no objective definition and practically impossible to quantify or measure. They are more likely to be effects of the primary economic variables and institutions rather than causes. Though social scientists often justify ideological goals, sociological thinking which has been around for centuries needs to be examined.

Herbert Spencer (1820–1903) tried to provide a rationale for the existence of classes though they were not clearly defined, by applying Darwin's principles to society and coined the phrase, "the survival of the fittest". He insisted this was nature's law and necessary for progress:

> Partly by weeding out those of lowest development, and partly by subjecting those who remain to the never-ceasing discipline of experience, nature secures the growth of a race who shall both understand the conditions of existence, and be able to act up to them. It is impossible in any degree to suspend this discipline.

William Sumner (1840–1910), who emphasized individual responsibility for poverty and wealth, success and failure, echoed this thinking. "The millionaires", he proclaimed, "are a product of natural selection . . . the naturally selected agents of society for certain work. They get high wages and live in luxury, but the bargain is a good one for society." His was the rallying cry for the conservatives and status quoists: "Let every man be sober, industrious, prudent and wise, and bring up his children to be likewise, and poverty will be abolished in a few generations".[11]

Thorstein Veblen (1857–1929) struck a different note, emphasizing that appearances count. He observed that in America the mere possession of wealth was considered a meritorious act. "Wealth is now itself intrinsically honorable and confers honor on its possessor". Work was a necessary evil: "Labor acquires a character of irksomeness by virtue of the indignity imputed on it". He coined the term conspicuous consumption referring to all elaborate, ostentatious, and wasteful expenditures which serve no other purpose than to demonstrate wealth. He spoke of conspicuous leisure as those behaviors deigned to demonstrate that the upper class was exempt from productive labor. Veblen felt that if shared values and common interests were emphasized, serious class struggles were unlikely since the lower classes would seek to emulate the upper class and not to overthrow them. The upper classes have learnt since Veblen's time to maintain a low profile and avoid conspicuous consumption and conspicuous leisure while encouraging the lower classes to do so.[12]

Vilfredo Pareto (1848–1923) claimed that in all countries at all times income was distributed in much the same way. Looking at elementary statistical data, including some early income tax returns, he noted that shares accruing to the rich and the poor remained basically unchanged. He attributed this unequal distribution of income to differences in ability and talent. In Pareto's law of income distribution, few were deserving of wealth compared to the multitude who deserved to be poor and very few indeed were deserving of great wealth. This provided for an invisible hand theory of income distribution as if normal inequality was justified by the distribution of initiative and talent in the population.[13]

Max Weber (1864–1920) attempted a synthesis of the cause and effects of the class structure. Property and lack of it, he said, were the basic categories of all class situations. "Property as such is not always recognized as a status qualification but in the long run it is, and with extraordinary regularity". Even in the economic sphere factors that influenced the class divisions depended on market situations such as employer from employee, creditors from debtors, buyers from sellers and landlords from tenants. He was aware of the political and social dimension to the class system. An example of it was the politics of the American South before the Civil War where poor whites tended to identify with rich whites rather than the poor blacks who shared their economic status. Though Weber correctly identified many of the factors involved in the class structures he failed to come up with a synthesis or theory of the class structure and his work resulted in voluminous but directionless studies by sociologists.[14]

Gerhard Lenski (1924), an American sociologist, provided insights into the political aspects of the class system. He considered self interest the prime human motivation: "When men are confronted with important decisions where they are obliged to choose between their own, or their group's interest and the interests of others, they nearly always choose the former—although often seeking to hide this fact from themselves and others". He explained the need for a democratic electoral process to legitimize the moral and legal basis for the controlling group:

> So long as (the elite) relies on force, much of the profit is consumed by the costs of coercion; . . . a large portion of the time, energy and wealth of the elite are invariably consumed in the effort to keep (the population) under control . . . Thus, those who seize power by force find it advantageous to legitimize their rule once effective organized opposition is eliminated.

The ruling classes legitimize their authority, apart from an electoral process, by rewriting history, recodifying laws or manipulating the other classes with propaganda.[15]

The other contribution of American sociology has been to complicate the discussion about class groups with class consciousness. George Lukacs refers to class consciousness as "the sense, become conscious, of the historical role of the class". Research into class consciousness involves an analysis of socialization, political propaganda, education and mass communications, of the ideas of the ruling class as compared to the events of daily life. Ernest Mandel puts it thus:

> In the last analysis the question boils down to this: Which force will turn out to be stronger in determining the workers' attitude to the society he lives in, the mystifying ideas he receives, yesterday in the church or today through TV, or the social reality he confronts and assimilates day after day through practical experiences?

The standard format of polling, in which respondents are asked to indicate their class identification or position, is of little value. Usually the results obtained depend on who is asking the questions and the questions itself. The ruling classes widely use sociologists and pollsters to set up the ideological road signs. As C. Wright Mills has said, if people do not grasp the class causes of their conduct, "this does not mean that the social analyst must ignore or deny them". Consciousness research is the only likely way of getting answers which one wishes to hear.[16]

It appears that the sociologists have been unable to clarify class system stratification or theory any more than the classical economists and politicians. Most acknowledge that the class system exists, but are unable to define it in a consistent and definite manner. Perhaps this has been because of the continuously shifting target. Therefore, contemporary opinions of different persuasion, including those of Nobel Prize winners, could help provide clues to the shape of the American class system.

Contemporary Thinking

Economists this century have bewailed the lack of a satisfactory theory of personal income distribution, that is, the theory of a class system. Irving Fisher says that "No other problem has so great a human interest as this (the distribution of personal income), and yet scarcely any other problem has received so little scientific study". Anthony B. Atkinson closed his book with the comment " . . . far too little is known about this central subject. This is an indictment of economics, but it is also a challenge." The existing theories are unsatisfactory, partial and piecemeal and supposedly income inequalities defy simple explanation. Part of the problem is the sensitivity of the subject because income equality has been the source of ideological wars and political revolutions. Nobel prize winning economists of the textbook, conservative and liberal leanings also reflect this disparate thinking.[17]

Paul Samuelson provides the textbook viewpoint, warning against the thinking that America's wealth is broadly shared by the majority. He explains the present income structure with an illustration: "If we made an income pyramid out of a child's blocks, with each layer portraying $1,000 of income, the peak would be far higher than the Eiffel Tower, but almost all of us would be within a yard of the ground". Samuelson realized that the dominant ideology tried to create a contrary impression and clarified:

> In the absence of statistical knowledge, it is understandable that one should form an impression of the American standard of living from the full-page magazine advertisements portraying a jolly American family in an air-conditioned mansion, with a Buick, a station wagon, a motor launch, and all other good things that go to make up comfortable living. Actually, of course, this sort of life is still beyond the grasp of 90 percent of the American public.[18]

Samuelson was aware of the historical stability of income distribution:

> Yet when we look at the crude statistics of income and wealth, we find that the last few decades have not much changed the proportions of total income going to the lowest and highest fifths of the population and to the fifths in between. The total of the social pie has grown. But the sharing of the separate pieces is much the same as in 1950. This is an uncomfortable fact that we tend to push out of our minds, perhaps comforting ourselves with the hope that the growth in the shared total will float more and more people out of the abject poverty that has characterized most of mankind in most of history.

Samuelson was close to the mark in saying America hoped that so long as the tide was rising it would lift all the boats.[19]

Samuelson provided a personal touch to his analysis, saying, "I belong to the middle group who thinks that improving minimum standards of living for those at the bottom is a desirable goal. And who think that a gradual reduction of inequality and expansion of equality of opportunity is both desirable and feasible". He was less clear on how the goal was to be achieved, shifting the onus to Congress and the government. "But my experience as a student of economics and of history does not permit me to think that the task will be an easy one . . . It is hard enough to persuade Congress to modify in any degree the gaping loopholes in our progressive income and death-tax structure". Samuelson understood the dilemma but would rather not say much, maybe to maintain his "middle group" credentials.[20]

Milton Friedman, a partisan of the conservative brigade, provides the upper class rationale. One approach is to trivialize the subject of income distribution. "In every society, however it is organized, there is always dissatisfaction with the distribution of income . . . The farther fields always looks greener so we blame the existing system. In a command system envy and dissatisfaction are directed at the rulers. In a free market system they are directed at the market." There is an underlying hint that those who feel there is better income distribution somewhere else better move there. America, love it or leave it.[21]

Friedman claims income distribution is determined by individual choice and chance and the free market:

> Chance determines our genes and through them affects our physical and mental capacities . . . Choice also plays an important role. Our decisions about how to use our resources, whether to work hard or take it easy, to enter one occupation or another . . . to save or spend—these may determine whether we dissipate our resources or improve and add to them. Similar decisions by our parents, by other benefactors, by millions of people who may have no direct connection with us will affect our inheritance. The price that the market sets on the services of our resources is similarly affected by a bewildering mixture of chance and choice.

Friedman is not perturbed by the fact that if the income distribution is determined by the free market and individual ability it would be normally distributed instead of an extremely skewed distribution in favor of the upper class.[22]

Instead of blaming the government for the skewed distribution of income he assails it for promoting equality: "Much government activity during recent decades in the United States and other countries that rely predominantly on the market has been directed at altering the distribution of income generated by the market in order to produce a different and more equal distribution of income". Friedman feels the Declaration of Independence refers to equality of men before God in the hereafter. Since the Civil War the governing principle has been "equality of opportunity in the sense that no one should be prevented by arbitrary obstacles from using his capacities to pursue his own objectives". "A very different meaning of equality has emerged in the United States in recent decades, equality of outcome". Friedman then reserves volumes to show that equality of outcome is an impossible dream because abilities are not equally distributed.[23]

In a classic ploy of creating maximum confusion, Friedman says the goal of equality of outcome is, "fair share for all, which reduces liberty. If what people get is to be fairness who is to decide what is fair?" Essentially Friedman is saying that unless there is a consensual theory of income distribution the status quo is as fair as one can get.[24]

John Kenneth Galbraith, the Harvard economist, has provided the liberal outlook on class struggle in the United States. "The class conflict is part of our cultural heritage. Moreover, in the last two centuries a great many employers have proclaimed fulsomely a new era of good feeling in their labor relations". Class struggle in his vision is a battle between capital represented by the big corporations and labor represented by the unions. Even if the rich enjoyed monopoly profits, the liberals went along so long as the labor represented by the unions and other skilled workers could participate in the game. The burden then shifted to the unorganized and unskilled groups in the class system. This provided a stable system, "under the rich cloak of democracy, a democracy in which the less fortunate do not participate". While the economy was growing and the tide rising, there was no point rocking the boat because in the "affluent society" that was America, poverty was not a major problem but "more nearly an afterthought". The liberals provided a rationale for the monopoly game. "With the passage of power to the corporate bureaucracy, to what I have called the techno-structure, the conflict is a good deal less stark". Galbraith had argued in the past that one cause of the Great Depression was the acute concentration of wealth whereby the people could not buy the abundant products generated by the economy of 1929. In the present context, neither Galbraith nor any other liberal has come forward to explain how inequality could be diminished or how the wealth of the very rich could be rechanneled to the poor and the deprived.[25]

It appears that from American Revolution onwards, economists, sociologists and politicians have been aware about the existence of the class structure but failed to define it. The British socialist John Strachey once observed that "the persistence and magnitude of income and wealth concentrations in capitalist society—despite all the efforts of democratic forces, reform legislation, transfer payments, and trade unions to reduce them—suggests that capitalism has strong, inherent tendencies to generate and perpetuate enormous inequalities". And certainly these inequalities are not determined by free market forces and inherent distribution of talents and abilities. The failure to come up with an income distribution model is glaring. Even the sociologist Schumpeter called for an imposing synthesis. "Our time revolts against the inexorable necessity of specialization and therefore cries out for synthesis, nowhere more than in the social sciences, in which the nonprofessional element counts for so much".[26]

A valid and useful theory of the American class system must meet a number of requirements. First, there should be a relatively high degree of consensus among the members in the system about the criteria, characteristics and dimensions of the different classes. The values supporting class should ideally fit in with other values held in society. Class consciousness should be evident in that individuals are subjectively aware of their own class and that of others in the system. The existing institutional infrastructure should mesh with the class structure. An American class system can now be defined and its implications in everyday life outlined.[27]

CHAPTER 2

CLASS SYSTEM THEORY

The modern history of economic theory is a tale of evasions of reality. –**Thomas Balogh**[1]

We have two classes of forecasters (economists): Those who don't know—and those who don't know they don't know.
–**John Kenneth Galbraith**[2]

The balance of power in a society accompanies the balance of property and land. –**John Adams**[3]

Class is a force which unites into groups people who differ from one another, by overriding the difference between them.
–**Marshall**[4]

"The rich are richer—and America may be the poorer—the widening income gap could cost the U.S. plenty," proclaimed a *Business Week* headline in late 1991. It explained the economic and moral dilemma of the last fifteen years:

> Simply put, growing income inequality and stubbornly high poverty rates threaten the country's long-term growth prospects. That's because inequality of income distribution and persistent poverty can put a damper on productivity growth, while stagnating incomes crimp consumer purchasing power . . .

15

The nation's savings rate was supposed to rise, but it didn't. And the swelling tide of income for a few was supposed to lift all boats, but it didn't.

Henry J. Aaron of the Brookings Institution says about the surge in income for the richest segment:

> It's impossible to attribute the sharp increase in income at the top of the scale to a drastic increase in the relative value of the services provided by people at that level, what we're observing is some rent-seeking activity, whereby lawyers, investment bankers and other professionals extract extra income for seemingly unique abilities.[5]

In March 1990, *The Christian Science Monitor* staff writer David R. Francis in an article titled "Wealth of a Nation" said, "The United States thinks of itself as a nation with a strong middle class. In terms of income, that remains true. But in terms of wealth—an individual's savings, investments and ownership of property—the middle class is relatively weak". Thomas Shapiro, a sociologist at Northeastern University in Boston, explains:

> Wealth is distributed a lot more unequally than we had thought. About one-third of households have zero or negative net financial assets. In other words, they have few if any savings or investments to fall back on should they lose their job or be incapacitated. Their only safety nets are relatives, government welfare or private assistance of some sort.

Melvin Oliver of the University of California, Los Angeles, noted, "Even the demise of the family car can precipitate an immediate economic crisis". The median American household had net financial assets of $2,599 in 1984—a financial cushion adequate for barely three months if the household lived at the poverty level. Sociologists Oliver and Shapiro explain that the reduction in capital gains taxes proposed by President Bush would have worsened the "maldistribution" of wealth toward those already wealthy. There was no increase in productive investments as a result of reduced tax rates for the rich during the Reagan years. To achieve the goal of "equality of opportunity, not results" sociologists suggest a small tax on wealth and tougher inheritance taxes.[6]

A theory of the American class system can help make sense of these media reports.

Theoretical Wealth Distribution

Wealth can be defined as stored-up purchasing power. It can also be looked at as accumulated savings at a point in time. Income, however, is the monetary gain over a period of time which is generally of twelve months. It is subject to variation and manipulation over time, while wealth is more stable. They are like the balance sheet and income statement for a business; the former gives better understanding of the size and power of the business. One of the reasons is that wealth can always be converted to income for consumption until it has been consumed. Wealth is the determining factor for understanding the class system.

Subject to confirmation, initially it will be assumed that the American class system consists of four classes based on net worth. The top ten percent of households comprise the upper class. Then come the next forty percent of households, constituting the middle class. The working class makes up the next forty percent of the population and the underclass covers the bottom ten percent of households. This defines the size and the position of the class groups, and the terms Upper, Middle, Working and Underclass have no relationship with conventional meanings and usages.

Motivation and control are two determining factors of the class system. In the absence of wealth and savings, a person has to work or starve. In America employers have traditionally found coercion resulting from zero savings useful in creating a motivated and pliant working class. Another method of coercion and control is to make the employee assume a debt like a home mortgage. Although the coercion is less drastic than the threat of starvation, it allows a cushion of only a few months before loss of shelter. Compared to starvation, the specter of mortgage as a weapon of control differs only in degree and is used for motivating the middle class. The class system conceals this coercion, making the individual believe he is responsible for his actions. A competitive threat from an underclass has to be created to control the working class. The underclass is also used to direct the hostility and frustrations of the working class. It is more useful if the underclass can be easily identified by race, color or religion. This gives most of the population someone below to kick. Politically the underclass, which is clearly different from the rest of the population, becomes an essential ingredient of the class system.

The class system legitimizes the coercion faced by different classes. From the beginning the economic system and the government were designed for control by the upper class or the elite, which comprises about ten percent of the population. An apparently democratic election, with universal suffrage, legitimizes their domination. The upper class needs the votes of at least forty percent of the population so that together they command a majority. The middle class voters generally support the upper class because the latter ensures that the middle class has visible and real advantages over the working class and underclass.

These economic, political and sociological principles are synthesized to obtain the theoretical class structure based on wealth distribution in Figure 1, which provides a Lorenz curve for the theoretical wealth distribution with the population percentage on one axis and the percent of wealth on the other. The starting point A assumes that to win an election only fifty percent of the vote is necessary and the winner takes all. This means that the winners in the election deserve all the wealth. As the losers were allowed to vote this legitimizes the power structure and decisions of the government. By not allowing any wealth or savings to the losers they are forced to work under the threat of starvation. Therefore point A establishes the two basic classes of the class system, the haves and the havenots.

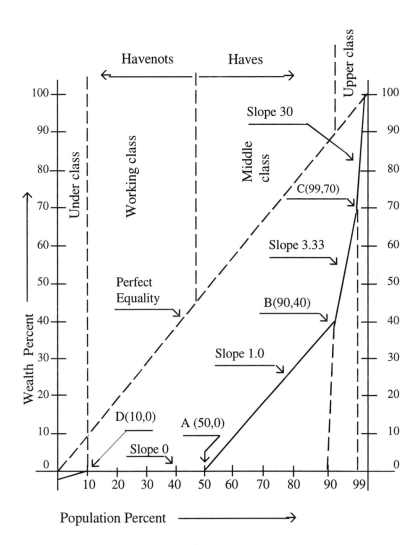

Figure 1 Theoretical wealth distribution (Lorenz Curve)

For point B it should be noted that the elite, the controllers, the shepherds in the total population are the top ten percent. For winning elections they need the votes of forty percent of the population who are not part of the elite or upper class. In a "fair" game the middle class, that is 40 percent of the voting segments, deserve 40 percent of the total wealth. Usually the upper class finds 40 percent of total wealth sufficient to obtain the loyalty and votes of the middle class. Therefore, point B establishes the split of the haves into the upper class, which is ten percent of the population with sixty percent of the wealth, and the middle class, which is forty percent of the population with forty percent of the wealth.

This principle of divide and rule can be applied at higher levels. Again the top ten percent of the upper class, which is the same as the top one percent of the total population, can be defined as the trustees. The total wealth of the upper class is split two ways, between the gatekeepers and the trustees. Therefore, the top one percent of the population gets thirty percent of the wealth while the gatekeepers, who are about nine percent of the population, get another thirty percent of the wealth. Here point C establishes the differentiation between the gatekeepers and the trustees within the upper class. This logarithmic division of wealth probably continues in the top one percent fraction of the population.

Coercion has to be concealed among the havenots. The impression of a competitive free market system has to be provided to control their discontent. This is done with an underclass consisting of ten percent of the population, defined by point D. As the underclass is not allowed to work and has to be fed to be kept alive, their numbers have to be restricted to generally less than ten percent. This can economically be justified because by providing competition to forty percent of the havenots who are the working class, the underclass reduces their demands and overall consumption. If the underclass can be racially differentiated then the fact that it has been artificially created escapes notice and they can be blamed for being lazy, racially inferior and causing problems for the working class.

The theoretical model of the class system divides the population into four classes with different degrees of wealth. This model defines the size and location of the four classes in the wealth distribution. For subsequent comparison with the actual distribution of wealth and the change of distribution with time, the size and placement of the four classes will be held constant.

Present Wealth Distribution

Data on the wealth distribution in America are vital to validate the theoretical wealth distribution. But details on wealth distribution are not collected intentionally because of its political implications. The most recent survey of household wealth was conducted by the Federal Reserve Board in 1983 and 1988, the one before that in 1962. Results from these surveys have been analyzed and reported by the Joint Economic Committee, U.S. Congress, in 1986. The data on wealth are only available in bits and pieces, which obscures the overall picture. Moreover the data are provided in a form related to income so that valid conclusions cannot be drawn. The total picture can be reconstructed by obtaining pieces of the jigsaw puzzle from different reports.

Several objections can be raised about the accuracy of the data. But it can be inferred that any error will be on the conservative side. This means that in reality the wealth distribution is more unequal than the estimated distribution.

In analyzing the actual distribution of wealth and comparing it with the theoretical distribution of wealth, the critical data to be noted are the shares of the working, middle and upper classes. As seen from Table 1, based on the Federal Reserve Study of 1983, the actual distribution of wealth very closely follows the theoretical distribution of wealth. Working and middle class shares of wealth are 3.4 percent and 33.2 percent compared to theoretical values of 0 percent and

40 percent. Similarly the upper class share is 63.9 percent against a theoretical share of 60 percent. However, this source of data is silent about the share of the trustees. Data on wealth by deciles of the population are not normally publicized.[7]

Table 1   Wealth distribution by net worth
(Federal Reserve Board Study 1983)

Wealth Decile	Mean net worth in thousands $$	Wealth %	Class	Wealth %
First	−3.8	−0.4	Under	−0.4
Second	−	−		
Third	1.5	0.2	Working	**3.4**
Fourth	8.6	0.9		
Fifth	20.7	2.3		
Sixth	35.4	3.9		
Seventh	53.0	5.8	Middle	**33.2**
Eight	80.1	8.7		
Ninth	136.0	14.8		
Tenth	585.9	63.9	Upper	**63.9**
TOTAL		100%		100%

Source: The American Profile Poster by Stephen J. Rose, 1986, Pantheon Books, p. 31.

The Federal Reserve Board collected data with an additional survey of high income families. To achieve a more realistic view of the actual distribution of wealth, these data are provided in Table 2, which combines the data provided by the Federal Reserve Bulletin for the bottom ninety percent of the families and that by the Joint Economic Committee of Congress study for the top ten percent of the families. It emerges that the concentration of wealth is greater than that estimated by theory under ideal conditions. It was found that the top one percent of the population owned almost forty percent of the wealth. The gatekeepers had almost a thirty percent share of the wealth, as predicted, while the middle class was short-changed because they held less than thirty percent, instead of a fair share of forty percent. The working class had almost no wealth. Overall it appears that the actual distribution of wealth follows the rules and guidelines of the class system theory. This can be seen from the Lorenz curves for the theoretical and actual distribution of wealth in Figure 2.[8]

Table 2 Wealth distribution by net worth [8]
(Federal Reserve Board Survey, 1983)

Class	Net worth Range $	Population Percent	Wealth Percent
Under	0	10	NEGATIVE
Working	1–32, 749	40	**3.1**
Middle	32, 750–206, 340	40	**27.2**
Gatekeeper	206, 341–1, 422, 599	9	**29.0**
Trustees	1, 422, 600 above	1	**40.6**
Total		100	100

What is included in the data and what has been left out should be explained. While households account for the vast majority of the nation's wealth, they do not account for all of it. Governments hold significant wealth in the form of land, buildings, infrastructure and defence establishments, which need not be taken into account because they do not affect the distribution of wealth among the classes and is property held in trust for the common good.[9]

Pension funds data have been excluded from the survey. Individuals ordinarily do not know how much they will benefit from pension funds because they do not know how long they will live. They frequently do not have any actual economic control over the investment or use of such funds until retirement. The management of pension funds is generally a fiduciary responsibility of corporations which, in turn, are controlled by the upper class.

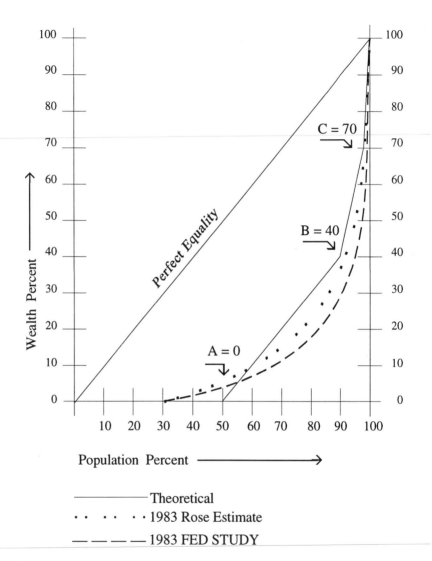

Figure 2   Wealth distribution (Lorenz Curve)

Exclusion of pension fund data can be justified as it would not change the wealth distribution. A special pension survey found that half the population had no pension plan at all. Another study found that the top one-fifth of the beneficiaries received annual payments more than six times as much as the bottom one-fifth. Also the total pension funds constitute only about ten percent of the nation's privately held wealth. Therefore it appears that the exclusion of pensions will not change the overall distribution of wealth or the class system.[10]

The Federal Reserve Survey data also excluded the value of household durables such as stereos, furniture and automobiles. A study by the Federal Reserve Board's Division of Research and Statistics found that the inclusion of automobiles would reduce the upper class share of wealth by only one percent.[11]

An obvious limitation of wealth data is that these underrepresent the upper levels, primarily because of the difficulty in obtaining the cooperation of a sufficient number of survey subjects. As wealth data are not collected by any agency and it is not necessary to disclose it, the collected data underestimate the actual wealth of the upper class. Moreover the wealth can be easily hidden by legal entities like corporations, trusts and foundations.

In the absence of surveys, the federal estate tax returns have historically been used for estimating wealth. Until 1976 all estates with gross assets of $60,000 or more were required to file a return. Since 1981, however, the filing threshold has been increased so that only estates with assets in excess of $600,000 are required to file a tax return. Statistically the federal estate tax returns can be used to validate the wealth data obtained by surveys, providing confidence in the Federal Reserve data on the actual wealth distribution.[12]

American families in the aggregate owned about $12 trillion in gross assets in the spring of 1983 when the survey of Consumer Finances was conducted. This was divided between a total of 83,918,000 households. Their net worth totaled

$10.6 trillion in holdings ranging from real estate through IRAs to business assets. Another $1.3 trillion was held in pension funds. Nongovernment entities such as nonprofit institutions, including foundations, schools and hospitals had a net worth of a little over $200 billion.[13]

Although individual family wealth is confidential information, not to be disclosed until a f ederal estate tax return has to be filed, each individual has a fairly accurate idea of his net worth. Table 2 provides the net worth range of different classes in 1983 dollar value. The underclass has a negative net worth and they have to meet the means tests to receive welfare. For the working class, the median net worth is $5,050 which means that the working class has practically no cushion against unemployment. They barely have two months' rent and security deposit for shelter and the bare minimum in furnishings. Their automobile is also probably financed. The median asset value for the middle class is $67,000, which means that most of their assets are in home equities. With a net worth of $ 206,341 a person enters the upper class. These figures allow identification of a person's place in the class system. As in real life only data on incomes are collected, the relationship between the income and wealth distribution needs to be examined.

Income Distribution

In the absence of regular wealth distribution data collection, income distribution perforce becomes a prime consideration. Income distribution is significant for understanding the class system insofar as it indicates the distribution of wealth. For this, the relationship between income and wealth distribution needs to be understood first.

Table 3 shows the distribution of income by class as per the Federal Reserve Survey of 1983. Although the median income range goes up from the underclass to the upper class, the size and limits of the classes are not easily visible from income distribution. There are several reasons why income distribution is used more to obscure the class system rather than clarify it. The first is that class is determined by the accumulated savings and inheritance rather than income. What can be saved from the income is more important than the income itself.[14]

Table 3   Distribution of income by class[14]
(Federal Reserve Survey, 1983)

	Annual Family Income Thousand $ Range					
Class	0–10	10–20	20–30	30–50	50–Above	Total
Under	100	–	–	–	–	100
Working	32	26	23	15	4	100
Middle	12	19	20	28	21	100
Upper	1	6	10	21	62	100

Data on income are especially distorted for the upper class. Income from municipal bonds mostly owned by the upper class are not reported. This distorts the income data for the upper class and the overall distribution of income. Another major source of income for the upper class is dividends from securities and capital gains. A significant part of the existing income distribution statistics fail to account for income earned in the corporate sector of the economy and not distributed to the owners. As Harvard economist William Crum puts it, "A group of wealthy directors owning stock in a closely held corporation may vote to retain earnings not so much because of the needs of the business as on account of large surtaxes for which they would be personally liable were these earnings disbursed".[15]

Other sources of income for the upper class which do not show up in the income statistics are the corporate fringe benefits and expense accounts. These can include company cars and airplanes, excellent medical care, country-club memberships, dining and entertainment allowances. This would explain in part why only 62 percent of the upper class made more than $50,000 a year in 1983. (Table 3)

As class is based on savings which depend on expenditures as well as the level of income, income statistics alone are inadequate. Expenditures are of two kinds, the basic one on food, shelter, transportation, and the other on taxes which have to be paid on income. Whatever the class grouping of a family, basic expenditure is central to a productive life. For this reason, if income statistics are to relate to class, the basic expense or standard deduction has to be reduced from all income. Taxes are a big expenditure. A major part of the taxes are hidden, of the sales tax type, while a small part is the visible income tax. Even the visible income tax treats the income of the working class, which pays rent, differently from the income of the middle class, which pays for shelter in the form of mortgage interest. These distortions make income distribution statistics of little use as indicators of wealth distribution and the class system. This also appears to explain why for two hundred years economists have failed to come up with a theory of income distribution and claim it is incomprehensible.

That the confusion and deception are not accidental can be seen from the dissemination of the income statistics. Most of the statistics reported by the government agencies, including the IRS, universities and the media are by quintiles. This is done though the basic data are collected as deciles. But with quintiles the boundaries of the class system are obscured. The bottom quintile merges the underclass with the working class, the middle quintile merges the working class with the middle class while the top quintile merges the upper class with the middle class. Gabriel Kolko recognized this process: "(Income Fifths) obscure important patterns of income distribution that appear only when the population is further divided into tenths".[16]

It appears that the purpose of income statistics is to make inequality appear less extreme than what it really is. This can be seen from Table 4 which tabulates IRS statistics on income. It shows that the upper class has only 40 percent of the total income while the middle class has 45 percent. This is in sharp contrast to wealth where the upper class has 70 percent of the total wealth while the middle class has only 27 percent of the wealth. While the general lack of meaning in income statistics for understanding or controlling the national economy is evident, income distribution data as a substitute for wealth data have to be relied upon as the only available approximation, keeping in mind the errors introduced by this procedure.

Table 4   Percentages of income by class[17]
(Internal Revenue Service, 1988)

Class	Income Range $	Income Total %	Wealth
Under	below 3,000	1	0
Working	3,000–18,000	14	3
Middle	18,000–60,000	**45**	**27**
Upper	60,000–above	**40**	**70**
Totals		100	100

The data on family income are not necessary for identifying its class status. Not only is class related to wealth but also with the nature of the assets such as equity in automobiles, homes, businesses, financial securities and commercial real estate.

Financial Assets Distribution

The key to understanding the American class system is the Financial Assets Distribution among the population. Net wealth can be subdivided into personal property like automobiles and home furnishings, residential property like equity in principal residence, income producing financial assets like small businesses, securities (including stocks and bonds) and commercial real estate. Figure 3 shows the distribution of different kinds of assets by class. Class will be considered by wealth deciles as defined earlier. From the bottom the first decile represents the underclass. The next four deciles together represent the working class. The middle class is represented by the next four deciles. The top decile represents the upper class which is split into the trustees, which is the top one percent of the population, and gatekeepers, who are nine percent of the population.[18]

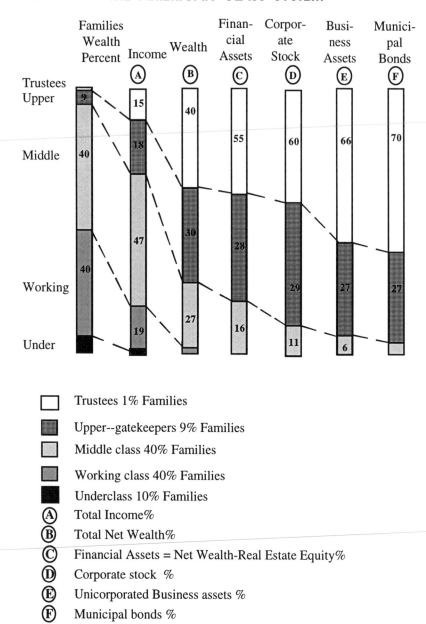

Figure 3 Distribution of financial assets

Column A represents the distribution of income. Earlier it was noted that the only function of income distribution was to obscure the class boundaries, which made most of the official statistics meaningless. Income distribution figures show that the upper class has only 33 percent of the income while the middle class has 47 percent of it. Conceivably, therefore, income is distributed based on the efforts and abilities of the individuals.

Although personal property like furnishings and automobiles technically count as wealth, in America they are consumables which have to be periodically replaced. They are insignificant in the total wealth picture. However, they constitute most of the wealth of the working class as automobiles are essential to get to work. So the wealth distribution in Column B eliminates the working class, which owns a couple of percentages of wealth. The wealth distribution also shows the importance of the trustees. Though the trustees constitute only one percent of the population they own 40 percent of the wealth. The rest of the upper class, the gatekeepers, own 30 percent of the wealth while the middle class owns only about 27 percent. Wealth distribution highlights the fact that the working class has negligible wealth and savings.

For the middle class, significantly most of their wealth is in home equities. A major part of their assets are illiquid and tied with home and shelter. Equity in principal residence provides some protection from inflation but it does not provide any earnings. Column C shows the distribution of financial assets which is the net worth minus the equity in real estate. It becomes clear that the net financial assets, that is income producing and productive assets, are concentrated in the hands of the upper class. Fifty-five percent of the net financial assets are owned by the trustees while the gatekeepers own 28 percent. Although the middle class own 16 percent of the financial assets, most of it is in bank related deposits in saving accounts or IRA or Keogh accounts. The upper class are the moneylenders to the economy, providing 83 percent of the net financial assets.

Contrary to the claims of "people's capitalism" as publicized by the New York Stock Exchange and the Advertising Council, stock ownership, like every other form of wealth and assets, is highly concentrated. Column D shows that almost 89 percent of all privately held stock in U.S. corporations is owned by the upper class, while the trustees own 60 percent just by themselves. In the Federal Reserve Board Survey only half the families with incomes of $50,000 or more reported owning any stock. An even smaller percentage reported owning shares in more than one company or having a brokerage account. The data understate the concentration of stocks controlled by the upper class because a large percentage of the stock is held by fiduciaries, foundations, etc., which are largely controlled by the trustees.[19]

Column E shows that the distribution of noncorporate business assets is even more lopsided where the upper class holds 93 percent of all these assets. They also own 97 percent of the municipal bonds, with the trustees owning 70 percent. This is indicated in Column F. Clearly capital gain tax benefits and benefits from municipal bond interest exemption go mostly to the upper class, especially to the trustees.

For matters of political expediency each person must know his own class and that of his neighbors and friends. This makes it imperative to examine class system characteristics and how they are reinforced, keeping in mind that income, wealth and asset holdings of individuals are only known to them.

Class Characteristics

Fundamental characteristics define the boundaries between the four classes. A major difference between the upper and middle class is the ownership of net financial assets which produce income such as securities, commercial real estate or businesses. Homeownership forms the distinctive division between the middle and working classes. The working class are generally renters because they have been unable to save or inherit a down payment for a home or qualify for a loan.

The distinction between the working class and the under-class is poverty and submission to welfare and means tested programs. Food stamps and to a certain degree race, color, or national origin are used to characterize the underclass. In each case the neighborhoods will be distinctive because people of the same status tend to flock together. Class consciousness is also created by school districts, and property tax deductions and mortgage deductions for income tax purposes.

Characteristics like educational achievement are strongly correlated to class. Other factors are job security, and marital status of the head of the household. The relationship between occupation and class based on responsibility or industry needs to be noted.

Figure 3 brings out that the upper class owns 83 percent of financial assets, 89 percent of corporate stock, 93 percent of business assets and 97 percent of municipal bonds. Though the rest is owned by the middle class, they are insignificant and tied in pension funds or in the form of cash with banks. Apart from being money lenders to the nation, the upper class trades in the stock market, having brokerage trading accounts for access to professional advice on investments. A keen interest or involvement in the stock market indicates upper class membership. This is equally true about a preoccupation with capital gains and tax-free municipal bonds. More than half the upper class income may be from investments in secu-rities and businesses. The upper class families, especially the trustees, are more likely to have inherited their assets instead of accumulating them by savings.

Table 5 Class and homeownership[20]

Class	Percent Homeowners	Asset (1983) Range $
Upper	**95**	200,000 and above
Middle	**93**	25,000–200,000
Working	35	0–25,000
Under	–	0
Total	64	

Source: Household Wealth and Asset Ownership: 1988 Series P-70, No. 22, U.S. Dept of Commerce p.19

Table 5 explores the connection between class and home-ownership. Homeownership of 95 percent and 93 percent for the upper and middle classes, who have net worth above $25,000, is to be expected because the tax laws encourage investment in a home as a first priority to obtain the mortgage deduction. Investment in a home provides protection against inflation with build up of equity.

Almost a third of the working class also own homes though they have low or net worth of a couple of thousand dollars. There are two ways of explaining this. One is government programs such as the Federal Housing Administration and Veterans Administration which allow purchase of homes with less than five percent down or no equity in the property. Such programs artificially try to increase the homeownership percentage for political reasons though the government bears all the risk of loss and foreclosure. Another reason for home-ownership with almost no equity is that the down payment has been borrowed from a parent or relative.

Homeownership is a characteristic the middle class shares with the upper class. This ensures that the middle class generally aligns itself with the upper class and against the working and underclass in political contests. The education system based on local property taxes and the property tax deduction is closely linked to homeownership and location. In this way the middle class can benefit from subsidies for homeownership and education.

Homeownership is used to divide the middle and working classes. As renters the working class are looked down upon as a separate class. Low interest rates for mortgages provide additional benefits to the middle class compared to the working class, who generally pay high interest for consumer loans. That this division between the middle and working class has been consciously created is evident from the design of the income tax laws.

The role of race in distinguishing between the haves and havenots is clear from Table 6A. Overall there were 11 percent blacks, six percent hispanics and 83 percent whites in the total population. Here hispanic by definition could be of any race. What it shows is that the upper class is exclusively white with a token one percent black presence. Hispanics come in between the blacks and whites but are more closely related to the status of blacks.

Table 6A Class and race distribution [21]

Class	Black	Percent Hispanic*	White	Total
Under	26	12	62	100
Working	13	7	80	100
Middle	6	4	90	100
Upper	1	2	97	100
Total	11	6	83	100

* Hispanic - any race

Highlighting the race factor is the way the black and white underclass are physically separated. Although 62 percent of the underclass are white, they are distributed in white working and middle class neighborhoods and cannot be distinguished from their looks. The only sure way to tell if a white person belongs to the underclass is if he uses food stamps in the supermarket.

The nature of racial discrimination becomes clear from Table 6B. Only 21 percent of the blacks can claim middle class status while 78 percent belong to under or working class. With a hispanic, there is a 72 percent chance that he is part of the havenot population.

Table 6B Race composition by class (1988)[21]

Race	Families Percent	Havenots Under	Havenots Working	Haves Middle	Haves Upper	Median Net Worth
White	83	9	38	43	10	43,279
Black	11	29	49	21	1	4,169
*Hispanic	6	24	48	26	2	5,524
Total	100	10	40	40	10	35,752

* Hispanic - any race

Though blacks are only 26 percent of the underclass they are segregated in neighborhoods by color.The blacks, because of easy identification, become the representatives of the underclass itself. The white underclass can be helped by charitable organizations as they can go into white working and middle class neighborhoods and churches. But for blacks the haves are only 22 percent and they are in no position to help the 29 percent underclass. The apparent identification of the blacks with the underclass comes in handy to the upper class to practice divide and rule.

Table 7   Class and education[22]

Class	Drop Out	High School Graduate	Junior College	College Graduate	
Under	**37**	28	21	14	100
Working	28	33	24	15	100
Middle	24	31	21	24	100
Upper	13	25	21	**41**	100
Total	**26**	31	22	21	100
Med. Wealth$	25,000	35,268	35,000	70,000	

It appears there is only a general co-relationship between class and education. One problem with Table 7 is that the data on college graduates do not indicate the proportion of postgraduates. The data are related to the education of the head of the household. The overall 26 percent of the population were high school dropouts while another 21 percent were college graduates. Also significant is that 41 percent of the upper class are college graduates while 37 percent of the underclass are high school dropouts even when there is free education in the United States. It may be possible that education is more a reflection of class status rather than the other way around. Therefore, factors related to food and shelter and economic class may be more important than spending on schools and teacher student ratios.

The relationship between class and job security is shown in Table 8. On the whole 7.4 percent are working part time or actively looking for a job while 13 percent are out of the job market. Generally the upper class has the greatest job security and the underclass has the least. Only 59 percent of the underclass work full time while 26 percent have given up hope of finding a job. The "not looking" category is not even counted in the official government unemployment figures. Fourteen percent of the upper class are not looking for a job, presumably because they no longer need to work. The middle class has more security compared to the working class as 5 percent of the middle class are working part time or looking for a job as compared to 9 percent for the working class. The "not looking" column also includes retired people.

Table 8 Class and job security[23]

Class	Working Full Time	Working Part Time or Want Job	Not Looking	Total
Under	**59**	15	**26**	100
Working	79	**9**	12	100
Middle	84	5	11	100
Upper	83.5	7	**14**	100
Totals	79.5	**7.4**	**13**	100%

Table 9 Class and marital status (1988)[24]

Class	Couple Household	Male Single household	Female Single Household	Total
Under	**31**	20	**49**	100
Working	48	21	31	100
Middle	67	11	22	100
Upper	**77**	10	13	100
Total	**56**	**16**	**28**	
Med. Wealth $	**57,134**	**13,053**	**13,571**	

Class and marital status have a significant relationship, which Table 9 looks at. Fifty-six percent of the households have a male-female couple in the family which means generally there are two incomes. Females head 28 percent of the total families while males head 16 percent of the total signifying a single income. The single males or females may be widowed, divorced, separated, or unmarried. The responsibility for the children generally falls upon the female household heads though they may receive some child support payments.

Table 10A   Occupation and class by wealth (1983)

Occupation of Family Head	Working	Middle	Upper	Mean $	Median $
A) Not Working	58	32	10	88,963	23,331
B) Service Work	72	27	1	28,539	11,245
C) Craftsman or Foreman	59	37	4	51,429	28,672
D) Clerical or Sales	62	33	5	52,228	21,202
E) Service Sector Managerial	53	37	10	83,205	30,136
F) Manufacturing Professional	43	44	13	129,641	55,055
G) Manufacture Business	26	37	37	525,370	120,172
H) Service Sector Business	37	39	23	344,515	69,827
I) Banking Insurance Real Estate	23	35	42	746,798	141,480
J) Lawyer & Accountant	39	32	29	375,055	95,202
K) Health Service Professional	25	30	45	412,462	200,156
Total	50%	40%	10%	133,502	30,553

Source: Financial Characteristics of High Income Families, Federal Reserve Bulletin, March 1986

Table 9 shows that almost fifty percent of the underclass families are headed by females. It probably results from government Aid to Families with Dependent Children (AFDC) policies in force. Generally 77 percent of upper class families are headed by couples, while that holds good for only 31 percent of underclass families, signifying that economic factors largely precipitate divorce, separation, abandonment and breakup of families. This causes a wide gap in family stability between the haves and havenots. By marital status the median asset value of couples is four times that of households headed by males or females only, yet another hint that the class system may lead to family instability and breakup.

Table 10A shows that occupation and class are significantly related. Labor, service work, clerical or sales activities requiring very little education or skills have the lowest median net worth and constitute major parts of the working class. There are craftsmen, foremen and service sector managerial personnel who have skills or supervisory responsibility and with a larger median net worth though most of them still are part of the working class. Manufacturing professionals, including engineers, small manufacturing business owners, and service sector business owners are more likely to be middle class personnel. The upper class is heavy with banking, insurance, and real estate occupations including lawyers, accountants and health service professions. In addition to education and responsibility, protection against competition and entry into the profession appear to be significant factors. For this health care service professionals have the highest median wealth and 45 percent of the members in this category are in the upper class.

Table 10B   Labor force participation of wives[25]

Class	Families%	Working Wives%
Under	10	**26**
Working	40	34
Middle	40	59
Upper	10	**66**

Table 10B looks at labor force participation of wives by class. The percentage of wives increases in big steps from 26 percent for the underclass to 66 percent for the upper class. One reason is that the classes in this figure are defined by income instead of wealth. Another factor is the occupation of wife in relation to the occupation of husband which is shown in Table 10C. It appears that the husbands and wives tend to be matched by education, skill level or type of occupation. For example, 51 percent of professional men are married to professional women or female managers, while 40 percent of the male managers are married to women who are themselves managers and professionals. As professional and manager level women are more likely to work and have a career instead of staying at home (they can afford baby sitters) this elevates the labor force participation in the upper class. If the data are collected by wealth and the upper class is divided into the rich and trustees it will probably show a decline in labor force participation of the wives of the trustees because they do not have to work and are likely to be involved in voluntary work or help their spouses with their careers.

Table 10C Occupation of wives by occupation of husband

Occup. of Husband %	Occup. of Wife percent						
	A	B	C	E	F	D	G
A-Manager	**16.5**	**24.6**	43.2	11.9	0.4	1.0	2.4
B-Professional	**10.7**	**40.4**	35.6	8.9	0.3	1.0	3.1
C-Clerical Sales	11.0	18.9	51.3	14.2	0.4	0.8	3.4
D-Skilled Mfg	6.4	13.4	41.5	28.3	0.4	3.2	6.4
E-Unskilled Mfg	5.0	11.7	35.8	37.2	0.7	3.0	6.5
F-Farmers	4.3	13.7	28.8	22.5	23.1	1.2	6.4
G-Unemployed	4.5	11.6	34.4	30.6	0.2	1.5	17.2

Class consciousness is created and made visible by divisions such as availability of productive assets, homeownership and race (including food stamps). The major effects of the economic class system show up as educational achievement, job security, family stability and labor force participation of wives. The constant attempts to hide class lead to a condition where the public can see and feel class effects but cannot define it.

Class System Stability

The American class system has been extraordinarily stable, lasting two centuries without any major threat. The importance of the distribution of wealth and economic stability was recognized since the inception of the Constitution. Jefferson, writing from France to Madison, noted that "property of this country (France) is absolutely concentrated in very few hands" with grave consequences for French society. More recently Galbraith has argued that one cause of the Great Depression was the acute concentration of wealth. The concentration of wealth affects the functioning of free markets with detrimental impact on the demand and supply of goods and services. However, the basic question is what characteristics make a given distribution of wealth just or unjust and how do they effect the stability of the economic system.[27]

Table 11A maps the changes in the distribution of wealth from 1962 to 1983 as measured by the Federal Reserve Surveys. The critical factor is the changes in distribution of wealth between the middle and upper class. In theory the middle class share below 40 percent would create an impression of unfairness and need for change. In reality this happens only when the middle class share falls below 30 percent. These changes in the distribution of wealth with the business cycle may also coincide with recessions and booms.

Table 11A Distribution of wealth by class (1962–1983)[26]

Class	1962	1970	1977	1983	Theoretical Limits
Upper	66	69	63	68	60
Middle	**30**	**29**	**35**	**30**	40
Working	4	2	2	2	0
Under	0	0	0	0	–
Total	100	100	100	100	100

Source: Survey of Consumer Finances, 1983: Federal Reserve Bulletin, December 1984, p. 862

Table 11B   Wealth share of Trustees (Top 1% of Families)
1958–1976 (Estate multiplier estimate)

Year	1958	1962	1965	1969	1972	1976
Wealth Share %	26.6	28.2	**31.3**	27.4	27.7	**19.2**

Source: The Concentration of Wealth in the United States, The Democratic staff of the Joint Committee, U.S. Congress, July 1986, p. 40–42.

A problem with the distribution of wealth is that the collection and dissemination of data has been made difficult. The Federal Reserve Surveys in 1962 and 1983 are the only available data on wealth. Even these are not freely accessible to the public and researchers. Traditionally only the wealth of the top one percent of the population has been estimated by the estate multiplier method from federal estate tax returns. The estimated wealth for the trustees (top one percent of the families) for the years 1958 to 1976 are shown in Table 11B. The data generally support the trends and information gathered from the Federal Reserve Board Surveys. After the last full fledged estate multiplier study in 1976, the IRS prohibited private researchers from gaining access to estate tax records. This put an end to further estate multiplier studies by private scholars or any verification of Federal Reserve Surveys.[28]

The wealth distribution theory, which in turn controls the distribution of income, subsidies and taxes, is closely linked to the actual working of the economy. Almost half the population has no net worth. The middle class has most of its net worth tied in home equity while the upper class controls most of the productive, income producing assets. Although the shares of the middle class have changed, the class system has survived booms and busts, and changes from an agricultural to an industrialized economy to an economy based on computers and communication revolutions. It is well worth examining how it has performed over the last two hundred years.

CHAPTER 3

HISTORY

Money, not morality, is the principle of commercial nations.–**Thomas Jefferson**[1]

Till there be property there can be no government, the very end of which is to secure wealth, and to defend the rich from the poor.–**Adam Smith**[2]

Although we are all of us within history we do not all possess equal powers to make history.–**C.Wright Mills**[3]

Even the greatest of all past civilizations existed on the exploitation of the misery of the many.–**Lyndon B. Johnson**[4]

Alexis de Tocqueville is the high priest of the traditional view of America as a democratic classless society. The young French aristocrat visited this country for nine months and published *Democracy in America* in 1835. He was amazed at a social setting where the word "servant" was taboo and advertisements were placed for "help". The working people dressed as well as merchants, statesmen proclaimed their humble origins, deferring to the masses, and everyone ate huge quantities of foods available in Europe to only few. Another observation attesting to the predominance of the masses was the vulgarity of manners—the public slouching, spitting, and rudeness—and the fact that "any man's son" could "become the equal of any other man's son".[5]

According to this thesis the United States in the first half of the nineteenth century was a society dominated by people of the middling orders. The near, if not perfect, equality of condition left little opportunity for vast accumulation of wealth. Most of the rich men in America were typically self-made, born to poor humble families. Nor did they hold on to their wealth for long. In this dynamic society riches and poverty were transitory, which explained the dwindling influence of the wealthy. The United States had eliminated all important restrictions on voting. In short, social democracy was an automatic consequence of political democracy; in a civilization that prized honest work over status, class barriers diminished in proportion as they were increasingly breached.[6]

Many historians have questioned whether De Tocqueville was describing the American reality or devising an abstract democratic model of his own marked by flights of fancy. Though the most important insights were based on marginal evidence the myth of a democratic classless society has survived to the present. The distribution of wealth and class through American history, starting with the Colonial period when the foundation was laid, needs a critical appraisal.

Colonial Period

A class system in the American colonies before the Revolution is not surprising because the colonizers were the British who had considerable experience with their own class system in England, which also had a King. The only difference was the economic environment in a far and undeveloped continent. While the home country had plenty of labor and infrastructure but little spare land, the new continent had almost endless virgin land which had to be cleared for cultivation but no labor force or infrastructure. This called for a new class system suited to the colonies based on black slavery, white indentured servants, a headright distribution of land and the corresponding political realities. The end result would be a class system which would provide the blueprint for the Constitution and subsequent events.

There was some experience with and acceptance of the English class system from the very beginning. In early New England, Harvard rosters classified each student as "gentleman" or just "Mr."—depending on his birth and station in life. At fetes in colonial America, the dancing order was arranged according to the net worth of the participants in the ballroom. The principal guest, usually a British naval officer, first danced with the richest girl, then going down the line as demanded by the protocols of wealth.[7]

Even before the Revolution, landed estates and colonial mansions in America mimicked the old world. From the earliest English settlements, men of influence were granted large parcels of land. By 1700, fewer than a dozen individuals owned three-fourths of the acreage in New York. In the interior of Virginia, 1.7 million acres belonged to just seven people. By 1760 most of the commerce, banking, mining and manufacturing on the eastern seaboard was controlled by fewer than 500 men in five colonial cities who also owned much of the land.[8]

For political control of far-off colonies the British created a control mechanism based on the principle of the king and the House of Commons and the House of Lords. There were to be elections for the legislature, along with a governing council and the governor. This gave the impression that the locals had a say in the government but in reality the actual governance was done to suit the interests of the king and the ruling class in England, represented in America by the governor and the governing council or senate.

Property qualifications were used as of 1787 as a first step to disqualify up to a third of the white male population from voting. The next was to make the property qualification for holding office so steep that most voters would be prevented from qualifying as candidates. Thus, to qualify as a member of the New Jersey legislature, a net worth of £1,000 was required, while state senators in South Carolina were required to have estates with net worth of at least £7,000 (more than a million dollars in today's worth). The practice of voice votes and the "absence of a real choice among candidates and programs" led to "widespread apathy". This allowed men of substance to monopolize important offices. Before the Constitutional Convention, the French Charge d' Affaires wrote to his Foreign Minister:

> Although there are no nobles in America, there is a class of men denominated "gentlemen" . . . Almost all of them dread the efforts of the people to despoil them of their possessions, and, moreover, they are creditors, and therefore interested in strengthening the government, and watching over the execution of the law . . . The majority of them being merchants, it is for their interest to establish the credit of the United States in Europe on a solid foundation by the exact payment of debts, and to grant to Congress powers extensive enough to compel the people to contribute for the purpose.[9]

The skewed distribution of land and the political design allowed increasing concentration of wealth during the Colonial period. Recent studies of scattered towns and villages confirm this. In Chester County, Pennsylvania, the richest 10 percent of the population controlled approximately 25 percent of the wealth in 1693. Over the course of the next century their share of the wealth increased to 40 percent while that for the bottom 60 percent of the population declined from 38 to 17 percent. Wealth was even more unequally distributed in commercial or seaport towns and the rate of change in concentration was swifter. In colonial Boston, the wealthiest one percent of the population owned about 10 percent and the upper 10 percent about 37 percent of the city's real and personal estate in 1687. By 1771 the upper 10 percent owned about 55 percent of the property of a Boston community that had become "more stratified and unequal". Broader studies have found that on the eve of the Revolution the richest tenth owned about 40 percent of the net wealth in the middle colonies of New York, New Jersey, and Pennsylvania; while in the Northeast as a whole the upper tenth owned about 45 percent of the wealth.[10]

The economic situation was configured in such a way that the great bulk of the working class had to live at a basic level. Most of the agrarian population comprised poor freeholders, tenants and indentured hands. The middle class consisted of small farmers who were burdened with heavy rents, ruinous taxes and low incomes. To survive the vicissitudes of the economy they borrowed money at high interest rates from the upper class by mortgaging their future crops. Newspapers reported an "increasing numbers of young beggars in the streets".[11]

That the stability limits of the class system and wealth concentration were being approached could be seen by the economic prisoners crowding the jails. In 1786, one county jail in Massachusetts held 88 persons, of whom 84 were incarcerated for debts or nonpayment of taxes. The people were increasingly beginning to feel that the revolution against the British Crown was a wasted effort. In many states armed crowds blocked foreclosures and freed debtors from jail. Violent and organized disorders came to a head when indebted farmers of western Massachusetts led by Daniel Shays took up arms in the winter of 1787. Although the state militia put down their rebellion with 11 men dead and scores wounded, it indicated the status of the class system in the year the Constitution was formulated.[12]

The American class system primarily seeks to make almost half the population work while keeping them at a basic level where they cannot accumulate savings or wealth. This was difficult during the Colonial period because land was in plenty and labor in short supply. Even white indentured servants had to be let off after completing their term in five to seven years if they did not run away earlier. The problem was resolved by instituting black Protestant slavery (denied humanity of black slaves). Not only did slavery restrict the consumption of the blacks but also that of the middle class whites who were forced to compete and survive in the tobacco commodity markets with inferior parcels of land and without slaves. As a result most of the savings and wealth ended up with the upper class.

There was a catch to this. The number of blacks in the population had to be restricted if they were not to become a majority and take over the country or threaten the stability of the economic system itself. At the time of the Constitutional Convention in 1787 Georgia and South Carolina had a black majority and it was being felt that limits had to be put on the black population. The American class system would have to change gears, and this would happen with the new Constitution.

Constitutional Foundation of Class System

At the Constitutional Convention in 1787 there were two schools of thinking which can be termed the class system Federalist and democratic Anti-Federalist viewpoints. Both sides were articulate and formulated their opinions in writing. The class system viewpoint was presented forcefully by James Madison and Alexander Hamilton while the democratic arguments were represented by John Adams and George Mason. In the end the Federalists succeeded in writing and ratifying the Constitution with an entrenched class design that would make a mockery of democratic principles, if not in letter then in spirit.

John Adams developed an exhaustive exposition of the rich-poor issues at that time. Adams felt society could be divided into two classes, a small group of rich persons and a large mass of the poor, while politics was founded directly on economic interests. These classes were engaged in a constant struggle, with the rich seeking to augment their possessions at the expense of the poor and the latter trying to despoil the rich. The instinct for acquisition was strong enough to override religious or moral considerations. Using their superior ingenuity, the rich, if unchecked, would absorb nearly all of the country's wealth. The Constitution had to represent the rich and poor as distinct orders with an independent executive enjoying a long tenure as a check on the contending classes.[13]

Daniel Webster later saw the basic conflict between democracy and the class system rooted in the haves and havenots of property. Universal suffrage, he declared:

> could not long exist in a community where there was a great inequality of property. The freest government, if it could exist, would not be long acceptable, if the tendency of the laws were to create a rapid accumulation of property in a few hands and to render the great mass of the population dependent and penniless. In such a case, the popular power must break in upon the right of property, or else the influence of property must limit and control the exercise of popular power.[14]

The class system advocates were perfectly aware of the conflict with democracy. Hamilton said the conflict between the wealthy and the needy should be the basic determinant of the government's structure:

> All communities divide themselves into the few and the many. The first are the rich and well born, the other the mass of people. The voice of the people has been said to be the voice of God; and however generally this maxim has been quoted and believed, it is not true in fact. The people are turbulent and changing; they seldom judge or determine right. Give therefore to the first class a distinct, permanent share in the government. They will check the unsteadiness of the second . . ."[15]

Hamilton was only agreeing with Madison, the father of the American class system, who enunciated the general principles in the tenth issue of the *Federalist:*

> The most common and durable source of factions has been the various and unequal distribution of property. Those who hold and those who are without property have ever formed distinct interests in society. Those who are creditors, and those who are debtors, fall under a like distribution . . . the regulation of these various and interfering interests forms the principal task of modern legislation, and involves the spirit of party faction in the necessary and ordinary operations of the government.[16]

Madison's efforts were directed at checking the "leveling impulses of the propertyless multitude that composed the majority faction. To secure the public good and private rights against the danger of such a faction and at the same time preserve the spirit and form of popular government is then the great object to which our inquiries are directed". Madison got right to the heart of the matter: how to keep the form of popular government with a minimum of the substance; how to construct a government that would not tamper with the existing class structure but still secure a degree of popular support; a government strong enough to serve the growing needs of the upper class while withstanding the democratic demands of the popular class. The inadequacy and instability of democracies were described: "Democracies have ever been spectacles of turbulence and contention; have ever been found incompatible with personal security, or the rights of property, and have in general been as short in their lives, as they have been violent in deaths".[17]

It has been argued that the American class system was based on individuals possessing talent and abilities in different degrees:

> The diversity in the faculties of men from which the rights of property originated, is no less an insuperable obstacle to a uniformity of interests. The protection of these faculties is the first object of Government. From the protection of different and unequal faculties of acquiring property, the possession of different degrees and kinds of property immediately results: and from the influence of these on the sentiments and views of the respective proprietors, ensues a division of the society into different interests and parties.

Those without property or any hope of acquiring property would use their franchise to vote themselves the property of others. Madison foresaw this danger and warned the convention delegates:

An increase of population will of necessity increase the proportion of those who will labor under all the hardships of life and secretly sigh for a more equal distribution of its blessings. These may in time outnumber those who are placed above the feelings of indigence. According to the equal laws of suffrage, the power will slide into the hands of the former.[18]

As a safeguard Madison suggested a Republican form of government and large political units:

The influence of factions leaders may kindle a flame within their particular states, but will be unable to spread a general conflagration through the other states. A religious sect may degenerate into a political faction in a part of the Confederacy; but the variety of sects dispersed over the entire face of it must secure the national councils against any danger from that source. A rage for paper money, for an abolition of debts, for an equal division of property, or for any other improper or wicked project, will be less apt to pervade the Union than a particular member of it; in the same proportion as such a malady is more likely to taint a particular county or district, than an entire State.[19]

The members of the Constitutional Convention in Philadelphia were, without exception, men of property. As leaders and representatives of their several states, they were accustomed to the deference of ordinary people—the yeomanry and tenants of the country, the mechanics, tradesmen and laborers in towns. Jefferson referred to the convention delegates as "an assembly of demigods". Agreeing to keep their deliberations secret, the Convention came up with a Constitution to protect property rights over personal liberty. Liberty to the founders meant freedom to invest, speculate and accumulate wealth and to secure its possession without encroachment by the public. Checks and balances were intended to operate against the will of the majority.[20]

To ensure a government of the wealthy for the wealthy and by the wealthy the Constitution created a Madisonian control tower. The legislative branch, Congress, was composed of two houses: a Senate in which each state would have two members irrespective of its population and a House of

Representatives in which representation was proportionate to population. The Senators from each state were to be elected indirectly by their respective state legislatures. An electoral college voted by the people but composed of political leaders and men of substance would choose a President who was the head of the executive branch. It was anticipated that the electoral college would normally fail to muster a majority for any one candidate, and the final selection would be left to the House, with each state delegation therein having only one vote. The Supreme Court Justices were appointed for life by the President after confirmation by the Senate.

An impression of a democratic form of government was created by allowing the people to elect the House of Representatives without property qualifications. But this was the outer limits of democracy, as the House could not act or pass any laws without the concurrence of the Senate. The Senate would be packed with the richest of the rich, as the state legislators electing them were themselves subject to property qualifications.

Even if by some improbable turn of events a law endangering the interests of the upper class was passed both in the House and Senate, the President could veto it. To override a presidential veto both the Houses would have to reconfirm it with a two-thirds majority. The founders were sanguine that only the wealthiest would reach the Presidency. Charles Pinckney suggested that no candidate be deemed fit for the office of the presidency unless he could prove a net worth of $100,000 which would exceed $10 million in today's value—though this property qualification was not adopted. If the legislature overrode the presidential veto, the Supreme Court provided another check. As the final interpreter of the Constitution, the Supreme Court could declare an act of Congress unconstitutional. Being appointed for life with the right political orientation, the judges, it was hoped, would ensure that property rights would take precedence over all other rights.[21]

Proof that property was well protected could be seen from the special accommodation of black Protestant slavery in the Constitution. Three-fifths of the slave population in each state were counted when calculating representation in the lower House. This would provide leverage for slaveholders compared with nonslaveholding whites, who were a majority. The import of slaves was given constitutional protection for a further 20 years. Slaves who escaped from one state to another had to be delivered to the original owner upon claim. This would confirm the subhuman status of the blacks, who were not considered citizens and therefore not subject to the protection of the law. This later created a dilemma because all states would pass laws to get rid of the blacks and there was no place for them to go.[22]

When Colonel Mason recommended that a committee be named to draft "a Bill of Rights," a task he said which could be accomplished "in a few hours," the other convention members voted unanimously against it after a perfunctory discussion. The deliberate omission of a Bill of Rights seemed to the democratic (Anti-Federalists) faction a damaging admission of the ulterior motives of their opponents. A Bill of Rights in the first ten amendments to the Constitution had to be included as the only way to have the Constitution ratified. Originally an eleventh Bill of Rights stated that the first ten would be enforceable in the states, but this was withdrawn. The Constitution was intended to protect the rights of the upper class from the federal government, while they could very much do what they pleased in the states.[23]

If the Constitution was a card deck stacked in favor of the upper class, how was it ratified? Initially most states opposed it. The property interests at the convention knew that once the Constitution was ratified they would always be in the driver's seat. Bribes, intimidation and other forms of discouragement were used against the opponents of the Constitution. The Constitution was never submitted to popular vote. Ratification was achieved by state convention composed of delegates who came from the affluent strata and no more than a sixth of the adult males voted. In five states it was "questionable whether a majority of the voters participating . . . actually approved the ratification." Overall the Constitution had only to be ratified in nine out of the 13 states to take effect.[24]

The Constitution's intention of entrenching the class system is evident from the procedures for amending it. According to J. Allen Smith, "All democratic constitutions are flexible and easy to amend. This follows from the fact that in a government which the people really control, a constitution is merely the means of securing the supremacy of public opinion and not an instrument for thwarting it". The American Constitution contrived an elaborate and painstaking amendment process, requiring ratification by two-thirds of both the Senate and the House, and three-fourths of the state legislatures. To the extent that the majority principle existed at all it was tightly locked into a system of minority votes, aborting swift and sweeping popular action.[25]

Using the powers granted by the Constitution, Alexander Hamilton lined the pockets of his friends and set precedence for using the Treasury for the enrichment of a select few. The first American Congress, in its first acts of legislation, set up a national bank and a settlement of the war debt that enriched the speculators (most of them Hamilton's friends) who had bought worthless Confederation bonds at deep discounts and cashed them at face value. By assuming this debt, the federal government used the public treasury to create a vast amount of credit for a propertied class that could then invest it in commerce and industry. The people would eventually have to pay for this assumed debt.[26]

Madison, in laying the foundation of the American class system, set an example of how economic interests could be used to divide and rule. It could be used to overcome the "factions", the cleavage of society into ideological camps divided by their basic beliefs. Economic conflict could be managed because economic interests are divisible, whereas political or religious beliefs are not. It is always possible to split an economic difference in two because half a loaf is better than no bread at all, as the American class system has proved in two centuries.[27]

Antebellum Period

Not only did the Federalists succeed in writing the class system into the Constitution with the protection of property taking precedence over democratic sentiments, they also appointed Federalists to the Supreme Court. Even when a Democrat like Jefferson won the Presidency in 1800 he could do little to contain the class system. It took a generation and the political revolution of Andrew Jackson before a shift could be effected in the thinking of the Supreme Court.

During the period between the ratification of the Constitution and the Civil War, the economy and the distribution of wealth developed along predictable class lines. The only difference was that the North abolished black slavery and developed a class system based on a white working class which had to work under the threat of starvation, with the blacks performing the role of the underclass. This put the North and the South, with conflicting class systems, on a collision course leading to Civil War.

The original Supreme Court appointed by George Washington consisted of property holders who shared the anti-democratic bias of the Federalists and the Constitution. John Jay, the first Chief Justice of the United States (1790–95), saw "the wise and the good" as locked in an endless struggle against "the wicked and the weak" and expressed his philosophy candidly: "those who own the country ought to govern it . . .". Justice James Wilson was the author of the constitutional clause asserting that "No state shall pass any . . . Law impairing the Obligation of Contracts". He was deep into land speculation and has been described as a "member and legal protector of the creditor class". John Rutledge had formerly served as South Carolina's governor and while holding the office vetoed a proposed State Constitution on the ground that it was too democratic. He resigned when it was adopted over his veto. Justice William Cushing presided over a number of Shays' Rebellion trials and earned the rebels' hatred. One commentator noted about the original six justices of the Supreme Court, "All were members or representatives of the propertied, creditor classes, and all believed that the purpose of government was to protect the rights of property against the covetous depredations of the lower classes."[28]

Replacing the original justices before the election of Jefferson in 1800 were Federalist judges who were no better in their attitudes. Samuel Chase expressed his attitudes in a statement to a grand jury: "The bulk of mankind are governed by their passions and not by reason. The establishment of universal suffrage will take away all security for property and personal liberty and our constitution will sink into a mobocracy, the worst of all popular governments".[29]

Jefferson broke ranks with the conservatives and resigned from his position as Washington's Secretary of State. He won the Presidential election in 1800, which signaled the initial victory of the first political party claiming to represent the American people. The *Colombian Sentinel* declared, "Tremble then in case of Jefferson's Election, all ye holders of public lands, for your ruin is at hand". John Taylor articulated the fears of the upper class. Taylor's analysis, like that of Madison and Adams, focused sharply on the class system and unequal distribution of wealth. Taylor viewed inequality as the result of exploitation, not of superior virtue: "He (Taylor) will not admit that the great difference in wealth, the abysmal division into rich and poor, are historically the product of the industry of the few and the sloth of many. On the contrary, he holds that the older aristocracies were begotten by exploitation, not by thrift and savings". The American aristocracy (upper class) was based on wealth achieved through manipulation of the financial system (stocks, bonds, currency, etc.) and the remedy against exploitation by the financial oligarchy was to use the political process to destroy the special privileges of this class.[30]

Jefferson not only felt personal revulsion at the methods of capitalism but also felt their development was incompatible with the perpetuity of American institutions. However, his political platform was not based upon the concept of a national government acting vigorously on behalf of the middle class but one of simply stopping it from granting special privileges to the upper class and returning to a basically laissez-faire system.[31]

Jefferson realized the upper class had a trump card in the Supreme Court: "The Federalists have retired into the Judiciary as a stronghold . . . and from that battery all the works of republicanism are to be beaten down and erased". John Adams' last important act was to appoint John Marshall as Chief Justice and Jefferson never succeeded in breaking the Federalist hold on the judicial system. Marshall took advantage of the favorable social climate to write his personal views into law that "had pretty well established the Constitution as a document which forbade government interference with private property, even on the ground of the public welfare".[32]

It took the terrible crash of 1819, which was blamed on the Federalist monster, the Bank of the United States, for Marshall's influence to wane. Only with the coming of the Age of Jackson did the pendulum begin to swing in the direction of democracy. Jacksonians explicitly sided with the havenots. Jackson's closest political advisor, Amos Kendell, summarized the new political philosophy:

> In all civilized as well as barbarous countries, a few rich and intelligent men have built up Nobility Systems, by which, under some name, and by some contrivance, a few are enabled to live upon the labor of the many . . . (These ruling classes) are founded on deception and maintained by power. The people are persuaded to permit their introduction, under the plea of public good and necessity. As soon as they are firmly established, they turn upon the people, tax and control them by the influence of monopolies, the declamation of priest-craft and government-craft, and in the last resort by military force.[33]

Marcus Morton, then serving on the Massachusetts Supreme Court, elaborated the Jacksonian position:

> My opinion is that the danger most to be feared and guarded against is encroachment by the powerful upon the weak—and by the rich upon the poor and not the reverse. My constant apprehension is that the weaker members of the community will be divested, or restricted in their rights. The greatest vigilance is needed to protect the common mass of the community—the industrious, quiet, producing classes of Society against the over bearing influence of the rich and powerful. If I am not always found on the side of the weak against the strong, whether in reference to Government, corporations or people it will be because I err in finding which that side is.[34]

The Jacksonian political revolution succeeded where Jefferson had failed with the appointment of Chief Justice Roger B. Taney to the Supreme Court in 1836. "Mr Taney is as sincere and thorough a Democrat as any in the country . . . He is a sound anti-monopoly Democrat," a newspaper of that time described him. Before his appointment he was a central figure in Jackson's administration and had drafted the veto message when Jackson vetoed the charter of the Bank of the United States. The message stated in part:

> It is to be regretted that the rich and powerful too often bend the acts of government to their selfish purpose. Distinction in society will always exist under every just government. Equality of talents, or education or wealth cannot be produced by human institutions. In the full enjoyment of the gifts of Heaven and fruits of superior industry, economy and virtue, every man is equally entitled to protection by law; but when the laws undertake to add to these natural and just advantages, article distinctions . . . to make the rich richer and the potent more powerful, the humble members of society—the farmers, mechanics and laborers—who have neither the time nor the means of securing like favors to themselves, have a right to complain of the injustice of their government.[35]

Taney's tenure on the Supreme Court saw a shift from the property position to the direction of democracy. Taney considered the primary purpose of government was to promote the happiness and welfare of the people at large, not to protect the accumulated property of the wealthy few:

> The object and end of all governments is to promote the happiness and prosperity of the community by which it is established . . . The continued existence of a government would be of no great value, if by implications and presumptions, it was disarmed of the powers necessary to accomplish the ends of its creation; and the functions it was designed to perform, transferred to the hands of privileged corporations.

According to historian Pfeffer, implicit in the opinion is the assumption that not merely are the interests of the community superior to the rights of the individual but also the protection of private property and the promotion of profit making are not necessarily the only or even highest and overriding ends of government. The significance of the opinion was not lost on Justice Story, who felt that it almost amounted to a repeal of the Constitution, since its fundamental purpose was to protect the rights of the wealthy from this type of attack. The thrust of the Constitution and the American class system could not be changed or deflected in the antebellum period, as an analysis of the actual wealth distribution reveals.[36]

Table 1   Distribution of noncorporate wealth by class [37]
             (Antebellum period)

Class	Population Percent	New York City 1828	New York City 1845	Brooklyn 1810	Brooklyn 1841	Boston 1833	Boston 1848
Trustees	1 %	29	40	22	42	33	37
Gatekeepers	9 %	–	–	37	36	42	40
Middle	40 %	–	–	39	21	25	23
Working	40 %	–	–	2	0	0	0
Under	10 %	–	–	0	0	0	0
Total	100			100%	100%	100%	100%

Philip Hone noted the extremes in wealth distribution even during the Jacksonian era. His beloved New York City had "arrived at the (unhappy) state of society to be found in the large cities of Europe in which the two extremes of costly luxury in living, expensive establishments and improvident waste are presented in daily and hourly contrast with squalid misery and hopeless destitution." Table 1 shows the changes in the distribution of wealth over time in New York City, Brooklyn and Boston, which can be considered typical. Here the figures are for noncorporate wealth. If corporate wealth were to be included the wealth distribution would be even more stark. With time, the concentration increased in all the three cities. In Brooklyn, there was a sharp reduction in the share of the middle class from 39 percent in 1810 to 21 percent in 1841. A committee of the Common Council had reported that persons "of very extensive capital paid taxes on personal property far less in proportion than those in moderate and low circumstances". Without real estate these figures indicate wealth distribution on the conservative side. The other point to note is that as the bottom 80 percent of the population had no wealth, the middle class share shown was held by the top decile of the class.[38]

These estimates at the start of the period became more glaring towards the end, as the share of the top one percent rose from roughly one quarter to onehalf. Nor was opportunity more equal than material condition. Notwithstanding the Horatio Alger myths, the rich with few exceptions had been born to wealth and comfort, owing their success mostly to inheritance and family support. Antebellum (pre-Civil War) urban society was clearly a class society.[39]

Upwards of a third of the population in the South and the cities cramped with immigrants were poor or destitute. Poverty and overcrowding in the north-eastern urban areas led to the cholera and typhoid epidemics of 1832, 1837 and 1842, when "the rich fled the cities, the poor stayed and died." The working class struggled under inhuman conditions. The press reported adolescent girls laboring from six in the morning until midnight for three dollars a week, women who fainted beside their looms, and children as young as nine and ten working 14-hour shifts, falling asleep beside the machines they tended, suffering from malnutrition, sickness and stunted growth. A worker complained in an address before "The Mechanics and Working Classes" in 1827: "We find ourselves oppressed on every hand—we labor hard in producing all the comforts of life for the enjoyment of others, while we ourselves obtain but a scanty portion, and even that in the present state of society depends on the will of employers".[40]

Civil War

Historians have vaguely acknowledged that the Civil War had something to do with slavery and was a form of class war. An understanding of the Civil War and its consequences is enhanced with an idea of the contrasting Southern class system based on black Protestant slavery and the Northern white wage slavery.

The Southern upper class was made up of aristocratic planters, where ten thousand families owned more than two million out of a total population of four million slaves. They were the top one percent of the population, the trustees. The two million other slaves were owned by the upper class. White yeomen farmers constituted the middle with marginal land holding or were tenant farmers. The four million slaves were the working class. At the bottom of the Southern class system were the poor whites who survived on charity as an underclass.

Southern Protestant slavery was based on race. The blacks were not granted citizenship rights. There were no courts or jails for the blacks. As the whites could breed with the black women, the mulattos had to be categorized as blacks. It was assumed that the blacks could never be freed and would have to be fed forever. This created a dilemma for the Southern class system. The black slaves lost their utility with soil degradation and new territories had to be found to keep them working. Neither could they be freed, and keeping them alive meant feeding them.

More damaging was that the white middle class was competing in the same market. The competition from the slaves forced them to bring down their standard of living to the basic level, at par with slaves. The white middle class wanted to move to free territories where they did not have to compete with black slaves and could accumulate wealth. Finally, the white underclass lived even worse than slaves. They could temporarily be deluded with dreams of white supremacy but white immigrants from Europe avoided the South. The South could not match the population growth of the North and stagnated, remaining an agricultural economy and politically because the import of black slaves was banned.

After abolishing black slavery, the North doubled its population with white immigration from Europe. Eventually there were so many poor Irishmen escaping the famines in Europe that they took up jobs previously filled by blacks in the Northeast. The blacks became the new underclass. The North developed a class system based on white wage slavery. Financiers, merchants and mill owners were the upper class. The middle class consisted of the farmers of the Northwest, the skilled craftsmen and small business owners of the Northeast. Unskilled white workers, working in textile mills and as construction gangs, were the working class. Most of the working class lived in urban slums at basic level. A wealth distribution study of ten urban areas in 1860 showed that more than fifty percent of the population had no material wealth, most of which was concentrated in the hands of the upper class.[41]

The stability of the Northern class system depended on the prosperity of the middle class farmers who did not have to compete with the black slaves because they grew food for the Northeast and the South, which specialized in cash crops. The working class in the North could dream of moving to the frontier and becoming independent farmers. So long as land was available in the Northwestern territories, the new middle class could be used by the upper class for political support, thus limiting the discontent among the working class, who had putative voting rights. The Northern class system required new territories free from black slaves for its stability.

This contained the germ of conflict between the two class systems. Both needed new territories, the South for planters with black slaves and the North for the white farmers. The new territories could either serve the interest of the rich and powerful minority planters or the majority of white yeoman farmers. The election of Abraham Lincoln on a platform of slave-free territories and homestead policies set the stage for drastic action. The South had to face the danger of a majority of white middle class yeoman farmers moving to new slave-free territories enticed with homesteads. The only way to keep the whites from fleeing was to secede from the Union because the Constitution could prevent Abraham Lincoln from interfering with black slaves in the South, but not the whites.

The colonial relationship explains why the North did not allow the South to secede. The growth of cotton was financed by the Northern merchants, who were owed two to four hundred million dollars. The cotton was exported to Europe and formed the major source of earnings for the country. The cloth was woven in the Northern mills and sold to the South along with food and other manufactured goods. The North not only financed and profited from Southern black slavery, but also the South constituted a source for raw materials and a market for finished goods. In the absence of a practical compromise which could resolve the dilemmas, war was the inevitable result.

The 13th, 14th and 15th amendments to the Constitution were put into effect at the conclusion of the war abolishing slavery, giving citizenship rights to blacks and providing the infrastructure of public order for everyday living. Once slavery was abolished, the question of guaranteed food and shelter for the blacks ended and they were now free to starve. There was no reason to give blacks precedence over whites in jobs and they entered the underclass. With citizenship rights blacks could gradually move to northern cities. As the Northern and Southern class systems merged the spread of blacks nationally created a permanent underclass. The Civil War was the result of the middle class who by sheer numbers, under Lincoln's leadership, broke the grip of the Northern and Southern upper classes on the political and economic life in America.

In January 1865, Karl Marx drafted an address from the International Workingmen's Association to Abraham Lincoln. It declared that the working men of Europe felt instinctively that "the star spangled banner carried the destiny of their class," and concluded:

> The Workingmen of Europe feel sure that as the American War of Independence initiated a new era of ascendancy for the middle class, so the American anti-slavery war will do for the working classes. They consider it an earnest of the epoch to come, that it fell to the lot of Abraham Lincoln, the single minded son of the working class, to lead his country through the matchless struggle for the rescue of an enchained race and the reconstruction of a social world.[42]

This was a picture which few Americans would have recognized. Less than a year before, speaking to a group of New York workingmen, Lincoln had discussed the working class stake in the war with an exposition of the American class system ideology :

> None are so deeply interested to resist the present rebellion as the working people. Let them beware of prejudice, working division and hostility among themselves. The most notable feature of a disturbance in your city last summer was the hanging of some working people by other working people. It should never be so. The strongest bond of human sympathy, outside of the family relation, should be one uniting all working people, of all nations, and tongues, and kindred. Nor should this lead to a war upon property, or the owners of property. Property is the fruit of labor—property is desirable—is a positive good in the world. That some should be rich, shows that others may become rich, and hence is just encouragement to industry and enterprise. Let not him who is houseless pull down the house of another, but let him labor diligently and build one for himself, thus by example assuring that his own shall be safe from violence when built.[43]

Lincoln provided an accurate picture of the America he knew. He represented the American middle class against the upper class, but it offered little comfort to the working class. The Civil War proved that for a stable class system, in the long run the working class would have to be of the same race as the majority while the underclass could be of separate race, color or religion. Limited to ten percent of the population, it could not threaten the dominant population. Once the fatal flaw in the Southern class system was corrected, the march of the American class system continued unimpeded.

Post-Civil War Nineteenth Century

A battle of wits between the upper and middle classes for a fair distribution of wealth continued for the rest of the 19th century. The upper class kept up the flow of immigrants from Europe, forcing the middle class into a competitive market where they had to survive at a basic level while lowering the wage costs in the industrial market. In defence, the middle class tried to organize into unions with sporadic uprisings and strikes. The upper class tried to regulate competition for themselves by monopolization, charging exorbitant prices for goods and services and increasing their share of the wealth. The upper class usually had its way because of its control over the government. When they could not totally control the legislative and executive branches, they turned to the Supreme Court to enforce their will.

While insisting that free markets and competition worked for all, the upper class tried to protect their interest with tariffs, public subsides, land grants, government loans, contracts, patents, trademarks and other methods provided by civil authority. During the late 19th century an enormous budget surplus collected by the government "from the consuming population, and above all from the poor wage earners and farmers" was paid to upper class investors in high premium government bonds. Almost half the present area of the United States, about a billion acres of land in the public domain, was given over to the upper class. Matthew Josephson describes how the government transformed common wealth to private riches:

> This benevolent government handed over to its friends or to astute first comers . . . all those treasures of coal and oil, of copper and gold and iron, the land grants, the terminal sites, the perpetual rights of way—an act of largesse which is still one of the wonders of history. The Tariff Act of 1864 was in itself a sheltering wall of subsidies; and to aid further the new heavy industries and manufactures, an Immigration Act allowing contract labor to be imported freely was quickly enacted; a national banking system was perfected.[44]

The surge of industrial activity set in motion by the Civil War continued with bouts of panic and depressions. By 1873 the postwar boom collapsed and was followed by a depression which lasted until 1880. This resulted in stronger monopolies as the weaker companies were driven to bankruptcy. John D. Rockefeller during this period put together his Standard Oil monopoly by destroying or taking over his competitors. The trend continued with the recession of 1883 and the depression of 1893.[45]

The upper class monopolization virtually impoverished the working class, their ranks swollen by large numbers of immigrants from abroad and migrants from rural areas, living in subhuman conditions and working for near starvation wages. Even the middle class was not immune to this transfer of wealth. The railroad strikes of the 1870s were followed by the farmers' rebellions and the industrial strikes of the 1880s and 1890s. The upper class control of the government ensured that public authority intervened to crush the strikes, first using the police and state militia and later federal troops. "The industrial barons made a habit of calling soldiers to their assistance; and armories were erected in the principal cities as measures of convenience". To prevent the regular army from being permanently garrisoned in industrial areas, the government took steps "to establish an effective anti-radical National Guard".[46]

The widening gap between the rich and the poor during the late 19th century exacerbated class tension, and the middle class turned increasingly to federal and state legislatures, seeking laws to regulate corporations and protect the average person. The upper class responded by turning to the Supreme Court to determine whether legislative regulation was an unconstitutional infringement of the liberty and property of persons conducting those activities. Historian C. Peter Magrath summarized the economic and legal issues:

> There was, for one thing, the whole question of economic regulation. By 1874, the outline of modern American society had clearly emerged; urban and industrial, it revealed great disparities of wealth and poverty, while small groups of men, accountable to no one, controlled the banks, railroads and industries which were the economic sinews of the new nation. As those at the bottom of the economic scale felt the burdens of irresponsible economic power, there came demands for public regulation. First to protest were the western farmers who believed themselves oppressed by the giant railroad corporations. Those to be regulated naturally fought back, attacking the regulatory legislation on many fronts, but especially in the courts. From this conflict came some of the Court's most significant and difficult decisions.[47]

In 1895 the Supreme Court issued a trilogy of rulings affirming the sanctity of the American class system and the dominance of the upper class, blocking all possibilities of reform. The Pollock decision denied the government the power to impose an income tax. The E.C. Knight decision denied government the power to regulate the activities of the great manufacturing corporations, including the monopolistic trusts. The Debs decision denied the rights of workers to strike collectively in support of their demands. Robert H. Jackson, a 20th century Supreme Court judge, highlighted the drastic effect of the three 1895 decisions on the reform movement:

> The central problem of democratic government became one of working out a tolerable balance among those forces (industry, finance, agriculture, and labor), of moderating the

always threatening power of those whom society permits to own or control its economic resources. Our history demonstrates that our legislatures saw the answer roughly in this way: first there must be a tax policy, based on ability to pay, sufficient to support social services for those upon whom systematic inequalities bore most harshly—in short, an income tax, secondly, there must be regulation of the power of wealth where the premise of competition failed, thirdly those without wealth must be protected in their efforts to organize.[48]

Justice Brown's dissenting opinion in the Pollock case showed who controlled the Supreme Court and the Constitution:

(The Court's decision) involves nothing less than a surrender of the taxing power to the moneyed class . . . Even the specter of socialism is conjured up to frighten Congress from laying taxes upon the people in proportion to their ability to pay them. It is certainly a strange commentary . . . that Congress has no power to lay a tax which is one of the main sources of revenue.[49]

At the end of the 19th century, the American class system was in total control of most of the nation's institutions. The progress of the system was assured as the country entered the 20th century. It would take a stock market crash and a major depression to reveal the limits of the American class system.

First Half, Twentieth Century

In the 20th century, as in the centuries before, the upper class manipulated the government to pull their chestnuts out of the fire: repressing democratic forces, limiting competition, regulating the market to their advantage, and in other ways capturing a larger share of the wealth. The upper class consolidated its hold on the national economy and government to override state and local laws. The concentration of wealth proceeded undisturbed from World War I till the stock market crash of 1929. World War II enabled America to come out of the depression, and for the next 50 years the country entered a permanent defence spending spree on a Cold War footing.

The period from the beginning of this century to World War I was known as the Progressive Era because of the much publicized and cosmetic legislation to control monopolies; the Sixteenth Amendment, which allowed for a graduated income tax and the Seventeenth Amendment, which provided for direct popular election of Senators. By 1915, many states had passed laws limiting the length of the workday and providing workers compensation for industrial accidents. Some states had passed minimum wage laws and 38 states had enacted child labor laws restricting the age and working hours for children. The upper class decided to change direction and strategy. To free themselves from the "vexatious" reformist laws of state and local governments they acted at the national level to control the agenda. As the utilities magnate Samuel Insull said, it was better to "help shape the right kind of regulation than to have the wrong kind forced upon (us)". Therefore, during this period federal market and price regulations in meat packing, food and drugs, banking, timber and mining were initiated at the insistence of the market leaders within these industries. The effect was to raise prices and profits for the large producers, weed out smaller competitors and increase monopolization of the economy.[50]

The upper class strategy was to extend some protection and benefits to the middle class to win their support. In an oligopoly-like situation the upper class did not lose much because increased costs were passed on to the consumers. The major sufferers were the workers without organization and leverage.In oligopolistic industries, the length of the work-day was limited to eight hours with time-and-a-half overtime pay. However, millions of the workers had to put in 12 to 14 hour days, usually six or seven days a week, and according to government figures two million children were still forced to work to supplement the family income. Much of the reform legislation was mere window dressing.[51]

The presidency during this period was firmly under upper class control. Theodore Roosevelt attacked the "malefactors of great wealth" and was hailed as a "trust buster". Yet he was hostile towards unionists and reformers, calling them "muckrakers," and was close to business magnates who were part of his administration. William Howard Taft and Woodrow Wilson did not see any conflict between their political goals and those of business. Wilson, while attacking the corrupt political machines and the big trusts, obtained most of his campaign funds from a few rich contributors, and worked closely with associates of Morgan and Rockefeller. "Progressivisim was not the triumph of small business over trusts, but the victory of big business in achieving the rationalization of the economy that only the federal government could provide".[52]

World War I helped the upper class contain class conflict. Popular attention was focused on the menace of the "barbarian rulers of Germany" supposedly threatening Anglo-American civilization. Patriotic feelings ran high and strikes were now treated as unacceptable interference with war production. Federal troops raided the Industrial Workers of the World headquarters and imprisoned those suspected of socialist sympathies. During the postwar period the government used the "Communist scare", resorting to mass arrests, political trials, deportations and Congressional investigations to suppress labor unrest and anti-capitalist ideas. The upper class shuddered at the Russian Revolution of 1917 and Secretary of State Robert Lansing told President Woodrow Wilson the revolution was setting a bad example for the common man in other nations, including the United States.[53]

The 1920s was the decade of big business. According to historian Mason:

> To the loud acclaim of the business world, Harding sounded the keynote of the next decade of Republicanism: 'We want less government in business and more business in government.'

The change was highlighted by placing Andrew Mellon, the top notch monopolist and multimillionaire, at the head of the Treasury Department. The Republican party regained leadership and practically gave over the government to business.

Table 2   Change in concentration of wealth over time[54]
(% of total wealth by top 1% families)

Year	1922	**1929**	1933	1939	1945	1949	1953	1958	1962
Percent Wealth %	31.6	**36.3**	28.3	30.6	23.3	20.8	27.5	26.9	27.4

Source: Figures calculated from estate tax returns.

Businessmen emerged as heroes of the popular culture. The prevailing belief was "What's good for business is good for the country". Prosperity was supposedly within everyone's grasp; stock speculations and other get-rich-quick schemes abounded. Table 2 shows that the share of total wealth for the top one percent of the families increased from 31.6 percent in 1922 to 36.3 percent in 1929. The upper class had never had it so good. However, the bulk of the population was without wealth. More than sixty percent of the families did not have enough income to provide for the basic necessities of life. In 1928, Congressman Fiorello La Guardia reported on his tour of the poorer districts of New York: "I confess I was not prepared for what I actually saw. It seemed incredible that such conditions of poverty could really exist".[55]

The stock market crash of 1929 brought on the Great Depression of the 1930s. Speaking about it, banker Frank Vandelip noted: "Capital kept too much and labor did not have enough to buy its share of things". Senator Hugo Black observed in 1932: "Labor has been underpaid and capital overpaid. This is one of the chief contributing causes of the present depression. We need a return of purchasing power. You cannot starve men employed in industry and depend upon them to purchase." Others blamed the Depression on its victims. Henry Ford said the crisis was caused by laziness: "The average man won't really do a day's work. There is plenty of work to do if people would do it". A few weeks later Ford laid off 75,000 workers. Hardship for the middle and working classes accompanied the Depression and a torrent of strikes involving hundred and thousands of harbor and textile workers, auto and mine workers swept the nation. Between 1936 and 1940 the newly formed Congress of Industrial Organizations organized millions of workers on an industry-wide basis after protracted struggles.[56]

The upper class response was again a mix of token programs and damage control during the first two terms of President Franklin D. Roosevelt's administration, called the New Deal. Central to the New Deal program was business recovery with the setting up of the National Recovery Administration comprising the corporate representatives in each industry to restrict production and setting up minimum price requirements to shore up the position of the giant corporations. To bolster production and employment the Reconstruction Finance Corporation lent $15 billion over nine years to big business and the upper class. The Civilian Conservation Corps provided jobs at subsistence wages for 250,000 of 15 million unemployed people to give the New Deal a human face. The Works Progress Administration reached about one in four unemployed with work of unstable duration. The divide and rule strategy was used to win over the middle class with the Social Security Act of 1935, which covered only half the population and provided no medical insurance and protection against illness before retirement. Old age and unemployment insurance applied solely to those in some industries who enjoyed sustained employment. Most of these programs were funded though regressive payroll deductions and sales taxes and the implementation left to the states, who could impose additional restrictions.[57]

Limited concessions were given to the middle class with the Wagner Act of 1935, which granted labor the right to bargain collectively and won over the labor leadership. John L. Lewis warned that "the dangerous state of affairs" might lead to "class consciousness" and "revolution as well" and pledged that officials of his own union were "doing everything in their power to make the system work and thereby avoid (revolution)".[58]

By 1940, unemployment persisted as a major problem and the level of consumption and national income was lower than that in 1929. Historian Bernstein analyzed the failure of the New Deal:

> The New Deal failed to solve the problem of Depression, it failed to raise the impoverished, it failed to redistribute income, it failed to extend equality and generally countenanced racial discrimination and segregation. It failed generally to make business more responsible to the social welfare or to threaten the business's preeminent political power. In this sense, the New Deal, despite the shifts in tone and spirit from the earlier decade, was profoundly conservative and continuous with the 1920s.[59]

The upper class dictated the national economic agenda through the Supreme Court during the New Deal. As Supreme Court Justice Jackson summarized the situation:

> Two kinds of power seem always in competition in our democracy: there is political power, which is the power of voters, and there is the economic power of property, which is the power of its owners. Conflicts between the two bring much grist for the mill. The basic grievance of the New Deal was that the Court has seemed unduly to favor private economic power and always to find ways of circumventing the effort of popular government to control it or regulate it.[60]

World War II enabled the United States to pull its economy out of the Depression. Thereafter a permanent war economy was necessary to maintain the tenuous prosperity and lower the Depression-era unemployment. For most of American history the population had rights to participate as voters, but the state with its judges, courts, police, army and bureaucracy remained at the disposal of the upper class. The upper class share of total wealth varied between 80 percent and 60 percent, with corresponding 20 to 40 percent shares for the middle class, through the booms and busts of the monopolistic, regulated economy. Before charting the progress of the American class system and its effects on the economy after World War II, it would be more pertinent to identify who constitute the haves, their guiding principles and their method of functioning and control.

CHAPTER 4

THE HAVES

If you destroy the leisure class (all those who can afford to hire a maid), you destroy civilization.–**J.P. Morgan**[1]

Whoever expects to walk peacefully in the world must be money's guest.–**Norman O. Brown**[2]

What I want to see above all is that this remains a country where someone can always get rich.–**Ronald Reagan**[3]

Our men feel that, although I may have my millions and the reward of their daily toil, still we are about equal in the end.–**William H. Vanderbilt**[4]

The American population is composed not of classes but of men and women of the middle, united as strivers and self betterers.–**Benjamin DeMott**[5]

John D. Rockefeller, a self-made man, had accumulated almost a billion dollars, his net worth, by 1913. His friend and advisor, Frederick T. Gates, warned him of the terrible danger ahead: "Your fortune is rolling up like an avalanche! You must distribute it faster than it grows! If you do not, it will crush you, and your children, and your children's children". Obviously Gates exaggerated, since Rockefeller's sons' sons have survived the fortune, which was estimated to be at least $6 billion in 1986.[6]

Eventually Rockefeller's sons learnt the tricks of the trade. In 1904 John D. Rockefeller Jr. said, "I was born into it (wealth) and there was nothing I could do about it. It was there, like air or food or any other element. The only question with wealth is what to do with it". Later the eldest Rockefeller's heir wanted just more than $1 million to snatch J. Pierpont Morgan's Chinese porcelains from the hands of Frick and Widener. Not having the cash handy he applied to his father for a loan and was turned down. Rather than lose the treasure, Rockefeller, then 41, wrote to his father pleading for funds: "I have never squandered money on horses, yachts, automobiles or other extravagances". Collecting porcelains ("the only thing on which I care to spend money") was a costly hobby but "quiet and unostentatious and not sensational". "The money put into these porcelains . . . is all there, and while not income producing, I have every reason to believe that . . . a sale under ordinary circumstances would certainly realize their full cost value, and, as the years go by, more . . .". He got his million—as a gift, not a loan.[7]

In another story *The New York Times* reported:

A Texas millionaire couple paid $500,000 some time ago to Harvard's Kennedy School of Government for titles that are "normally reserved for instructors and administrators". The agreement required that in return for the donation, Charles C. Dickinson III and Joanne W. Eaton Dickinson of Wichita Falls, Texas, would be "appointed to appropriate positions in the School of Government that will afford them status as officers of the University with the privileges associated therewith . . ." The *Associated Press* quoted Mrs. Dickinson: "Charles and I need an identity. We cannot very well say we are philanthropists at cocktail parties. We want to be affiliated with Harvard".[8]

The haves are the top fifty percent of the population which consists of the upper and middle classes. As these stories illustrate the upper class is trying to conceal its status behind a facade of a middle class image. The upper class can be easily identified by their disproportionate share of wealth, which results in a further categorization of the class into the gatekeepers and the trustees. Not only does this class have assets many times that of the middle class but also it almost exclusively controls the productive, income producing assets. Other characteristics of the upper class include inheritance and their status as creditors for the national economy. One way to view this class is as shepherds to the national economy with the other three classes making up the sheep.

The middle class can primarily be identified by the homeownership characteristic. Homeownership is a characteristic the middle class shares with the upper class and is used for mutual support. In the 1992 primaries George Bush's solution to the middle class riddle was, "redefine it as anyone who votes". Voting is a trademark of the middle class because the upper class wants middle class votes in return for the sharing of national wealth.[9]

It is important to achieve a precise definition of the upper and middle classes and identify their characteristics because the terms have been used loosely by politicians and the media, creating confusion.

The Shepherds

The top ten percent of the households in terms of net wealth comprise the upper class, distinguished from the middle class and the other strata by the share of wealth at their disposal. In theory the upper class can own sixty percent of the nation's wealth and give the appearance of a fair game. Table 1 shows that in 1983, according to the Federal Reserve Study as reported by the Congressional Budget Office, the upper class had 71.7 percent share of the nation's wealth, seven times the fair share of wealth which is theoretically due to the middle class. It was intended from the very beginning that this thin upper crust would be the shepherds to the nation, keeping the flock together.

Table 1   Upper class identification (1983)[10]

Characteristic	Upper Class	Gatekeepers	Trustees
Households - %	10	9	1
Households - Thou.	8400	7560	840
Net Wealth - %	**71.7**	29.9	**41.8**
Corporate Stock - %	**79.3**	29.3	**50.0**
Productive wealth- %	**83.2**	30	53.2
Unincorp. Bus. Assets %	**93.4**	27.4	66.0
Municipal Bonds %	97.7	27.5	70.2
Minimum Net Worth - Thou. $	**206**	206	**1,422**
Average Net Worth - Thou. $	**904**	**419**	**5,276**
Minimum Ann. Inc. - Thou.$	60	60	280
Inequality (Times Middle Class)	7.2	3.3	**41.8**
Social Register (Families Thou.)			40(5%)
Forbes 400 (Families Thou.)			0.4(.05%)

In 1983 there were 8.4 million households nationwide in this class. The minimum net worth of the shepherds was $206,000 while the average net worth was $904,000. As wealth figures are not collected or publicized and are only known to the householder, the minimum annual income for the shepherds was $60,000. However, as all income does not have to be reported to the Internal Revenue Service (IRS) and various kinds of income are treated differently, income statistics are fundamentally flawed and subject to manipulation and can only indicate a reference point.

As wealth distribution is deliberately skewed in the extreme and changes logarithmically, the upper class is again divided into the gatekeepers and the trustees. The trustees are the top one percent of the nation's households or the top ten percent of the shepherds, controlling more than half the upper class share of wealth. The rest are the gatekeepers. This definition estimates 7.5 million gatekeeper households with an average net worth of $419,000 in 1983. And though this is only thrice the average middle class wealth, it gives the gatekeepers a solid standing in terms of neighborhoods and living standards.

The minimum net worth for the 840,000 trustee households in 1983 was $1.4 million and the average net worth $5.2 million. They owned approximately 42 percent of the nation's wealth and their average wealth was 42 times that of the middle class.

Table 2 divides the trustees into millionaires, decamillionaires, centimillionaires and billionaires. There were 1.2 million millionaires in 1987, 82,000 decamillionaires, 1,200 centimillionaires and only 49 billionaires. This marks the outline of the control pyramid. The Social Register, which details about 40,000 families, includes only five percent of the trustees, while the *Forbes* 400 richest families lists only one-twentieth of one percent of the trustees. These figures reveal what the media conceal, that there is indeed a class system. Estimates have been made for the wealth of the trustees for the last two centuries and these vary between 30 and 40 percent of the nation's wealth.

Table 2   Trustees[11]

Year	1 Million	10 Million	100 Million	Billionaires
1981	600,000			
1982		38,855	400	13
1983			500	15
1984			600	12
1985	832,602		700	13
1986			900	26
1987	1,239,000	81,816	1,200	49
1988	1,500,000	100,000	1,200	51

Apart from the quantum of upper class wealth, its nature is as important in understanding the class structure. Most of the upper class wealth is in productive assets generating income. Table 1 shows that 79 per cent of the publicly traded stock is owned by the upper class, with the trustees owning 50 percent. This gives them control over the large corporations and the total economy. Once the home equity component of the wealth is taken out, the upper class ownership of the productive wealth amounts to 83 percent, the share of the trustees being 53 percent. Unincorporated business assets are even more concentrated; the upper class owns 93 percent of it while municipal bonds with tax free interest are almost wholly owned by the shepherds.

Economists and sociologists have failed to agree on the basic definition of the upper class because data on wealth are not collected. When studies are conducted based on the Social Register, the focus is confined to the top five percent of the trustees. These families can be called the super-rich, which means that in 1983 they had a net worth exceeding $10 million. Supporting the super-rich is a scaffolding of social institutions—private schools, elite universities, the "right" fraternities and sororities, gentlemen's clubs, debutante balls, summer resorts, charitable and cultural organizations, and such recreational activities as fox hunts, polo matches and yachting. Educating the children of the super-rich is only one function of the private schools. They serve to bring together the families which are spread over the country. These schools assimilate the brightest of the other classes. Sweezy calls them "recruiters for the ruling class, sucking upwards the ablest elements of the lower classes and performing the double function of infusing new brains into the ruling class and weakening the political leadership of the lower classes". The exclusive schools and social institutions exist to make the identification and networking of the super-rich easier.[12]

The upper class, to stick together, has to act together and countless studies have been done based on the education from private schools, universities, membership in exclusive clubs or interlocking directorships to define a group which may be hatching a national conspiracy. With no such group emerging, the very existence of an upper class is denied. A conspiracy is not essential to ensuring class interest and loyalty. Wealthfare and privilege are distributed based on the wealth pyramid, which ensures the stability of the system. If there are over a million millionaires, then adding another hundred millionaires a year through lotteries will not change the system. It in fact helps the American class system by introducing an element of chance which masks the unchanged essence of the system.

The one thing that can be said with any certainty is that the upper class does not generate this wealth exclusively through wages and salaries. A major source of wealth is profit from productive assets. Hidden government subsidies is another route to wealth accumulation. Since income saved is wealth, minimizing taxes for the upper class is important. The special tax treatment for the upper class comes with tax-free fringe benefits, capital gain treatment of certain income and tax exemption of interest income from municipal and state bonds. For individuals, taxes are pared with deductions for mortgage interest, charitable contributions, state and property taxes. These are designed to give the impression of a progressive tax structure, with the upper class being subject to higher tax rates, when in reality the total tax structure is highly regressive. Other ways of protecting the upper class from taxes are through corporations, trusts and foundations. Finally, to preserve wealth in perpetuity for the upper class, estate taxes have been so structured as to amount to a voluntary tax.

Table 3   Outstanding federal debt-year end 1981 to 1990
(In trillions of dollars)[13]

Debt	1981	1983	1985	1987	1989	1990
Gross	0.99	1.37	1.82	2.35	2.87	3.20
Government	0.21	0.24	0.32	0.46	0.68	0.79
Public	0.78	1.13	1.50	1.89	2.19	2.41
Foreign	0.14	0.17	0.22	0.30	0.39	0.40
All Classes	0.64	0.96	1.28	1.59	1.80	**2.01**
Upper Classes	**0.53**	0.80	1.06	1.32	1.49	**1.66**

Table 3 provides an example of how the shepherds act as money lenders for the national economy and the owners of most of the productive assets. It shows the outstanding federal debt at year end for the period 1981 to 1990 in trillions of dollars. After deducting the securities held by foreigners, it appears that the federal debt held by the upper class increased by $1.13 trillion from 1981 to 1990 using a conservative upper class share of productive assets of 83 percent.

They had to get $1 trillion from somewhere to lend it to the government. The shepherds used the simple strategy of extracting this amount from the national economy and lending it back to the government to earn interest.

In addition to extracting wealth from the national economy, protecting it from taxation and passing it on to future generations, the shepherds need to control the government and institutions such as the press. This is necessary so that decisions and policies give precedence to class interests over that of the country.

Control of the legislative and executive branches of the government is achieved through campaign contributions with lobbying. Through these, especially the Senate, this class controls the regulatory agencies, the military, the FBI and CIA. Using charitable contributions and funding from corporations and foundations, the upper class keeps universities and opinion molding associations such as the Council on Foreign Relations, the Foreign Policy Association, the Committee for Economic Development, the Business Advisory Council and the National Advertising Council under control. The press is kept in check so that it reflects the interests of the upper class by providing stable funding through advertising.[14]

The Middle Class

The middle class can be defined as 40 percent of the households from the sixth to the ninth decile when all population is considered by net worth. Forty percent is the share of national wealth the upper class allocates for this segment of society. For middle class standing, one requires a net worth of between $30,000 and $200,000 in 1983 dollar value, including equity in the home, based on the Federal Reserve Board Survey. In terms of income, which is only an approximate and inexact indicator, middle class families had a range of between $25,000 and $65,000 in 1989 dollar value before taxes. Taxes and subsidies are a major factor in controlling class and obtaining the desired proportions.[15]

The class system allows the middle class to accumulate savings and become homeowners. Homeownership, in turn, triggers a set of rights and duties for the middle class. It allows the middle class to borrow money at specially low interest rates and have some protection from inflation. With homeownership, the middle class can at least stay even because the home prices go up with inflation, increasing their equity. With time home equity provides a cushion in adverse circumstances and some stability for the middle class. In return, the middle class has to vote for and support the policies of the upper class even if they are unfair, wasteful and inefficient.

Savings and homeownership go together and have a special role in the class system. The national economy provides long-term mortgages at interest rates which are half the consumer interest rates, with low down payments. Mortgage interest is allowed as a deduction in determining the income tax. This encourages the middle class to invest their savings in homeownership at the first opportunity, as otherwise the income will be lost in additional taxes.

Homeownership provides the connecting link between the middle and the upper class. Homeownership is a double-edged sword in the control of the middle class. To participate in homeownership the middle class has to qualify for mortgage loans which require steady employment potential. Once they get the loan it requires a monthly mortgage payment throughout the working life. Loss of a job, if not temporary, will result in mortgage default and loss of shelter and savings. Therefore, homeownership goads the middle class to be compliant, loyal employees.

The shepherds use homeownership to ensure that the middle class is on their side during political tussles and elections. Once the shepherds are elected with middle class votes they give themselves privileges and wealthfare checks which barely touch the middle class such as capital gains, charitable deductions and municipal bond interest exemptions. In the end the middle class is lucky to get its share of the wealth because the shepherds are constantly trying to increase their share without creating instability in the class system. The deduction for mortgage interest and property taxes for income tax purpose is an example of how the upper class reduce their taxes on multiple homes valued up to a million dollars.

Homeownership also sets the two classes apart. Most of the middle class assets are tied to home equities, which means they are not very liquid. Homes primarily provide shelter and not income. Therefore, most middle class assets are nonproductive. Home equity is usually highly leveraged with a mortgage loan which can create a volatile situation, especially with a stagnant economy and uncertain employment situation. This can be contrasted with the shepherds, who have a major portion of their assets in income generating assets. The middle class are net borrowers, taking into account their mortgages, while the upper class are net creditors for the economy. The relationship between them is that between creditors and debtors or employers and employees.

The difference between the middle class and the working class again pertains to savings and homeownership. The working class is not allowed to accumulate savings and cannot participate in homeownership. The difference between the two classes is one of degree at the boundary. The middle class has more savings, more job security and more family stability. When it comes to a choice, it sides with the upper class and against the working class.

Voting sets the middle and working classes on different course. The middle class are avid voters but not the working class.Only 53 percent of the electorate bothered to vote in the 1984 presidential election and 50 percent in 1988. According to election analysts the voter turnout for the middle class was 75 percent compared to 25 percent for the working class.[16]

Sociologists have traditionally tried to demarcate the boundary between the middle and the working classes by the types of jobs, such as white collar/blue collar, skilled/unskilled, professional/supervisory or business/employee divisions. Actually, the major difference relates to job security and protection from competition. Professionals are solidly middle class because professions such as engineering, accounting and teaching limit competition with educational and licensing requirements, controlling entry and overall numbers. Small business owners are usually middle class because of the savings requirements to start and run a business. Even college graduates are not guaranteed middle class status because it depends on the field of specialization and the degree of control possible. For skilled, semiskilled or service jobs the status will depend on the industry and the degree of unionization. The same worker with the same set of skills may be in the middle class if he is part of a unionized work force and end up as working class if he is working on his own.

Unions in America are middle class organizations, controlled by the upper class within the parameters of the system. In monopolistic or oligopolistic (shared monopoly) industries the upper class is prepared to share some of the monopoly profits with unionized workers for industrial peace and reduced risk.

American unions are unique in representing a small minority of the labor force. Usually the earnings of union members exceed those who are outside its ambit by a wide margin. The earnings differential was 51 percent for carpenters, 35 percent for mechanics and repairmen and 23 percent for craftsmen. However, for semiskilled workers, union membership provided a premium of as high as 56 percent. Therefore, as part of the middle class, union members receive benefits which are denied to the working class.[17]

Sociologists have noted the identification of the unions with the middle class values and abandonment of the working class. Union workers are concerned with homeownership, mobility for themselves and their children, savings and insurance and other typically middle class aspirations. American unions have at times rejected and ridiculed the participation of working class elements such as blacks, Chicanos and the poor. William Gould argues that these organizations have a vision that "does not extend further than the next wage increases for their white memberships".[18]

Middle class votes are bought by transferring benefits, direct and otherwise, to it with special privilege or controls which are not available to the working and the under-classes. Direct benefits may include special wage laws like the Davis–Bacon Act for federal projects, federally insured loans and mortgages, special income tax deductions and special medical insurance benefits. Indirect benefits are provided through government expenditures on defense, crime control and education.

The Davis–Bacon Act of 1931 requires contractors on federally assisted projects to pay the wages set by the Department of Labor. This meant that the federal projects had to hire carpenters in Boston in 1981 at $19 an hour when private contractors were paying only $13.34. A study by Oregon State University in 1982 found that the Act drove up construction costs in rural areas by 26 to 37 percent. It has been estimated that it comes to as much as $1 billion a year in added construction costs. The unions control the hiring. As the program is limited and does not apply to all construction projects, it involves the transfer of $1 billion a year to the middle class.[19]

The Federal Housing Administration and Veterans Administration guarantees loans and mortgages with very little down payment or none in some programs. These are supposed to assist the middle class in buying starter homes. This is an ideal way of buying middle class votes because there is no downside risk for the home buyers and the lenders. If the home values go up the middle class can build up equity in the home. If the home values go down the owner can walk away and hand over the home to the government. The upper class lenders cannot lose because of the federal loan guarantee. During the construction, the middle class gets jobs at premium wages while the upper class contractors make guaranteed profits.[20]

The middle class is promised the best health care in the world with no limits at minimal cost. In theory the middle class can choose their personal physicians, sue them for millions if anything goes wrong, and with no limits on the cost and duration of care while paying a minimum. These dreams are realized with hidden subsidies and waste of national resources. *Time* magazine reported in 1993 that "Taxpayers spend about $84 billion a year subsidizing tax-free medical care for the mostly middle class and upper class corporate workers".[21]

Middle class votes are also bought with defense spending which helps the upper class grab their share through the military-industrial complex. About two million people serve in the U.S. armed forces, one million civilians work for the Pentagon, and four million people are employed by firms working mostly on military contracts. Though many of the foot soldiers in the armed forces may be of the working class, most of the employees in industry are middle class.[22]

Crime is manufactured to purchase middle class votes. The United States led the world in 1992 for the number of persons in prison per 100,000 population. It costs $50,000 to $70,000 per bed to build a prison and about $20,000 a year to operate it. There is a lot of money to be made in building prisons and buying middle class votes by giving them jobs. In New York State, attempts to slow prison growth and cut back long mandatory terms for drug criminals led to protests by politicians, especially Republicans from rural areas, which have more than 80 percent of the state's prisons. Assemblyman Daniel L. Feldman, a Brooklyn Democrat, said, "Prisons are the best political plum there is in those communities, and they're not just saying lock them up, but lock them up in my district".[23]

Another method of obtaining middle class support is providing educational facilities for the underclass. It is evident that learning cannot take place on an empty stomach. This apparent anomaly can be understood once it is realized that low income district schools are not meant for educating the children but providing jobs to the middle class.

Ideology and Image

The upper class needs some kind of ideology to make the visible policies seem plausible and get the benefit of doubt for itself. Where the facts are too damaging, the error of omission or unavailability of information does the trick. The shepherds have learnt from Thorstein Veblen, who brought into vocabulary the terms conspicuous consumption and conspicuous leisure, that a low profile is the best camouflage.

Right from the founding of the country the upper class has justified its existence with the argument of differing abilities and talents. The criterion of ability is money making, which gives it superior ability. Using acquisitiveness as a sign of ability and then using ability to explain wealth is nothing but playing with words. What it does not explain is why the average wealth of the gatekeepers should be three times that of the middle class and the average wealth of the trustees is 30 times that of the middle class. It also does not explain why 50 percent of the population has no wealth, because surely they have some ability. For this reason ideology requires that all discussion of wealth be omitted.[24]

An ideological defence of the upper class is the lack of information and a problem of definition. Andrew Hacker says:

> On wealth itself we have no reliable information. Neither the census nor Internal Revenue has ever asked people to declare their holdings. What you own is nobody's business while you still have breath in your body, the only exception being if you happen to run for or hold office in a jurisdiction where disclosures are mandatory. Among our rights to privacy, this one seems paramount.

It is not a question of privacy, because in an income tax audit the IRS can be involved with the minutest detail of a family's daily life and activities. Again Mr. Hacker has trouble defining the rich: "Which Americans should we call rich? The richest five percent of our population holds 40 percent of the nation's wealth. Domhoff—concentrates on the top one percent. The trouble with both estimates is that they include too many people who, while well off, are still what we think of as upper middle class". In the absence of wealth data the discussion turns to impressions and how people respond in surveys.[25]

Forbes annually provides a survey of the 400 richest men in America. The minimum net worth was $260 million in 1990. Information about the total distribution of wealth is withheld. The reader is supposed to form his own impression about the status of the population based on this one-in-a-million sample. Another article in *Forbes* noted, "Politicians may talk about raising taxes only for rich people, but to raise any significant amount of revenue the politicians would have to attack the middle class". The impression is again that the rich are a tiny fringe with almost no demarcation between the rich and the middle class.[26]

Thorstein Veblen in his book *The Theory of the Leisure Class* highlighted the importance of image for the upper class. The walking stick as evidence of conspicuous leisure was described as:

> The walking-stick serves the purpose of an advertisement that the bearer's hands are employed otherwise than in useful effort, and it therefore has utility as an evidence of leisure.

Conspicuous leisure was the distinction gained by idleness in a world where almost everyone has to work. The rich man might work himself, but he gains distinction from the conspicuous idleness of his women. J.P. Morgan justified the leisure class on much the same line, balancing their sublime role of preserving civilization with the ridiculous dividing line of their being able to "afford to hire a maid".[27]

The rich, according to Veblen, flaunt their badge of superiority: "The only practicable means of impressing one's pecuniary ability . . . is an unremitting demonstration of ability to pay". After Veblen published his book, the rich could scarcely engage in spending with abandon without it being ridiculed as conspicuous consumption. Corporate jet-setting and other lavish festivals associated with business conventions are provided with a protective cover of corporate service or need. Politicians take pains to pass themselves off as members of the middle class. During the 1988 primary season

Senator Al Gore disputed his upper class status by saying he had mucked out pig barns in his youth. The upper class has realized how well a low profile suits them.[28]

Robert Heller in his book *The Age of the Common Millionaire* notes, "Any student of the wealthy, and of the means by which they acquired their wealth, must return to the lack of rational relationship between the riches of the Common Millionaires and their actual achievements. It is true that to him to whom much is given, too much is given". In a way the shepherd's life is more exacting than that of the sheep. Unlike the latter, who know no alternative other than toil, the shepherd must choose the purpose of his life—he must decide to what end to spend his days. There is truth in the saying, "From him to whom much is given, much shall be required".[29]

There is a constant tussle between the middle class and the upper class for a fair share of the nation's wealth. When the middle class share decreases to less than 30 percent, the rich are blamed for being greedy and wasteful and the Democratic Party finds favor in elections. When the middle class share of wealth gets close to 40 percent, the unions are blamed for waste and inefficiency and the pendulum swings towards the Republicans.

With the 1992 election the middle and the upper class ideologues presented their arguments in strength. Prof. Douglas Massey of the University of Chicago argued that a concentration of wealth would lead to a concentration of demand: "As you narrow the base of demand, you end up with such a narrow segment of the economy responsible for such a large percentage of purchasing power that the economy begins to fall apart". Kevin Phillips analyzed the situation as, "(Income inequality) has been most damaging to Bush. He has been hurt by the growing perception over the last two years that he favors the rich . . . He hasn't had any real empathy with the middle class".[30]

What the politicians on both sides of the divide would not admit was that the conflict is about sharing the spoils. The real victims of the American class system are the fifty percent of the population who comprise the havenots.

CHAPTER 5

THE HAVENOTS

Between the rock and a hard place.–**Anonymous**

The wealthy have little desire to govern the working people, they simply want to use them.–**Alex de Tocqueville**[1]

How the hell we gonna be rehabilitated when we ain't never been habilitated in the first place.
 –**Black survivor, Attica prison inmate rebellion**

The new poverty is constructed so as to destroy aspiration; it is a system designed to be impervious to hope.
 –**Michael Harrington**[2]

Every man has a right to life; and this means that he also has a right to make a comfortable living. He may by sloth or crime decline to exercise that right; but it may not be denied to him.–**Franklin D. Roosevelt, 1932**[3]

On March 11, 1993, the *Wall Street Journal* reported:

> Lou Capozzola worked 10 years at *Sports Illustrated*, jetting from Super Bowls to the Olympics as a lighting specialist. He was on the road 180 days a year, working 15–20 hours days.

92

In February 1990 he was called into his boss's office and informed that his job was being eliminated but that he could continue as an independent contractor. His base pay would be halved to $20,000. His overtime pay would be cut by as much as two-thirds. And he could forget about his $20,000-a-year benefit package, including medical coverage.

Then he was asked to leave town on assignment. "They say 'We value you and your skills. We're just going to pull the rug out from under your feet because we want to save $20,000' " he says.

In spite of the low pay and benefits, he agreed to stay on. He was the sole supporter of his wife and two children. "What could I do? They offered me some form of employment, I had to take it," he says.

This is the 1990's workplace. After spending years at one company, more American office and factory employees are getting transplanted overnight to a temporary or subcontracting nether world. They do the same work at the same desk for less pay and with no health insurance or pension benefits.

In another story the *New York Times* reported the case of a Texas prisoner who was convicted of three non-violent crimes that netted him $230.11:

William James Rummel was convicted of purchasing $80 worth of automobile tires on a stolen credit card in 1964, of forging a rent check for $29.36 in 1969 and of cashing a $120.75 check in 1972 without completing the repairs, for which the check was an advance payment.

Because Texas law mandates a life sentence for the third felony conviction, a state district court sent Mr. Rummel to prison for life in January 1973. On the two earlier charges, he had served a total of 16 months in prison. Mr. Rummel was 34 and had a 10th grade education.[4]

These reports illustrate the conditions before the havenots in 1993. The debate on economic security and individual freedom for the working class has been continuing from the turn of the century. In a 1910 speech, Theodore Roosevelt said:

No man can be a good citizen unless he has a wage more than sufficient to cover the bare costs of living and hours of labor short enough so that after his day's work is done he will have time and energy to bear his share in the management of the community, to help in carrying the general load. We keep countless men from being good citizens by the conditions of life with which we surround them.

The American class system is designed to provide a working class based on wage slavery, which means they must toil at the threat of starvation.[5]

The working class is allowed to accumulate very little savings or wealth. They are given enough to keep working and to produce the next generation of wage slaves for the system. The income given by one hand is taken away with the other, leaving them like rats on the treadmill. Their income is determined by competition in the free market. The working class is made to pay for social security, health, food, shelter and transportation at inflated levels so that it is left without savings. It is like the old share-cropping system where at the end of the season, after paying for seed, food, and shelter at the company store the farmhand owed more to the landowner than what he started with. The existing system is different only in that it is enforced at the national level.

The United States leads the world in terms of per capita citizens in prison, with the total prison population exceeding one million. Official unemployment figures in 1993 are around seven percent, and unemployment is accepted as a permanent feature of America's economy. Most of the large cities have black ghettos with violence, crime and decadence, making civilized living impossible. Los Angeles has just celebrated the 25th anniversary of the Watts riots. All indications point to the fact that the underclass is a permanent feature of the American class system and has been designed into the economic structure. Being the richest economy in the world with the resources to obtain an income distribution of its own choosing, this raises a number of questions. Having 10 percent of the population unemployed, in prisons or in urban ghettos is a tremendous waste of resources and economic inefficiency. Why is this permitted to happen?

Identification and Characteristics

Together the working class and the underclass constitute the havenots. Sociologists have described the working class by occupation, such as blue collar workers or manual, unskilled workers, while economists have used income categories. The working class is defined as 40 percent of the population between the second and fifth decile based on wealth or net worth. The fundamental feature of the working class is the inability to accumulate savings or wealth.

At the higher end of the working class the boundary with the middle class is determined by homeownership. The inability to qualify for a home loan generally puts a person in the working class category. At the lower end of the class, the boundary with the underclass is determined by assistance from food stamps.[6]

The bottom half of the working class has zero or negative financial assets. They have no savings to fall back on should they lose their job or become sick and are unable to work. Their only safety nets are relatives, government welfare, or some sort of private assistance.[7]

In terms of family income the range for the working class in 1989 was approximately between $7,500 and $25,000. Family income can be deceptive because it usually includes two incomes for married couples, who have additional expenses for raising children. Therefore, a single-income household with children will fall to the bottom of the working class while a single income household with no children may only make it to the top of the class. It would require a marriage with two incomes and the discipline of a delayed family to limit expenses before a couple could qualify for home mortgage and move into the middle class.[8]

The first level of control for the working class is competition in the free market. This means there must always be excess labor so that more people are looking for jobs than what are available at any time. In the normal course of events the incomes of the working class would be pressed down. However, there is a floor below which the wages cannot fall. As Adam Smith noted, "A man must always live by his work, and his wages must at least be sufficient to maintain him. They must even upon most occasions be somewhat more; otherwise it would be impossible for him to bring up a family, and the race of such workmen could not last beyond the first generation".[9]

These principles of competition to keep the working class at a basic, replacement level have been followed from colonial times to the present day. Only the methods of enforcement have changed over the last three centuries. In the latter half of the 20th century, the upper class has started exporting jobs overseas. As a result there will again be an excess of workers for the available jobs.

Jared Taylor says the term underclass did not exist before the civil rights movement. There were poor people and criminals, but they were the lower class. Definitions of the underclass were vague and thought to be a class among whom crime, poverty, ignorance and illegitimacy all combined to produce more of the same.[10]

The identification of the underclass in relation to income is possible only by decoding the language of the American class system. First, the government defines the official poverty line for a family of four. In 1993 this was anything less than $13,924. This figure is selected so that usually 25 percent of the population is below the poverty line before cash transfers and in-kind transfers. The objective is to show to the public the dramatic reduction in poverty caused by government transfers in cash and in-kind. After cash transfers the poverty level is reduced to 15 percent of the population and after in-kind transfers poverty is reduced to approximately 10 percent.[11]

Cash transfer payments include social security pensions and unemployment compensation. The former usually help the aged and the retired. Unemployment compensation is restricted to the workers who meet certain work requirements and is limited in time. Cash transfer payments are made to the working class to keep them at a reproducible level through changes in the business cycle. In-kind transfers include food stamps, Medicare and rent subsidies. Medicare goes mostly to those who have retired. Therefore, the underclass, by income, can be defined as the bottom 10 percent of the population below the poverty line after taking into account the government in-cash and in-kind transfers.[12]

A more accurate definition of the underclass is by wealth, that is the bottom 10 percent of the population by savings. That means the underclass must be desperate and hungry enough to submit to a means test for assistance. Food stamps assistance requires that a family of four cannot have more than $2,000 in savings. In 1992 food stamps helped feed 10.4 percent of the population. Studies have found that only 60 percent of those who qualify for food stamps sign up for it. The rest are unaware that they qualify or stay away from the program for fear of being stigmatized. Though there may be some cheating involved, food stamps overall are a sure visible indicator of the underclass.[13]

Another way to identify the underclass is by making adjustments to the official unemployment rate. A worker who sought work and described himself that way to the interviewer from the Bureau of the Census would appear in the statistics as officially unemployed. But if the worker accepted a part time job as a temporary expedient, he was recorded as employed though he wanted to work full time. If the worker ceased to look actively for work and admitted as much to the interviewer, he would be recorded as a "discouraged worker" rather than unemployed. Thus for a true measure of economic hardship it is necessary to take into account the unemployed, the discouraged workers and people working part time but who want full time jobs. Sar Levitan, a leading manpower expert, devised an Employment and Earnings Inadequacy Index to measure unemployment and subemployment. Over the years this index has hovered around 10 percent of the workforce. According to the Bureau of Labor statistics, in May 1993 there were 8.9 million unemployed and 7.7 million were working part time or discouraged workers. The economic hardship rate was almost twice the official unemployment rate of 6.9 percent and represented a part of the underclass.[14]

An important characteristic of the underclass is its racial composition and the concentration of blacks in high visibility ghettos. A third of the underclass is black, but the blacks form only 12 percent of the population. The white underclass is distributed throughout the country, indistinguishable from the whites of other classes.[15]

Mickey Kaus confirms, "It's simply stupid to pretend that the underclass is not mainly black". According to a large ongoing survey at the University of Michigan, blacks make up 55 percent of those who are consistently poor and more than 60 percent of those who stay on welfare for a long time. This reinforces the stereotype that most of the underclass is black. In 1980, of the 1.8 million ghetto residents in America's 100 cities, some 68 percent were black (21 percent were hispanic and only 10 percent white.) As a result, blacks are identified with major social problems such as high dropout rates from schools, crime and families headed by women.[16]

Working Class

Job insecurity and exploitation hold the key to the status of the working class. It is given the purchasing power necessary to buy goods and services at a quality and quantity considered to be the culturally defined minimum for existence, with little possibility of accumulating savings. Job insecurity is created by giving employers the option of firing workers at their convenience. As health benefits are usually tied to the employer, loss of job entails loss of health benefits as well. The latest trend is to deny health benefits to the working class in the first place. This is done with part time employment or independent contractor status.

Only 17 percent of the total labor force was unionized in 1992. Most of the unionized workers are middle class while most of the working class are nonunion. Surveys conducted by the University of Michigan found that a majority of the working class would like their wages and working conditions to be protected by a union contract. But the laws are stacked against unionization and labor. Thomas Geoghegan, a labor lawyer, explains the outcome:

> A new profession of labor consultants began to convince employers they could violate the Wagner Act (enacted in 1935), fire workers (attempting to organize a union) at will, fire them deliberately for exercising their legal rights, and nothing would happen? . . . May be after three years of litigation the employer would lose, and have to pay a few thousand bucks, if that much: a cheap price, though, for keeping out the union.[17]

Periodic unemployment is a built-in feature of the American economy as part of the business cycle. The majority of the periodically unemployed are the working class. Most of them are not covered by unemployment insurance. Unemployment benefits are designed for short recessions and payable only for 26 weeks. A majority of the working class exhaust their benefits before re-employment and the limited payments force them to exhaust savings and borrow money with charge cards.[18]

William Greider provides as an example the 500 office buildings in Washington, D.C., to show how the owners and managers have developed an efficient system to control the working class and deny them job security or benefits. Each owner hires an independent contractor to service the building and the competitive bidding ensures that the firm that pays the least to the janitors gets the contract. If the workers try to unionize and demand legal rights the building owner fires the unionized contractor and hires a new one who is nonunion and the process is repeated as many times as necessary.[19]

The independent contractors protect themselves by only giving part time work to the employees. They hold the workers to a four-hour shift each night by doubling the size of crews so that legally they can exclude the employees from all benefits payable to fulltime employees including health insurance, pensions, paid vacations or paid sick leave. The employees typically shuttle each day between two or three similar part time jobs which lack basic benefits. Instead of calling it exploitation the upper class justifies it on the specious ground of economic efficiency.[20]

The New York Times had a headline, "New jobs lack the old security, in time of 'disposable workers' ". Robert Reich thought that about 30 percent of the workforce was composed of contingent workers.Thus about 80 percent of the working class are disposable throw-away workers with meager benefits. Toledo, Ohio, was given as an example of the national trend. About 25 temporary help agencies displaced most of the permanent placement agencies.They provided welders, assemblers, electricians and other workers for small factories as well as clerical workers for offices.Their clients only paid wages, unemployment insurance and workers' compensation. Health and pension benefits were excluded as the competitive market could not bear the cost.Mr.Claus, owner of a temporary agency, noted that some companies in Toledo were using services like his to provide their entire work force: "I call it the new American sweatshop. It's four people who are owners or managers in a shop that has 200 people. They might have 12 permanent employees who are making $6.50 an hour. All the others are paid $4.75 and they're all temporaries."[21]

In addition to keeping the working class insecure, close to the minimum wage and without benefits, the life and limb of the worker is also expendable. The *Wall Street Journal* reported that some companies tried to avoid liability for contract workers. In an internal memo, Du Pont's Consolidated Coal unit told its employees they should not interfere with a contract employee doing something dangerous unless company property or the employee were endangered. According to the company the memo did not encourage employees to look the other way, but established the contractor's obligation to ensure the safety of its own employees. In 1992, three contractors and one employee were killed in a West Virginia coal mine explosion. The contractors were welding a pipe in an area known to be heavy with methane gas. Federal and state authorities cited the contractor and the company for failing to ventilate the area and to examine for methane gas. The company planned to appeal against all citations and pass the buck to the temporary agency supplying the contract workers.[22]

The trend is clear. According to predictions in *Time* magazine, temporary or disposable workers will increase from 75 percent of the working class in 1988 to 100 percent by the year 2000. After two years of record profits, the Bank of America announced in 1992 that thousands of employees would become part timers. Manpower Inc., with 560,000 workers, is the world's largest temporary employment agency as General Motors (367,000 workers), IBM (330,500) and other industrial giants are shrinking their payrolls. The number of people employed by Fortune 500 companies has shrunk from 19 percent of the workforce in the 1970s to less than 10 percent in the 1990s. Working class members are liable to be treated as second class citizens by the upper class employers and middle class permanent employees. Says Manpower Chairman Mitchell Fromstein: "The U.S. is going from just-in-time manufacturing to just-in-time employment. The employer tells us 'I want them delivered exactly when I want them, as many as I need, and when I don't need them, I don't want them here' ". The impersonal market forces of the new global economy are blamed for the situation. Americans must now compete for jobs with the growing legions of skilled workers in developing economies from Asia to Eastern Europe in the global "wage slave" market. The American class system gets access to the basic level reproducible working class as predicted by Adam Smith.[23]

Economic insecurity results in family instability and divorce for the working class. The Census Bureau reported that poverty was a major factor in the breakup of American families. Stresses associated with economic insecurity and financial needs make dissolution of families more likely. Donald J. Hernandez, the Census Bureau demographer who wrote the report, noted, "Poor two parent families were twice as likely to break up as were two parent families not in poverty". He also pinpointed the causal relationship between economic insecurity and family breakups. "Over the last decade or two, there has been a lot of emphasis on the rise of one parent families as a cause of poverty. But this report shows that the opposite process is important. When two parent families fall into poverty, that significantly increases the chances that the family will break up". The shepherds are blaming the victims when families break up because of premeditated economic insecurity enforced on the working class.[24]

A major factor in keeping the working class at a basic, reproducible level is the effect of racism and the underclass. The race card ensures the control and exploitation of the working class. An understanding of the economics of racism is helped by tracing the original motivation of bringing the blacks into the colonies. The principles once established remain valid to this day.

White laborers had to be brought in as indentured servants in the 1600s as there was a shortage of labor in the colonies. The only problem was that the term of the white indentured servants lasted for only five to seven years and they could run away before that. The only way of keeping them at a basic, replacement level was by importing blacks and legally defining their subhuman status. The shepherds created a mobile labor force that operated at a basic, replacement level. The majority of the white workers were forced into competition economically with the black slaves through the cash crop tobacco and cotton economy of the South. To survive in the cotton marketplace the white workers had to peg their standard of living at the level of black slaves because of their inferior land compared to the plantation owners, who also benefitted from the economics of scale. By acknowledging the subhuman status of the blacks and going along with the slave import, the white workers dug their own graves. Understanding dawned on them late and the new immigrants from Europe avoided the South. But the precedent had been set and the shepherds fine-tuned their racist ideological appeal to last for centuries.

The operation of the American class system was simplicity itself. First use the blacks to set a subsistent, replacement level baseline established on the notion of black inferiority. Then force the white workers into economic competition with them down to the baseline. Black children were legally denied education before the Civil War and had to work in the fields starting at age ten. Though white workers could in theory allow their children to attend school, in reality they had to help their families grow cotton because the price of cotton sales did not permit hired help. The ultimate objective of racism is control of the white workers, and discrimination against the blacks is only the means to an end.

This is again evident when comparing the regional income statistics for whites in the southern states, where race discrimination was more rigid, compared to the northern or western states. In 1969, the per capita income of southern whites was $433 or about one-eighth less than elsewhere in the country. Aggregated over a southern white population of 47.6 million, this added up to a total loss of $20.6 billion in annual income. According to Victor Perlo that was the "privilege" of upholding the myth of white supremacy. Whatever advantages whites may gain from their racial monopoly on better jobs in the South, they lose more because of the existence of a low baseline. The black population is used by employers to lower the incomes of all workers, on all kinds of jobs.[25]

A particularly striking case is that of bus drivers in the South. Until the repeal of Jim Crow laws in the South in the early 1960s, white bus drivers enforced apartheid on the blacks, who provided a disproportionate share of the bus passengers because many of them could not afford other means of transportation. By the end of 1960s, black workers had jobs as bus drivers in the South, and in large numbers in the North. Statistics for 1969 show that the median earnings of white male bus drivers were $4,753 in the South and $7,137 in the rest of the country. On the other hand the median earnings for black male bus drivers were $3,767 in the South and $8,335 elsewhere. White southern bus drivers had median incomes about $1,000 more than the pitiful incomes of the black southern bus drivers. But the white southern bus drivers received about $2,830 less than white bus drivers of North and $3,582 less than northern black bus drivers. In the North, black bus drivers earned more than white drivers not because of "reverse discrimination" but partly because the black bus drivers are concentrated in big city routes, with good union contracts, and often with municipal ownership. More white bus drivers work as part-time school bus drivers in smaller towns, which is also true of southern bus drivers. The great majority of southern bus drivers were subjected to poverty wages and they paid this price for generations of rigidly segregated transportation arrangements.[26]

What is true about the South holds true for the rest of the country, though the difference is in the degree of racism. In addition to the downward drag on earnings, discrimination against blacks affects working conditions for whites. During the early 1970s, when the auto industry was experiencing a boom in Michigan, there was an accelerated hiring of blacks accompanied by a statewide racist campaign against school busing—that is, for segregated schools. Thomas Dennis describes how this related to the auto industry:

> As employment of black workers expanded in the automobile industry, employers concentrated them in worst jobs, such as the foundry, paint department, body shop, and on worst stations on the assembly line. The super exploitation prevalent in the foundries was extended to the production line via stepped up speedup. What happened at Chrysler was a good example. Jobs which were done by three or four white workers were given to two, maybe three, black workers. Production standards were raised dramatically when large number of black workers were put on the job. Then the company put black foremen over black workers to get even more work out of each worker. This move alone got 10 percent to 15 percent more production than before. It was like old times with black slave drivers keeping the slaves in line on the plantation.
>
> The fight of the black workers against the speedup was not supported by the union leadership or the white workers. The

racist antibusing campaign made it easier for the company to play the old divide and rule game—white against black. The amount of work put out by the black workers became the norm. White workers who complained about the greater work loads were told that if they couldn't do the job there were people who could. Thus this extra speedup became the way of life for the white worker also.[27]

It is not surprising that the southern states have the smallest percentage of unionized workers. Racist organizations like the Ku Klux Klan are used to beat up union organizers; state and local governments use the police and the National Guard to break strikes, and white workers are as much victims as the black workers. The social and job separation of black and white workers makes labor unity difficult. Most southern states have "right-to-work" laws, which prohibit the union shop and make it extremely difficult to establish a trade union in a plant. Many northern manufacturers and foreign industries are setting up shop in the southern states to take advantage of the racism and low wages.[28]

The Underclass

Herbert Gans has suggested that we have a large underclass and as we refuse to do anything about it, it must provide benefits other than getting the "dirty work" done by people who have no choice. The underclass provide job competition for keeping the working class in control and keep their wages at basic level. A "pariah group" based on racial lines gives a feeling of superiority to and limits the working class discontent. The cost of keeping the underclass alive without work is ultimately borne by the working class.[29]

The primary function of the underclass is to provide a working class for the shepherds at the lowest possible wages. Thurow explains:

> As long as there are a lot of unemployed people waiting in a job queue, the employer gets used to the idea of high turnover and does not bother to attach workers to the firm on

a long-term basis through training, fringe benefits, and so on. He would rather cut costs to the bone, be able to lay off at will, and, when needed, hire somebody else.

He then dwells on the creation of a permanent underclass: "If all low-paying jobs were held by people as stepping-stones, as opportunities to start work and then move up as the incumbents gained in skill and experience, then such jobs would not create a permanent under class of people stuck in poverty".[30]

Human societies compel most of their members to work, to produce the goods and services that sustain the community. Societies define work their members must do and the conditions under which they must do it. Only the American class system uses the underclass to provide competition to the working class so that they perform their assigned tasks under basic reproducible conditions. The underclass are treated in such degrading and punitive ways as to instill fear in the working class of the fate that awaits them should they relapse into beggary and pauperization. For the working class the fear of ending up on "the welfare" with the accompanying cruelties and indignities makes any job at any wage a preferable alternative. The issue is not the relative merit of work itself; it is rather how the working class can be made to work for the least reward.[31]

The role of the underclass in disciplining the working class has been historically recognized by the American class system. If the underclass was allowed to subsist without pain or stigma, why would the working class have worked? Bernard Mandeville in his famous *Fable of the Bees* warned that the working class laborers "have nothing to stir them up to be serviceable but their wants, which it is prudence to relieve but folly to cure." The original Poor Law of 1601 in England required service in a workhouse—deliberately designed to be unpleasant and degrading to discourage dependence and enforce wage labor. One member of the Poor Law Commission wrote, "I wish to see the Poor House looked to with dread by our laboring class, and the reproach for being an inmate extend downward from father to son . . .".[32]

The virtual identification of blacks with the underclass acts as a lightning rod for the frustrations and hostilities of the working class. Blacks are frequently used to perform the dirtiest dead-end jobs, partially mitigating a potential source of working class frustration and resentment against the class system.[33]

A dispassionate cost benefit analysis of the underclass is a revealing testimony of the American class system. It has been estimated that it would cost an additional one percent of the GNP to close the poverty gap, the difference between what the underclass now has (including existing income transfers) and what they need to maintain minimum standards of living. There are even more efficacious ways of eliminating the underclass. But in reality the costs of maintaining the underclass are minimal while the benefits to the ruling class are enormous. The benefits of the underclass are so overwhelming that the shepherds would have had to create one if it did not exist.[34]

The shepherds have a clear strategy for creating and controlling the underclass. The strategy unfolded in the development of the Full Employment Act, the minimum wage laws and programs for Aid to Families with Dependent Children (AFDC). Each of these programs is couched in idealistic terms which cannot be enforced and is subject to bureaucratic and judicial interpretation, giving the shepherds the levers of control. The sheep have been constantly deluded by the passage of laws with noble preambles and well-meaning presidential proclamations which were not enforceable and intended to leave the festering problems alone.[35]

The debate about the creation of the contemporary underclass started with President Franklin D. Roosevelt's State of the Union Address in the winter of 1935, deep into the Depression. At that time 20 million people were on public assistance in the form of direct relief—a cash dole or barely disguised "make work". Roosevelt told Congress that any form of handout sapped the morale and spirit of the unemployed:

> Continued dependence upon relief induces a spiritual and moral disintegration fundamentally destructive to the national fiber. To dole out relief in this way is to administer a narcotic,

a subtle destroyer of the human spirit . . . I am not willing that the vitality of our people be further sapped by the giving of cash, of market baskets, of a few hours of weekly work cutting grass, raking leaves or picking up papers in public parks. We must preserve not only the bodies of the unemployed from destitution but also their self-respect, their self-reliance and courage and determination.[36]

Roosevelt proposed a new public works program in place of "direct relief" that would be "useful in the sense that it affords permanent improvements in the living conditions or that it creates future new wealth for the nation". Those who could not work, the aged, the blind and the like would still get cash relief. But there would be no cash aid for Americans who were considered capable of joining the labor force. "Work must be found for the able bodied but destitute. The federal government must and shall quit this business of relief," Roosevelt declared.[37]

What FDR had outlined in his speech to Congress would be the condition of the underclass in the American class system. The solution he had proposed would destroy the class system by eliminating the underclass and its effects. This the shepherds would not tolerate. They went on the offensive. Businessmen opposed work relief because of its cost, and because any project, even ditch digging, was defined as government intrusion into competitive business. To make sure that little relief would result, the upper class fell back on a familiar ploy, insisting that relief be a local responsibility. In the end the work relief program was stymied and was soon aborted as Roosevelt gave in to the upper class.[38]

The next turning point in the underclass debate came with the end of World War II, along with war industries, and as great numbers of servicemen were returning home clamoring for jobs. There was widespread fear of unemployment during the transition to a peacetime economy. A full employment bill giving every American a right to work was introduced in Congress in 1945. If someone could not find a job, the government would be committed to finding or creating jobs for "all Americans able to work and willing to work". The shepherds retaliated to preserve the underclass. Senator Robert Taft of Ohio insisted that the term "right" be changed to "opportunity" and the word "full" be deleted from the title. That good sense had prevailed and the American class system survived was evident when Senator Taft assured his colleagues that they could vote for the final version of the Bill without qualms because "there is no full employment bill anymore".[39]

Thirty years later another challenge came from Congressman Augustus Hawkins representing the Watts district of Los Angeles, which had erupted into four days of rioting in 1965. Hawkins introduced his full employment Bill in Congress in 1974 along with Senator Hubert Humphrey, who sponsored an identical Bill in the Senate. The Humphrey–Hawkins Bill stated, "The Employment Act of 1946 is amended to declare that all Americans able, willing and seeking work have the right to useful paid employment at fair rates of compensation". It called for long-range economic planning to help people find jobs in both the private and public sectors, with the government being the employer in the last resort.[40]

The response of the shepherds was predictable. Arthur F. Burns, then head of the Federal Reserve Bank, noted in hearings on the Bill in 1975 that jobs created by the government should have wages that were, "unattractive, deliberately set that way to provide an incentive for individuals to find jobs themselves," conveniently ignoring the question how such jobs could be found when eight million Americans were out of work. It was hoped that the Bill would die of neglect. After the death of the co-sponsor, Senator Humphrey, a memorial full employment Bill was passed in 1978 after deleting the provision mandating the government as an employer in the last resort. The Act did say that Americans had a right to a job but not how it was to be enforced. Hawkins filed a nine-point indictment in the summer of 1979 against President Carter for failing to implement the Humphrey–Hawkins Act. He was silenced by benign neglect as most of the press and television stations did not bother to report his charges.[41]

The role of the minimum wage legislation in the creation of the underclass is indisputable. As an editorial in the *Wall Street Journal* stated: "Every economist knows that the minimum wage causes unemployment. The only economists that defend it are those who do so on sociological grounds". A minimum wage is an intervention in the free market for labor. If the minimum wage legislation was accompanied by a job guarantee it would provide a mooring to the workers and eliminate the underclass. As it is the minimum wage law, which does not apply to imported goods, exports jobs overseas so that there is no employment for the underclass and they remain the reserve labor army. The result is that a portion of the underclass is permanently unemployed with no provision for food and shelter or a welfare safety net. For the blacks among them who do not have access to private charity the minimum wage law is legislation for forced starvation and their basic food and shelter needs are met only in prison.[42]

Another possibility is the elimination of the minimum wage which would create a free-for-all competitive labor market for the havenots. This would result in the elimination of the boundary between the underclass and the working class and the shepherds would lose the benefits of divisive policies. They support the minimum wage law to create an underclass which offers a visible threat to the working class and blame it on the unions to camouflage the working of the class system. Originally the labor unions supported minimum wage legislation, as it helped the middle class wage structure from the bottom up. As David Smith, New York City's business development commissioner and a former aide to Senator Kennedy, explained:

When the minimum wage was 50 percent of the average manufacturing wage, as it used to be, you could really push the wage structure up from the bottom. But, when the minimum wage is now only 26 or 27 percent of the manufacturing wage and there are virtually no minimum-wage workers in factories except for the garment industry, the gap between the labor unions (middle class) and the working poor (working class) is wider. If we push up the wages of cleaning people and security guards and nursing-home attendants by $1.50 an hour, we're still not bumping up against the bottom of the industrial wage structure.

The unions have lost interest in the minimum wage level as it now does little for the wages of their membership.[43]

Aid to Families with Dependent Children (AFDC) is a logical outgrowth of the underclass which is, in turn, the fulcrum for the American class system. FDR's original aid plan was intended for families in which the breadwinner was "dead, disabled or absent". The assumption was that every able bodied person willing to work would have access to a job because direct relief was to be stopped. The old, the disabled and the widowed were to be taken care of by social security. The able bodied black and white members of the underclass and their children were left to fend for themselves. But the white underclass would get first preference in jobs and a private charity safety net controlled by tax deductible upper class contributions was created for them. The black underclass would be segregated into urban ghettos and divided into males, and females with children. It was only a matter of time before the unemployed males went to prison where they could be kept alive at minimum cost. Taking charge of prisoners would provide the middle class jobs and political and ideological benefits to the shepherds.[44]

It was not practical or cost effective to lock up black females and children. A woman, if made to starve, will in the last resort engage in prostitution. If the women are to be jailed for prostitution, who will take care of the children? Having women in prisons and children begging on the streets would batter the image of the richest country in the world. Therefore, once the essential role of the underclass has been rationalized, the AFDC program is the most cost-effective way to keep the women and children alive and make the underclass reproduce from generation to generation.

AFDC programs were made the responsibility of the states though funds were provided at the federal level to control costs. In 1960 three million people were on AFDC and it was the largest federal assistance program. For decades eligibility tests such as residence laws, man in the house rules and employed-mother rules kept costs low. Harassment of welfare recipients was commonplace. "Midnight raids" were staged to catch welfare mothers in the act of receiving "male callers," enforcing the notorious "man-in-the-house rule". Certain basic rights for the welfare recipients were created in the 1960s with the help of Office of Economic Opportunities and the National Legal Aid and Defenders Association. The rights to due process, rights to representation and protection against unlawful searches were created by court decisions and precedent. As a result the AFDC population increased from 3.1 million in 1960 to 10.8 million by 1974. The big change was in percentage of families that actually applied for and received welfare, from perhaps 33 percent in the early 1960s to more than 90 percent in 1971.[45]

Whatever the outward appearances, the shepherds have essentially created black ghettos in urban areas which violate all human rights and norms of civilization in the richest country. There is a causal relationship between the establishment of the ghettos and their effect on the black inmates. As Jared Taylor notes, an American has less than one percent chance of ending up in a ghetto if he manages to do three things: "finish high school, get and stay married and stick with a job, even a minimum wage job—for at least a year". But black ghettos are created by enforced unemployment and destruction of family life which make education a farce.[46]

One necessary condition for organizing black ghettos is racial segregation. A black person is easily identified. With a centuries-old tradition of slavery, it becomes politically convenient to enclose them in ghettos. A Berlin wall is not necessary because white security forces, historical stereotypes and unwritten rules will prevent escape from the ghetto. As Kardiner and Ovesey note, "There is no time in the life of the Negro, that he is not actively in contact with the caste situation".

Cornel West, a black intellectual, relates his experience driving through upstate New York to lecture at a New England College a few years ago. West was pulled over by a policeman who took him for a drug runner because of his flashy clothes, jewelry and sporty Camaro. When West protested that he was a professor of religion, the officer scoffed, "Yeah, and I'm the flying nun. Let's go, nigger," and hauled him to jail. It took a telephone call to the college to secure West's release. Segregation is a necessary condition for enforcing the boundary of the ghettos.[47]

Enforced unemployment which leads to loss of food and shelter is another necessary condition for black ghettos. The result, according to James Tobin, Nobel Prize-winning economist, is that:

> People who lack the capacity to earn a decent living need to be helped by minimum wage laws, trade union wage pressures, or other devices which seek to compel employers to pay them more than their work is worth. The more likely outcomes of such regulations is that the intended beneficiaries are not employed at all.[48]

How will those with no jobs and income and who have been legislated into starvation survive? Private charity is not available to blacks. There is no welfare cushion for them. Obviously they are expected to commit a crime and gain admittance to prisons. A 1965 study by the Pennsylvania Board of Parole found that 74 percent of convicted robbers were unemployed at the time of arrest. The President's Commission on Crime in the District of Columbia noted that 60 percent of adult criminal offenders had no regular history of employment, and among those employed, 90 percent earned less than $5,000 per year. A survey of research concluded that there is "a significant correlation between adult property [crime] arrests . . . and the rate of male unemployment".[49]

American prisons are concentration camps for black males. The United States in 1993 had a larger portion of its population behind the bars than any other country. Incarceration rates for the United States are three to five times higher than in other industrialized countries. Although males constitute 48 percent of the population they make up 95 percent of the prisoners. Blacks are 11 percent of the population but 48 percent of the prisoners.[50]

That American prisons are part of the class system setup is borne out by the lack of correlation with crime. As Todd R. Clear, a Rutgers University criminal justice scholar, noted, the growing prison population did not bring down the crime rate. The doubling of prisoners in the 1980s led to serious overcrowding, exacerbated by the rising number of inmates who are either classified as "habitual" criminals or serving minimum mandatory sentences. According to a legislative report in Florida, the number of prisoners classified as habitual offenders by 1996 was expected to grow to 50 percent of the prison system's current capacity.[51]

A deadly combination of guns, alcohol abuse and unemployment controls the number of black males in prisons. *The New York Times* reported that nine out of 10 Americans polled supported the Brady gun control bill but the shepherds through the National Rifle Association (NRA) have resisted all efforts to control the availability of guns. There were 37,000 deaths in 1990 from handguns alone. Guns play a special role in the ghettos. Anyone who needs a pistol for the weekend in Washington, D.C., can rent one for a few dollars. As a result the murder rate for black men between 15 and 24 rose by 68 percent and the rate for black youths between 15 and 19 doubled in the same period. One out of every 1,000 black men—10 times the number of whites in the same age bracket—is doomed to a violent death each year. Robert Broehlke, principal author of the Centers for Disease Control in Atlanta study, noted, "It is now more likely for a black male between his 15th and 24th birthdays to die from homicide than it was for a U.S. soldier to be killed on a tour of duty in Vietnam". Adele Harrell, a researcher at the Urban Institute in Washington, says, "you have a lot of weapons on the street, and on the street, violence is the standard way to settle a dispute".[52]

The ghettos makes normal civilized life impossible. Residents of the District of Columbia in 1988 and 1989 were more likely to be killed than people living in El Salvador, Northern Ireland, Kashmir, or even Lebanon. Some ghetto children start carrying guns by the time they are 10. In Detroit, which is 74 percent black, 365 children under age 16 were shot by other children in 1986—an average of one child a day. In New York City, crimes in schools against teachers were up 25 percent the first half of the 1989 school year. Violent crimes against elementary school teachers were up 54 percent. There was an increase of 15 percent in rape arrest for boys under 18 from 1983 to 1987.[53]

Malt liquor in 40-ounce bottles, with the promise of more alcohol for less money, lubricates the unendurable stress of living in ghettos. In 1991, Heilman Brewing came under fire from civil rights organization after introducing Power Master, its most powerful malt liquor at 5.9 percent alcohol, and targeting black drinkers. Later Heilman aimed at the young black consumers with an advertising campaign for Colt 45, linking black success with malt liquor. The 40-ounce bottle was introduced in the mid-'80s as a "retailer and consumer convenience", according to Ron Richards, a spokesman for the Miller Brewing Company. The industry took advantage of impoverished youngsters in search of a cheap high. According to Takani Thaemba, a public policy specialist for the Marin Institute for the prevention of alcohol and other drug problems, teenagers in poor neighborhoods now see malt liquor as alternative to drugs. Drinking a 40-ounce bottle of malt liquor for breakfast enroute to school was not unusual, said a Bronx teenager, and guzzling 40 ounces for intoxication is a major attraction at "hooky parties". Officially the shepherds are for a drug-free America but do not mind keeping the ghetto inmates sedated but alive.[54]

When black males in the ghettos have no jobs and are expected to go to prison, black families and marriages do not happen. What a reporter noted at a Chicago housing project is not surprising: "Most of the inhabitants said they had never been to a wedding. Several said they did not even know any married people".[55]

Black women can fend off starvation with the AFDC and food stamps programs. To obtain food and shelter they, however, have to bear children. There is one catch in the strategy. In 1986 an average AFDC family of one adult and two children was allotted $382 per month to meet their needs along with $228 per month in food stamps. There are no cost of living increases for AFDC allowances and they depend on the number of children in the household, which must not have an able bodied responsible male. Therefore, to make ends meet for food and shelter the ghetto women is forced into single motherhood and the role of a broodmare as during slavery before the Civil War.[56]

The female camp inmates have to engage in prostitution to survive and drugs to endure the pain of being mothers by the time they are 16, grandmothers when 32 and so on. Once the ghetto inmates are hooked to drugs, succeeding generations of crack or alcoholic babies get a head start in the ghetto culture. From 1985 to 1990 in New York State, crack addicted parents produced 467,000 children. Dr. Judy Howard of UCLA estimates that 40 to 60 percent of the students in ghetto classrooms will eventually be crack children.[57]

Ideology and Answers

The American class system is trying to conceal that there is a dual labor market in America. One part of it is the middle class whose votes are essential for the shepherds. The other is the working class who are kept at the basic, replacement level.

This denies the working class basic needs while insecurity results in a lack of human capital investment in the working class, destabilizing the family and denying basic preventive health care and education. The United Nations Human Development Report of 1993, with a Human Development Index based on life expectancy, educational standards and individual purchasing power, placed the United States sixth with Japan topping the list. Even this listing averaged the conditions of the working and middle classes. What it did not reveal was that 50 percent of the American population cannot earn an income needed to make choices because it contradicts the basic goal of the American class system.[58]

The shepherds paint the American unions in scary colors, though only 17 percent of the labor force is unionized and the unions can operate within strict limits. Most of the unionized workers are middle class. The working class and underclass have no institution to represent them and the economy is a gangup of the haves against the havenots.[59]

A way out of this dilemma is to provide the havenots with a voice. This could restore the system of checks and balances which is essential for the long-term survival of the economy. As surveys have shown, the working class wants to be represented by a union contract and wages. If their wishes are respected the unions could represent a majority of the workforce. Once this happens, the upper class cannot ride piggyback on the majority. A voice for all, where all groups sink or swim together in the global economy, can temper the demands of individual factions for long-term gain and stability. Though the destination of unions is clear, reaching there is another matter.[60]

The answer to the underclass problem, if it is considered a problem, has been known and attempts made to implement it since the Depression. The general population recognizes that minimum wage laws without guaranteeing jobs is a prescription for forced unemployment and starvation. Consider the following poll results:

A. It has been proposed that instead of relief and welfare payments, the government should guarantee every family a minimal annual income. Do you favor or oppose this idea?

Favor 19%   Oppose 67%   No opinion 14%
                              –(Gallup, 1965)

B. At a time when work is hard to find, the only human thing to do is to give the unemployed productive jobs so their families can eat.

Favor 93%   Oppose —   No opinion —
                                –(Harris, 1975)

C. When people can't find any jobs, would you be in
favor of the government putting them on the payroll
and finding work for them such as helping out in hospitals or cleaning public parks or would you be against
this idea.

Favor 89%   Oppose 8%   No opinion 3%
                                –(Gallup, 1972)

It has been known since the time of FDR that the economically efficient and human solution to eliminating the
underclass is to provide jobs for those willing and able to
work. The shepherds have opposed the solution for centuries.
The first task of upper class ideology is to make sure that the
subject of jobs for all is generally omitted from discussions.[61]
Providing a false choice is another ideological defense. The
way to reform the welfare mess, get rid of the black ghettos
and eliminate poverty is providing a minimum guaranteed
income or a negative income tax. It would only cost two
percent of the GNP to end poverty in America. Nixon suggested such a family assistance program in 1971 and President Ford in 1974 under the guise of welfare reform. Providing
a minimum guaranteed income for the underclass when the
shepherds are not even ready to provide a guaranteed job for
them is a hoax. A guaranteed minimum income for the
underclass is a false choice if the working class which constitutes 40 percent of the population is forced to work at a basic
reproducible level. For this, according to the Gallup poll cited
earlier, 67 percent of Americans opposed guaranteed minimum incomes for the underclass. This provides the shepherds
with the excuse not to implement the welfare reform proposal.
By floating the minimum guaranteed income idea periodically

the shepherds and their think tanks execute a masterful ideological stroke because it focuses attention on trivia and prevents discussion about guaranteed jobs.[62]

Another line of argument is that there are plenty of jobs but the lazy underclass is not interested in work. In a January 1982 press conference Ronald Reagan said he found pages of help wanted advertisements in the Sunday newspapers. Systematic studies of unemployment advertisements for New York State found that 85 percent of the positions required college training or special skills. For the remaining 1,305 "entry level" openings, 29,136 people applied. If jobs were going a begging it would be less expensive to guarantee jobs to anybody willing and able to work rather than provide welfare. But the cheapest solution is to have the media deny the nonavailability of jobs. The middle class voters who have jobs then believe and act on the message. Even in the middle of the recession in January 1976, *Business Week* ran an article entitled "A Million Jobs With No Takers" and *The New York Times* reported that "jobs, skilled and unskilled, go begging in many cities".[63]

Disinformation molds the middle class voters' opinion. According to a Harris Poll in the mid-1970s some 42 percent of the Americans agreed with the notion that "if people really wanted they can find jobs". The poll indicated the enduring strength of the notion among the haves that there are "plenty of jobs in the want ads" for anyone seriously seeking work. An unskilled worker with a high school education who scanned the want ads in Atlanta in June 1976 did find some 805 jobs being offered. Of the 518 non-sales jobs advertised that day, fully 486 required education or several years' experience. Overall 85 percent of the jobs were beyond the job seekers' reach. In fact, any job which the underclass can perform has been exported overseas and the remaining few can be so easily filled that they need no advertising.[64]

As a last resort, the shepherds play the game of blaming the victims, accusing the underclass of lacking in family values. This is the "Flawed Character" argument which appeals directly to the middle class voter psyche. If the poor are poor because of innate flaw in their characters, the middle class must have superior values which justify their position and privileges. To deny the flawed character argument is tantamount to questioning the status of the middle and upper classes.[65]

For this reason George Bush tried to blame the condition of the underclass on the lack of family values in the 1992 presidential election. The idea is to pin responsibility on the ghetto inmates for choosing a lifestyle of welfare cheating, drug abuse, crime, single motherhood, prostitution and violence. The middle class voters believe this and credibility is reinforced with media polls which accept and promote the reality of the American class system. The *Wall Street Journal* reported that "Americans feel families and values are eroding" but they disagree over the causes and solutions. To the question "Are social and economic problems that face America mainly the result of a decline in moral values, or mainly the result of financial pressures and strains on the family?" 45 percent agreed with financial pressures and 43 percent chose decline in moral values. This indicates that the middle class agrees with the ideology of the shepherds.[66]

Once ideology has been set apart what is the answer to the underclass riddle? It has been around for centuries. In the late 1790s the town of Hamburg initiated a public works program designed (in the words of Baron Kaspar Von Vought, the chief author of the scheme), "to prevent any man from securing a shilling which he was able to earn himself . . . for if the manner in which relief is given is not spur to industry, it becomes undoubtedly a premium to sloth and profligacy". To deter profligacy while dealing with vagrancy, the respectable citizens of Hamburg decided that, "six-sevenths of our poor being women and children" they should be set to work spinning flax in their homes. Men and boys were to make rope, clean streets, or mend roads. Relief payments were deliberately kept below market wages. "It was our determined principle, to reduce the support lower than what industrious man or woman could earn . . ." the Baron wrote. Finally he could report: "For the last seven years . . . hardly a beggar has been seen in Hamburg . . . We not only did much toward the relief of the poor, but . . . we gained some steps toward the more desirable, yet but slowly attainable, end, the preventing some of the causes of poverty".[67]

In 1992, Mickey Kaus proposed the guaranteed job solution for every able bodied person willing and able to work. All welfare programs of assistance in cash or in kind would be replaced by an offer of employment for every adult in a useful public job at a wage slightly below the minimum wage for private sector work. These jobs would be available to everyone, men as well as women, single or married, mothers and fathers alike without qualification. There would be no need to target the program for the poor or needy. The low wage itself would guarantee that those who took the jobs would be those who needed them, while preserving the incentive to look for better work in the private sector. With this system there would be no incentive for bearing unwanted children. Individuals would prefer birth control so that their earnings can be spent in meeting personal needs. In the long run the economy would benefit by investing in the human capital of the underclass for greater productivity.[68]

Yet the eminently sensible solution provokes the shepherds' ire because it will shake the foundation of the American class system. But the emerging global economy will put an end to the isolation of the American class system. This now requires an understanding of the operation of monopoly and free markets in the American economy.

CHAPTER 6

MONOPOLY AND FREE MARKETS

Heads I win, tails you lose.–**The Monopoly Motto**

People from the same trade seldom meet together, even for merriment and diversion, but the conversation ends in conspiracy against the public or in some contrivance to raise prices.–**Adam Smith**[1]

All amassing of wealth or hoarding of wealth above and beyond one's legitimate needs is theft. There would be no occasion for theft and no thieves if there was wise regulation of wealth and social justice.–**M.K. Gandhi**[2]

The market needs a place and the market needs to be kept in its place.–**Arthur M. Okun**[3]

The mere amassing of wealth is one of the worst species of idolatry.–**Andrew Carnegie**[4]

Early in 1962 Robert F.Kennedy, then Attorney General in his brother's administration, travelled around the world as a good-will ambassador of sorts for the United States. On his return he addressed the annual luncheon of the Associated Press. In his talk, printed in *The New York Times* of April 24, he related an incident:

I was introduced in Indonesia to another large student body and a boy at the end of my speech got up and asked a question. In the course of this question he described the United States as a system of monopolistic capitalism. And when he said that expression, half the student body applauded.

So I said, "Well, now, I'd like to find out. I am a representative of the United States here. What is it that you mean by monopolistic capitalism?"

And he had no answer. And I said "Well, now, anybody who clapped, anybody who applauded when this gentleman used that expression—what is it that you understand by monopolistic capitalism." And not one of them would come forward.[5]

If Kennedy thought that the refusal of his audience to debate the subject of monopoly capitalism indicated ignorance about it, he was sadly mistaken. Students in underdeveloped countries have seen the ugliest face of monopolistic capitalism and suffered the consequences of its policies in their own lives. If Kennedy had lived until the 1990s he would have been able to see for himself the results of monopoly capitalism in America.

Monopoly capitalism describes one facet of the American class system. The shepherds basically want monopoly control for themselves, while competition and free markets are directed at the sheep. The idea is that the shepherds should control most of the productive assets along with the savings. The shepherds have institutionalized monopoly in the American economy.

Purpose and Objectives

A prime objective of the American class system is to ensure upper class ownership and control over most of the nation's productive wealth. Most of the country's productive wealth is held by private and publicly traded corporations. The upper class owns 83 percent of corporate stock and 93 percent of nonincorporated business assets in America. Though the rest is owned by the middle class they are insignificant and tied in pension funds and financial institutions which are controlled by the upper class. The upper class thus controls the supply of goods and services in the economy while the sheep are consumers who supply their labor.[6]

The class system makes use of the monopoly and free market concepts. Shepherds control the income of the sheep by forcing them to exchange their labor in a competitive market. The upper class has developed a monopoly market to control the prices of consumer goods. The combined interaction of the income received by the sheep and what they have to pay for consumption gives the shepherds control over the distribution of savings and wealth for the nation.

All the savings due to increased productivity, technological advance or sale of mineral resources flow into upper class pockets. Robert Kuttner confirms this in *Business Week*: "As everybody knows, rich people own a disproportionate share of the nation's total savings supply—since the poor consume most of what they earn. Only the well-off save and invest a large fraction of their incomes". John Kenneth Galbraith explains the savings outcome in another way:

> The small volume of saving by the average man (middle class), and its absence among the lower-income masses (working class), reflect faithfully the role of the individual in the planning system (class system) and the accepted view of his function. The individual serves the planning system (class system) not by supplying it with savings and the resulting capital; he serves it far more by consuming its products.[7]

Once the nation's savings are concentrated in the hands of the upper class, their objective is to control the investment and flow of the savings. The first step is to maximize reserves for depreciation which remain under the direct control of the corporations and also count them as costs of doing business, reducing the earnings on which taxes are based. Investment tax credits are also used to reduce taxes. After minimizing taxes the upper class wants to retain most of the earnings for investment and only pay a part as dividends. Retained earnings remain concentrated and under the direct control of the upper class to be invested when and where convenient.

Another upper class objective is to control the funds paid as taxes, the idea being to get back what was paid to the government. This is done by diverting resources to defense spending, which is ideal for getting the money back from the government because it is intrinsically protected from competition and shrouded in secrecy. This game was played to the hilt in the 1980s when the Reagan administration was borrowing money to pay for defense. For the year 1992 corporate taxes amounted to $89 billion compared to $313 billion in military spending. The upper class could get more money back than what was paid in corporate taxes and then lend it back to the federal government as federal deficit and earn interest.[8]

Investment of savings in retained earnings directly under upper class control must meet certain objectives. Most important among these is the return on investment. If the rate of profit drops due to saturation of the local market the investment is directed overseas to achieve higher returns. The transfer of American technology and jobs overseas is overlooked.

Another important upper class investment objective is risk avoidance. If technological change or any other reason makes a product or mode of production obsolete it is best to write it off, thus reducing the taxes owed to the government. In effect, the sheep bear the losses for all mistakes or oversights caused by the shepherds. However, all profits accrue to the latter; it works out as a game of "heads I win, tails you lose".[9]

Along with risk reduction another upper class objective is portfolio diversification. It is pointless taking risks with individual companies or industries. To preserve their capital the upper class looks for a market return which keeps pace with inflation. Return on investment and security of capital is better protected with a shared monopoly rather than competition between companies in the same industry or between industries.[10]

Monopoly is a dirty word according to classical economics. In theory it leads to inefficiency and waste and misallocation of resources. When the American economy consists of hundreds of companies in different industries, the only way to achieve a monopoly economy is to institutionalize the ground rules so that the objectives of the shepherds are met.[11]

Institutional Monopoly and Control

Pure monopoly control of the economy is undesirable because it would reveal two sets of rules, competitive market rules for the sheep and monopoly rules for the shepherds. If the shepherds adopted free market competition rules for themselves the upper class would lose control over the distribution of wealth. The way out is to have institutionalized monopoly control of the economy while giving the appearance of competition. In the end it is like giving a choice of three television news channels while presenting identical news and sometimes with the same commercial being shown on more than one channel at the same time.

It is not difficult to set up an institutional monopoly control system because the upper class has common shared goals. All the individual players know that monopoly best achieves their goals and that they could never match the results by individual performance contests. They also know that individuals cannot manage the economy and the government, including regulation, defense spending, and foreign policy, on their own. The class system ensures that individuals are handsomely rewarded and protected in line with the responsibility given to them.

If an individual player steps out of line despite the careful grooming and selection process, the institutional control system can hasten his removal because the game of monopoly is inherently illegal and against national interest. The system can operate only by understanding the unwritten rules of the monopoly game, which are learnt by experience and training and not by what they teach in business schools.

The foundation of institutional monopoly control is based on the rule of thumb that though pure monopoly is illegal, shared monopoly, that is oligopoly, is acceptable. This means that a small set of companies, the big three or big five, dominate the direction and decisions for the particular industry, sharing the revenues and profits. Galbraith has noted, "The power exercised by a few large firms is different only in degree and precision of its exercise from that of the single-firm monopoly. If they compete with one another they do so less in terms of price than in terms of 'product development', advertising and packaging". Explicitly or implicitly major decisions are made taking into account the concerns of individual members. There is no need for an overt conspiracy and certainly none that can be proved. Decisions are made by individual producers based on their perception of the reaction of other producers and the ground rules of institutional monopoly. The institutional guidelines are provided by the board of directors and the managements are familiar with them.[12]

Standard economics books note that there is not much difference between monopolistic and oligopolistic economies:

> Oligopoly suffers from being particularly rigid and unresponsive to market conditions. They are also particularly compelled to dissipate economic resources in advertising and in meretricious variations in product characteristics . . . The prevalence of monopoly and oligopoly is a serious defect in the free market system of organizing economic activity.

Professor Paul Samuelson notes:

> The economic evils of [oligopoly and other market imperfections] transcend the mere matter of monopolistic profits . . . monopolistic and oligopolistic pricing . . . brings distortion of resource allocation (inefficiency and nonresponsiveness) even if the firms involved have their excess profits taxed or competed away . . . To reduce imperfections of competition, a nation must maintain perpetual vigilance.

The message is loud and clear. Whatever the textbooks might say, what is inefficient for monopolies is efficient for oligopolies. Therefore, in the case of oligopolies, because of precedent, the antitrust laws will be circumvented.[13]

The industrial concentration in the American economy is striking. Four firms accounted for more than half of the sales in the iron and steel industry. In copper, three firms accounted for 65 percent of sales; in aluminum a similar number produced 90 percent. Automobile production was dominated by three firms; the production of heavy electrical equipment by two, and aircraft by three, while computers, photographic equipment, and telephone equipment were produced by virtual monopolies. Three or four firms produced the majority of petroleum products, chemicals, drugs, soaps, dairy products, cereals and soups.[14]

In a traditional competitive market the producer is supposed to adjust his production and operations in response to the price, which is determined by competition among the suppliers of the product. With institutional monopoly the producer of goods is not a "price taker" but a "price maker". The price is determined in a way that after allocating funds for cost, depreciation, taxes, and dividend payouts enough is left for new investments. Not only does institutional monopoly allow the upper class to dictate prices but also to collect them from the consumers. Income this way is transferred from the sheep to the shepherds.[15]

Setting prices in theory would be considered illegal. If a firm could dictate prices then by definition its market share is monopolistic and it would be broken up on antitrust grounds. This is where the invisible arm of institutional monopoly intervenes and provides immunity to individual firms. A *Business Week* article described the basic approach of large corporations:

> The traditional model for pricing by large industrial corporations was codified in the management system introduced at General Motors by Alfred P. Sloan in the 1920's. Pricing was essentially static. Companies set a price that they believed

would provide a desired long run "target rate of return" at a given production volume. Although management was obviously forced to deviate from this pricing ideal by competition, the aim nevertheless was to create a pricing structure that was programmed to change gradually and predictably and to stick to it. Even though price-cutting occurred at the fringes of the market, the corporate establishment looked on it with disdain, as "chiseling" and sometimes disciplined the offender.[16]

In the case of GM, an impressive 19.3 percent rate of return was achieved during the postwar period compared to a target of 20 percent established by Sloan himself. This was substantially higher than the average rate of return of about 12 percent and there was talk of breaking GM into a large number of competing firms. But institutional monopoly made sure that GM would never be in serious danger because, "What is good for GM is good for America".[17]

What is true of the auto industry also holds good in other segments. "The endless manoeuvering for leadership position between Ford and General Motors is an almost classic instance of competition within oligopoly. Somewhat the same situation prevails in the electrical field where General Electric and Westinghouse are continuously in tacit agreement and continuously at war". Instead of price competition the individual firms are permitted to engage in sale promotion: advertising, variation of the products appearance and packaging, "planned obsolescence", model changes, credit schemes, and the like. The net result is reduced uncertainty and risk for the producers and consumers have to pay distribution costs which amount to 35 to 40 percent of the average prices of commodities sold at retail.[18]

A major source of risk and uncertainty for the upper class producers is worker demands and unions disrupting corporate plans. Institutional monopoly has been successful in dividing and segmenting the labor force and setting up procedures and precedents that make the unions impotent as a strike force. The labor force was first divided into two groups: those engaged directly in the monopolistic core of giant corporations and those working outside. Another division was achieved for the core group by industry-wise segmentation so that there was no interaction and cooperation between unions in different industries. Within industries more divisions were created between professional, skilled and unskilled workers. When convenient, race hostility was stirred up to deflect class conflicts into race conflict. During critical periods, some 30,000 to 40,000 blacks were imported as strikebreakers in a matter of weeks. The net result was, "The unionism that emerged was a mosaic of selfish sectional-minded groups, loosely organized in a relatively weak federation, hostile to the state, wedded to collective bargaining as the exclusive method of change, and frankly predicated upon a permanent acceptance of the capitalistic order".[19.]

The masterful stroke of institutional monopoly was the Taft–Hartley Act of 1947, which put the unions on a tight leash. Key provisions of the Bill were drafted with inputs from the Brookings Institution, The National Association of Manufacturers and the Twentieth Century Fund. Even the Wagner Act of 1934 which legitimized unions created the National Labor Relations Board (NLRB) as the arbitrator of conflicts between unions and management. The government, through the appointments made to the NLRB by the President, could shift power between labor and management. The result is that union membership has declined to less than 20 percent of the labor force in the 1990s. Unions are unable to organize new members to replace those lost. Every year before 1974 more than half the representation elections were won by unions. Their winning percentage dropped year by year to 44 percent in 1982. Even where unions have won the right to bargain, an AFL-CIO study shows that one-third of the elections have not resulted in a signed contract five years after workers have voted for a union. In the 1980s decertification elections to eliminate a union were on the rise and successful in three tries out of four.[20]

The institutional monopoly strategy for labor peace is to allow workers in oligopolistic companies to unionize by industry, so that the wage gains and benefits for all the companies are coordinated and synchronized. The producers can recover the increased costs by passing them on to customers as increased prices. As each oligopolistic industry is a "price maker" recovery of the increased cost are assured. The net sufferers in the plan are the working class and other wage earners who are not unionized and lack economic leverage. This basic formula was worked out in negotiations between the UAW and GM and has been in force since 1948.[21]

When the negotiations began the war time price controls were still in effect and President Truman's executive order prohibited any wage increase. Walter Reuther, president of the UAW, saw this as an opportunity to make company's prices and profits a part of collective bargaining. As a transcript of the negotiation reads:

> REUTHER: We are prepared to settle this demand for less than 30%, provided you can disprove our contention that wages can be increased 30% without increasing prices and you can still make a profit. If you can prove that we can't get 30%, hold prices, and still make a nice profit, we will settle for less than 30%.

The response from General Motors was blunt:

> COHEN: (Howard Cohen, assistant director of personnel for General Motors) Why don't you get down to your size and get down to the type of job you're supposed to be doing as a trade union leader and talk about money you would like to have for your people and let the labor statesmanship go to hell for a while . . . It's none of your damn business what GM does about prices.[22]

After a long strike resulting from the impasse President Truman pulled the rug from under Reuther by allowing steel companies to raise their prices in order to pass on the cost of a wage settlement in an equally bitter dispute in their industry. In the precedent setting settlement General Motors agreed to maintain the standard of living for union members with a stable pattern of wage increases while the union would not challenge its right to maintain the target rate of return. Ultimately the UAW would help the auto oligopoly with pattern bargaining and synchronized contracts and institutional monopoly would hold the unions responsible for all the ills befalling the industry.[23]

The playing field for all the companies must be level for a successful institutional monopoly and the industry itself must write the rules and interpret them. The shepherds "Did not merely pervert or take over the regulatory agencies— they planned and developed them as an alternative to public ownership, destructive competition, and uneven state regulation". According to Michael Parenti, institutional monopoly regulation:

> limits entry into a market, subsidises select industries, sets production standards that only big companies can meet, weakens smaller competitors, and encourages monopoly pricing. This kind of regulation has long been the rule in agribusiness, telecommunications, energy, oil, drug, rail and (until recently) trucking and airline industries.

The entire regulatory infrastructure was constructed in response to the needs and demands of the business community.[24]

Independent regulatory commissions make quasi-judicial rulings against which the only appeals can be in courts. Regulatory laws are written in a way that often everything is negotiable in the fine print. By substituting tentative declarations of intent for clear guidelines the meaning of the laws can be corrupted with changing targets and goals, acceptable tolerances and negotiated exceptions, discretionary enforcement and discretionary compliance. The corporations can choose which laws they want to honor. The cost of circumventing a law is often quite modest compared to that of compliance. What looks like a legal contest on the surface is really a political struggle. William D. Ruckelshaus, first administrator of the Environmental Protection Agency in 1971, described the continuing uncertainty of law he found when he returned to the job in 1983:

When I came back to EPA, I hadn't been in office twenty four hours when I was sued three times. I asked the general counsel to study it and he found that 85 percent of the decisions made by the EPA administrator that are appealable were appealed. Each case takes three to five years to work out in court and the way it's worked out is a settlement negotiated between the industry and the environmentalists with the government sitting on the sidelines as an arbitrator.[25]

It is a generally accepted principle that regulatory commissions will promote and protect the industries they have been established to regulate. This is understandable because some industries, including the radio industry, the airlines, the railroad and trucking industries, and the oil companies have actively sought regulation. When abolition of the Interstate Commerce Commission was proposed a few years after it was established the U.S. Attorney General wrote to a railroad president:

> The Commission . . . is, or can be made, of great use to the railroads. It satisfies the popular clamor for a government supervision of railroads, at the same time that the supervision is almost entirely nominal. Further the older such commission gets to be, the more inclined it will be found to take the business and railroad view of things.

Industry organizations strongly support their respective regulatory agencies. *Railway Age* in 1948 noted that transportation "has a natural tendency to become monopolistic and that the only sensible policy for government is to recognize this [and] regulate accordingly". The Interstate Commerce Commission continues to serve the railroad companies; the Federal Communications Commission is devoted to telephone companies and the media networks; the Federal Elections Commissions safeguards the two-party monopoly; the Food and Drug Administration is more interested in protecting the profits of the food and drug companies than in the health of the people; the Securities and Exchange Commission regulates the stock markets mostly for the benefit of large investors.[26]

Institutional monopoly control spreads its reach to other units of government. The modus operandi is exemplified by the Business Advisory Council which was formed in 1933. Officially the council was to advise the Department of Commerce and its membership was restricted to 60 active members predominantly drawn from large corporations. The Celler Committee investigating the BAC in 1955 observed that among the active and graduate members of the Council at that time:

> were representatives from 2 of the 4 largest rubber manufacturers, 3 of the 5 largest automobile manufacturers, 3 of the 10 largest steel producers, 4 of 10 largest companies in the chemical field, 2 of the 3 largest manufacturers of electrical equipment, 2 of the 3 largest manufacturers of textiles, 4 of the 16 largest oil companies and 3 of the largest manufacturers.

Usually, the representatives for the firms were board chairmen or presidents.[27]

The Council met six times a year in Washington or exotic locales and the expenses were met by private contributions. It was customary for senior government officials to attend these meetings and discuss important public policy with the Council. The press and uninvited members of the public were excluded because officials presented confidential advance economic information at such meetings. Apart from the meetings, BAC prepared reports on important topics of public policy such as labor policy, foreign trade, manpower mobilization, monetary policy, fiscal policy and antitrust policy. Most of the reports were not made public. One of the important functions of BAC was to recommend men to serve the government, including two or three Assistant Secretaries of Defense.[28]

The majority of the Celler Committee saw through such activities of BAC as a means of avoiding constraints of the antitrust laws. In 1961 when Ralph J. Cordiner of General Electric was the Chairman of BAC his firm was indicted for price fixing in the electrical industry. Given this criticism the

Secretary of Commerce suggested changes in the Councils's operation so that it became an independent body, changed its name to Business Council and took the office space outside the Department of Commerce. However, the same group of top business leaders continued to have the service of the same staff, which they continued to pay, and benefitted from the same access to the same government officials. As noted by the Celler Committee, "its advice and recommendations do reach into the farthest confines of Washington's bureaucratic structure". Essentially institutional monopoly had created a directorate of big business effectively controlling the economic policy of the nation.[29]

Advertising and sale promotion expenditures have a special role in controlling entry of new firms into the market and protecting the existing market shares. The role of advertising has been understood as that of hidden persuaders. But in a mature institutional monopoly economy advertising expenses are a fixed percentage of the sales price and included in the "price making" of the product. Therefore, shelf space and distribution of a product is controlled by the advertising budget. Any new entry to the market is discouraged because of their inability to meet the advertising budget of the existing products. The actual merit of the products or their competitive features are of secondary importance, if they cannot be ignored completely. Advertising has become an integral part of the corporations' profit maximization policy and serves at the same time as a formidable wall protecting monopolistic positions. An advertising agency noted that for many a corporate enterprise advertising expenditures are "a must for survival".[30]

It is a basic assumption of institutional monopoly that the prices should be set so that after costs, taxes, dividends have been paid there is enough for new investments or for replacing worn and obsolete machines. Most large companies have a target dividend rate around 50 percent which remains constant over long periods of time. Even when profits rise, the earnings are allowed to stabilize at a higher level for several years before the dividend payout is increased. The system minimizes the taxes paid by the shepherds. Retained earnings can directly go into investment without the need to pay taxes on dividends. The stockholders still benefit from the retained earnings because the price of the stock goes up and if necessary stock can be sold to meet individual requirements. When the stock is sold only capital gains taxes need to be paid, which is an additional incentive for stockholders.[31]

From an institutional monopoly control point of view each firm is guaranteed funds for survival and expansion and there is very little transfer of savings between firms or between industries. Firms almost always reinvest their internal funds and seldom make long-term loans or invest in other firms. This framework provides security to individual firms whose management has a well defined turf and does not need to worry about competitive attacks from other firms. The message for the management of individual firms is that cooperation within the monopolistic framework is more rewarding than inter-industry rivalry. Driving home the point further, individual managers are allowed to diversify their personal portfolios and need only token ownership of stock in the companies they manage. The managers are guaranteed high salaries and benefits even when individual firms show losses in the short run so that they go along with the system. In the end institutional monopoly rewards the shepherds at the expense of the sheep and inefficiency of the total economy.[32]

Institutional monopoly control constantly reduces risk for the shepherds so that they come out as winners. This is primarily achieved through the corporate income tax, which is a fudge factor to be included in the calculations when prices are determined. If equipment becomes obsolete or losses result from bad management decisions, the convention is to write off the losses for tax purposes, which in turn will reduce the income tax to be paid.

The use of accelerated depreciation and investment tax credits help distort economic realities. In the 1980s for example, the connection between accelerated depreciation deduction and the "useful life" of business plant and machinery was completely broken. A fictitious depreciation formula was created with 10 year write-off for buildings, five years for machinery, and three years for light equipment such as automobiles, known as 10–5–3. This resulted in a cut in corporate income taxes by more than $50 billion a year for the deep pockets of the shepherds. The process was shrouded in capital formation ideology as explained by Charlie Walker to the Senate Finance Committee on October 22, 1979:

> Mr. Chairman, nothing demonstrates more vividly just how far the country and Congress have come in the capital formation movement than to cast our minds back to the early 1970's and ask: How would the proposal for 10–5–3 have been received at that time? In all probability, it would have been subjected to extreme criticism and even ridicule. Tax purists would have attacked the scuttling of the useful life concept with respect to capital cost recovery as heresy. The static revenue cost would have brought forth forecasts of huge increases in Federal deficit. And the whole exercise would have been castigated as a "Fat Cat" plot to provide a "bonanza" for business by further "stacking" the Federal tax system in favor of the rich and against the poor. The fact only a few voices are now raised in objection to 10–5–3 testifies to the great progress that has been made.

The experience of the 1980s demonstrates that the upholders of institutional monopoly control knew exactly what they were up to.[33]

Once institutional monopoly control has created a mechanism for orderly transfer of savings to each individual firm for investment and minimized business risk for the shepherds, the stock market is needed only to distribute liquid wealth and as a channel for distributing income whose accumulation for capital purposes is not required. This way individual upper class members can spend their dividends or sell their shares according to their own personal needs and requirements. Dr. Paul Harbrecht summarizes the operation of institutional monopoly control:

We have evolved a new wealth-holding and wealth-circulating system whose liquidity is maintained through the exchanges but is only psychologically connected with the capital gathering and capital application system on which productive industry and enterprise actually depend. If this is the fact, one effect of the corporate system has been to set up a parallel, circulating "property wealth" system in which the wealth flows from passive wealth-holder to passive wealth-holder, without significantly furthering the functions of capital formation, capital application, capital use or risk bearing.[34]

Institutional monopoly control also spreads its tentacles in corporate pension funds. By awarding shares to the middle class employees in the form of retirement pensions, the shepherds create the myth of widely dispersed stock ownership while concentrating control, both through their own blocks of stock and the domination of pension funds. Instead of treating the pension funds at arms length as a fiduciary responsibility, the rules are framed for maximum flexibility and manipulation by the shepherds. By 1989 the $1.1 trillion in private pension funds and $727 billion in public pension funds represented the largest unregulated, untaxed pools of capital in the nation. Managers may invest the money almost anywhere they choose. The pension funds are not fully funded. In the merger and acquisition mania of the 1980s pension plan funds were raided and in many cases followed by plant closings and elimination of jobs. From 1980 to 1987 average assets per participating worker in pension funds for Exxon and Gulf & Western Corp. were reduced by 81 percent and 70 percent after raiding.[35]

The institutional monopoly control system stages another raid on the Treasury with the shepherds pocketing the funds and the sheep contributing through taxes. The shepherds have given themselves insurance from larceny through the Pension Benefit Guaranty Corporation, which guarantees retirement payments to beneficiaries after they have met all qualification tests. According to new rules approved by Congress companies can raid pension funds to pay health insurance premiums. After the pension funds run dry the shepherds can get money from the Pension Benefit Guaranty Corp. which is keyed into the public Treasury and the sheep. A repeat performance of the savings and loan scandal and the Federal Deposit Insurance scam is assured.[36]

There is an Anti-Trust Division for appearances but institutional monopoly protects individual firms by precedent and lack of enforcement of the laws. "Despite the strength of the argument for the antitrust policy, however, it is apparent that no thoroughgoing application of it is likely or even possible". Anti-trust policy has had no bearing on concentration in the economy because two-thirds of industrial production in the United States is in the hands of the thousand largest corporations. Coordination between the companies and industries is provided by the overlap of directors. According to the Patman Committee report of the mid '60s, the top 49 banks had 768 directors who also sat on the boards of 236 of the top 500 corporations, for an average of three per corporation board. For example, Mellon National Bank and Trust Company of Pittsburgh with $7.6 billion in trust assets was on the board of 21 major corporations with 74 interlocking directorships. To circumvent the Clayton Anti-Trust Act's restriction on interlocking directorship in the same field of production, Morgan Guaranty brings together the major automobile companies and commercial airlines. Further the big banks, insurance companies and financial institutions have interlocks amongst themselves. Chemical Bank of New York as an example had ties with 12 other banks, 13 insurance companies and 10 other financial institutions.[37]

Institutional monopoly has helped the concentration of capital with the merger process. Large scale merger movement began at the turn of the century, was pushed further in the 1920s and witnessed another upsurge after World War II. In 1968 there were 206 mergers involving acquired firms with assets exceeding $10 million. Of these,173 mergers were of the conglomerate type offering such reasons as immediate financial gain, tax writeoffs, integration of production and distribution, consolidation of market position, spreading of risk, getting in on cost-plus military contracts, entering a fast growing field. Diversification of risks had become necessary because the centralization process had already been carried to near monopolistic stages. The conglomeration trend peaked in the 1980s as giant companies were bought up by the supergiants. Mobil Oil purchased Montgomery Ward, Coca Cola swallowed Paramount Pictures and Texaco took over Getty Oil for $10.1 billion. The largest corporate mergers in history occurred during the 1981–85 period and some $100 billion of corporate cash resources changed hands.[38]

During the 1980s the risks were minimized for the shepherds owing to concentration, and conglomeration and institutional monopoly control proceeded to the next phase of the heads I win tails you lose game. The corporations were stacked with debt in corporate raids and management buyouts that increased leverage for the shepherds. Both were accomplished in essentially the same way—by borrowing money against the asset value and credit of the corporation. Monopoly prices charged by the corporation for new investment could be used for payment of debt, while the borrowed money could be raked off by the shepherds as payment for the stock. While engaging in financial manipulations and churning corporations the shepherds paid themselves exorbitant fees for legal, underwriting and financial guidance.[39]

In the concentration, merger monopoly game individual managers and chief executives have to submit to the institutional monopoly control. The management in return is generously rewarded with bonuses and golden parachutes. When LIN Broadcasting merged with McCaw Cellular Communications the combination triggered LIN stock options for chief executive Donald A. Pels to the tune of $186 million. For Steven J. Ross Time's merger with Warner Communications led to a $75 million bonus. The management and directors of big corporations are insiders who set the rules and understand the monopoly game. Institutional monopoly control brings to reality what individual managers can only dream of. But in the long run it is impossible to get something for nothing and consequences and problems of institutional monopoly have to be faced.[40]

Consequences and Problems

With successful institutional monopoly control the savings of the nation have been appropriated by the shepherds. The shepherds practically stopped investment in the U.S. economy and directed government spending into defense, ignoring infrastructure investments. The shepherds through the corporations have become a sovereign state whose interests control the U.S. economy even if it results in killing the goose that lays the golden egg.[41]

In the absence of a free market for the allocation of capital between industries and companies each company has to invest in its own industry and tries to maximize its profitability. A Special Report in *US News & World Report* noted:

> America as the "land of opportunity" is beginning to lose that title in the eyes of many U.S. businessmen. These businessmen increasingly are deciding that markets abroad—not those in this country—offer the biggest potential for future growth. The feeling grows that the U.S. market, while huge, is relatively "saturated".
>
> It is overseas that businessmen see the big, untapped market with hundred of millions of customers wanting—and increasingly able to buy—all kinds of products and services.
>
> To go after this market, U.S. firms are building and expanding factories all around the world. Since 1958, more than 2,100 American companies have started new operations in Western Europe alone . . .

An official of Colgate Palmolive Company outlined the motivation: "You are in a saturated market here in the U.S. where new products are the only answer to growth. Abroad there are millions of people each year who reach the stage in their cultural, social, and economic development where they buy toothpaste among other things we sell". The survey also noted that "Profit rates abroad generally are higher than those in similar activities in the U.S. Many firms report a percentage return 'twice as high abroad as in America'. Most cite lower wage costs overseas—and less competition."[42]

Business Week explains:

> In industry after industry, U.S. companies found that their overseas earnings were soaring, and that their return on investment abroad was frequently much higher than in the U.S. As earnings abroad began to rise, profit margins from domestic operations started to shrink . . . This is the combination that forced development of the multinational company.

As a result, long-term private investment abroad increased from $32 billion in 1960 to more than $71 billion in 1970. There was a mass exodus of manufacturing from the United States to countries with cheap labor. "Between 1957 and 1967 G.E. built 61 plants overseas . . . By 1974 about 75 percent of the assets of the American electric industry were located overseas". In other industries at that time "about one-third of the total assets of the chemical industry, about 40 percent of the total assets of the consumer goods industry . . . about one-third of the assets of the pharmaceutical industry, are now located outside the United States".[43]

Capital was initially exported and manufacturing facilities built overseas to obtain higher profits by meeting the needs of overseas consumers. The process continued with products manufactured overseas being imported for sale in the United States. American car companies and electronics manufacturers have been importing cars and VCRs for sale in the home markets. As a result manufacturing jobs were being lost in the country. *The New York Times* reported that in 1957, 22.7 percent of the world's manufacturing was carried out in the United States by U.S. multinationals and by companies operating only domestically; by 1983, the total was 13.9 percent. Yet during the same period, U.S. multinationals held on to 17.7 percent of the world's manufacturing business with less and less of that manufacturing undertaken domestically. These figures make clear an enormously negative effect on the U.S. economy caused by the American multinationals and their investment strategies.[44]

The new role of the American corporation is explained by Robert Reich:

> America's core corporation no longer plans and implements the production of a large volume of goods and services; it no longer owns or invests in a vast array of factories, machinery, laboratories, warehouses, and other tangible assets; it no longer employs armies of production workers and middle level managers; it no longer serves as gateway to the American middle class. In fact, the core corporation is no longer even American. It is, increasingly, a facade, behind which teems an array of decentralized groups and subgroups continuously contracting with similarly diffuse working units all over the world.[45]

As a result of corporate strategies and role in the global economy the U.S. trade deficit from 1984 to 1988 has ranged between $112 and $159 billion annually. This has occurred as a direct result of institutional monopoly control of the economy. Without it, the savings would be distributed among the sheep and they would use them with prudence. Allocation of capital in the U.S. economy based on free market principles would not see its diversion overseas to meet the narrow goals of the shepherds to the detriment of the U.S. economy.[46]

Officially the corporate income tax in 1993 was 34 percent, reduced from 45 percent in 1985. There were accelerated depreciation, investment tax credits, carryover of losses and many other loopholes created as incentives for corporations to increase their cash flow and invest in jobs. But in reality there is no connection between reduction of corporate taxes and the increase in domestic investment and creation of jobs. One survey by conservative economist Pierre Rinfret revealed that 75 percent of major corporations said they would not change their previous investment plans in response to the reinstatement of the tax credit in 1971. In fact nongovernmental investment in plant and equipment as a percentage of the GDP has declined from 13.5 percent in 1981 to 10 percent in 1991. The net result of the loopholes and manipulations is to reduce the actual corporate tax paid to the government. During the Eisenhower years corporate income taxes contributed about 28 percent of the budget compared to about 12 percent in 1980 and eight per cent in 1992. In short, the shepherds have pocketed an increasing share of the nation's savings instead of paying taxes, thus preventing investment in the country's infrastructure and contributing to increased federal deficits.[47]

Allocation of resources for the national economy has been even more distorted by military spending. In 1992 military spending amounted to $313 billion, which was 22 percent of the federal budget. Defense spending provides a windfall for the shepherds and protection for their foreign investments. For the national economy, however, defense is a squandering of resources, as it does not provide any direct benefits in consumable items or improvements in productivity from infrastructure investments. If the same funds were diverted to national infrastructure investments, more jobs would be created and productivity would improve.[48]

Institutional monopoly control has discouraged civilian public investment: from 1.5 percent of the GNP during the 1953 to 1969 period it came down to 0.4 percent in 1970 to 1986. American infrastructure has deteriorated to a point where half the bridges in New York State and 75 percent of those in New York City reportedly can no longer carry their intended loads. When several water mains burst before the 1989 municipal elections Bob Hope said, "New York doesn't need a mayor, it needs a plumber". Much of the stagnation in U.S. productivity and industrial decline can be blamed on scanty public investment. In 1981, the Council of State Planning Agencies looked at the condition of the country's infrastructure including roads, bridges, railroads, electric power grids, ports and water resources and issued a landmark report titled "America in Ruins". Estimates for infrastructure repair varied between $2 trillion and $3 trillion, with another $2 trillion needed to modernize industry. This is comparable with the trillions spent on the defense buildup of the 1980s alone.[49]

During the 1992 Presidential election candidate Clinton said he could bring as much as $13.5 billion a year into the Treasury through beefed-up enforcement in transfer-pricing of goods between subsidiaries of multinational corporations. The corporations try to minimize income and taxes paid in the United States. This is a replay on a global scale of a business practice that was popularized in the 1960s. During that decade U.S. companies began playing off one state against another, one city against another to locate a new plant or relocate an existing one in whatever area would offer the greatest tax incentives, minimizing the state and local taxes and employee wages and fringe benefits. Now the practice has gone global as corporations play off one country against another, one national tax system against another, one country against its possessions. In the *Wall Street Journal* there are headlines, "Foreign firms' income in U.S. is understated". But these games have been invented and used by U.S. multinationals for decades. About 25 percent of all U.S. exports and 15 percent of all U.S. imports are actually transfers between parents of multinational corporations and their affiliates abroad. Investments and profits of the U.S. companies have a higher priority than the health of the U.S. economy. The fact that the shepherds control the U.S. government and the presidency becomes obvious from President Bush's 1991 annual report to Congress on the state of the economy:

> The benefits of global economic integration and expanded international trade have been enormous, at home and abroad. United States firms gain from access to global markets; United States workers benefit from foreign investment in America . . . Competition and innovation have been stimulated, and businesses have increased their efficiency by locating operations around the globe.[50]

Institutional monopoly control gives the shepherds license to reward themselves with magical figures. In 1991 *Business Week* reported that the total pay of the 30 highest paid executives ranged from $ 5 million dollars to $26 million. The average chief executive's salary, bonus and long term compensation was $1.95 million in the *Business Week's* survey. During the 1980s chief executive officers' compensation jumped 212 percent. In 1953 corporations paid their executives $8.8 billion in salaries, stock bonuses and other compensation while corporation income taxes amounted to $19.9 billion. By contrast, corporations in 1987 paid their officers $200 billion in compensation and $83.9 billion in federal income taxes. That means business paid $2.3 in taxes for every $1 paid in executive salaries in 1953. On the other hand the pattern was reversed in 1987 because business paid $2.4 in executive salaries for every $1 in taxes.[51]

The consumers pay directly for institutional monopoly controls. *The New York Times* reported that monopoly control through bid rigging is common in the milk industry: "In a typical case, a Federal prosecutor in Florida said bid rigging has raised milk prices by 14 percent". Federal and state investigations found that executives at the nation's largest national and regional companies had conspired—sometimes for decades—to rig bids on milk products sold to schools and military bases.[52]

The report in the *Wall Street Journal* about Abbott Labs settling anti-trust litigation over the marketing methods of its infant formula is illuminating. The operational methodology of institutional monopoly control was revealed because Nestle, a foreign multinational, tried to enter the infant formula market through Carnation, its American subsidiary. The American Academy of Pediatricians was given $1 million annually for cooperating with the infant formula makers. By settling litigation without admitting any wrongdoing institutional monopoly control limited damage and resumed operations as usual. Abbott Labs raised the wholesale price of a 13 ounce can of Similac concentrate to $2.26, 53 cents a can more than Nestle/Carnation's Good Start formula. This amounts to a 30 percent premium for institutional monopoly control the sheep have to pay. The ideology used by institutional monopoly control to justify its goals and the possible answers to restoring the health of the U.S. economy need understanding.[53]

Ideology and Answers

The function of ideology is to divert the attention of the sheep from reality. This is done by repeating shibboleths like free markets, free trade, performance, double taxation, capital formation and jobs like a mantra over and over again. The idea is that the sheep will believe what they are told and blame one another for the travails.

The myth of the free market is the centerpiece of the ideology. Lewis Lapham notes:

> Maximization of profits would imply an operation run according to the arithmetic of performance, which would wreak havoc on everybody's comfortable arrangements. Let the rabbit of free enterprise out of its velveteen bag and too many people have to be fired, too much ideology exposed to light of judgment or ridicule, too much vanity sacrificed to the fires of efficiency. Such a catastrophe obviously would threaten the American way of life, to say nothing of the belief in free markets.[54]

Owing to tight school budgets instructional materials in American schools are provided by industry with largely self-serving publications. Free classroom materials are produced by 64 percent of the 500 largest American industrial corporations, and 90 percent of the industrial trade associations and presented through the Advertising Council, a business group. The predominant classroom economics lesson is the message of "free marketplace" and nonregulation of business. Another example of the ideological avalanche relates to the federal judiciary. Conservative foundations give judges and their families all-expense-paid trips to Miami so that they can take courses in the laissez-faire doctrine of Milton Friedman focusing on the need to leave the corporations alone. By 1980 one-fifth of the federal judiciary had taken advantage of the offer.[55]

Free trade ideology is only slightly less important than free markets. That free trade assumes full employment is not mentioned. The ground rules have changed in a world with excess capacity and large scale unemployment and under-employment. A rule of thumb in trade negotiations is that domestic purchasing power ought to produce domestic employment. But the American upper class has consistently undermined the domestic economy by diverting investments overseas even when there is unemployment at home. Today, nearly half the world trade is conducted between units of multinational corporations. Though the American economy is getting clobbered the shepherds continue with the free trade methodology to protect their overseas investments. Nancy McLernon of the Organization for International Investments representing multinationals said, "It would be crazy to think that these antics (Bill Clinton going after foreign companies to raise $45 billion over four years) have no effect on internal investment. It would also be unwise to think that America's own investments abroad would not be harmed by silly strikes against foreigners at home". In the end the interests of the shepherds take precedence over the American economy. *The New York Times* warned in a stern editorial denouncing domestic content legislation, "Protectionism might mean a few jobs for American auto-workers, but it would depress the living standards of hundreds of millions of consumers and workers, here and abroad".[56]

While the conservatives deny the existence of a planned monopoly the liberals represented by Galbraith acknowledge its presence and provide a rationale for giant corporations. According to him giantism, "gives them advantages in planning their future and assuring their own survival". He claims that a split between the management and ownership of corporations means monopoly control holds no dangers because the managers will continue managing the corporations in the public interest. But one percent of the American families own 50 percent of all publicly traded stock. Splitting of blocks of stock among family members for tax purposes, or the placing of the stock in professionally managed trusts and investment companies, where identities can be obscured, can hardly be regarded as dispersion of stock ownership. Most company directors are members of management in the largest industrial corporations and the directors are neither a passive group nor at odds with the basic policies and interests of the upper class. As the ownership and management of the corporations is based on institutional monopoly control there is no reason for managing the corporations in the public interest. The myth of separation of ownership and control was invented to provide a facade to live with monopoly control of the economy along with its consequences.[57]

With the myth of a free market economy comes the illusion of executive compensation tied to management performance. Some sort of rational explanation is necessary because the average CEO of a large American corporation earns about $2 million a year. According to United Shareholders Association president Ralph V. Whitworth, "Executive pay is irrational. There is no connection between pay and performance. Instead, compensation is based more on the size of the company, and that only encourages empire building". This confirms that executive pay is tied to institutional monopoly control. Steven Kaplan of the University of Chicago graduate school of Business says that on an average a chief executive has a 10 percent chance of losing his job in an average year. If his stock price is down 50 percent relative to the whole market, his chances of being dismissed rises to 15 percent— and 17 percent if his firm is in the red. Detroit's Big Three provide a good example of the lessons of institutional monopoly and executive pay. In the 1980s, auto makers raked up years of record earnings justifying even more lucrative pay packages for the CEO's. But much of the profit was the result of voluntary restraints set by the Japanese. As a result the chairmen of the Big Three automakers in the U.S. received $7.3 million in 1990 while the Big Three Automakers in Japan received $1.8 million including bonuses.[58]

To sum up the pay for performance debate Richard Darman, as Deputy Secretary of the Treasury in November 1986, told an audience at the Japan Society in New York that the conventional business establishment was "bloated, risk averse, inefficient and unimaginative". Executives paid $1 million a year, he said, "devoted less time to research and development than on reviewing their golf scores". He observed most of the upper management owed their places to "the strength of their demeanor and a failure to make observable mistakes".[59]

Blaming the consequences of institutional monopoly on the victims is a hallmark of the shepherds' ideology. Ross Perot declares, "We need to replenish our national savings pool so that we have capital to invest. We are saving at a rate of 4 percent compared to the Japanese at 18 percent and the Germans at 10 percent". The implication is that if only the average American saved like the Germans and Japanese there would be automatic investment in the U.S. economy and the problems would be solved. The Department of Commerce's national income accounts divide gross private savings into gross business savings and personal savings with only 20 percent being personal savings, the balance being the undistributed cash flow of businesses. This clearly shows that the sheep are not allowed to save because monopoly prices siphon off the savings into the corporations. Also $300 billion of savings are annually wasted in defense with no accompanying benefits. The savings and capital formation ideology is basically a diversionary tactic to prevent facing up to the real issues.[60]

Part of the capital formation and investment ideology was the argument against double taxation of dividends. The lack of investment in the U.S. economy could be blamed on the U.S. government because corporate earnings were taxed first at the corporate level and then individuals had to pay taxes again on the dividends received. But when tax reformers started taking the issue of double taxation of dividends seriously and voiced the need to eliminate the corporate income tax the capital formation lobby quietly dropped the subject from discussion.[61]

With institutional monopoly control, the U.S. economy is in decline. A solution must restore the efficiency of a competitive economy by tying rewards with risk and management performance and allocating the nation's resources and savings for optimizing the overall economy instead of catering to the interest of the shepherds. This may involve reigning in the multinationals with home bases in the U.S. or abroad and putting the American economy first.

A suggested solution is the replacement of the corporate income tax with a Value Added Tax (VAT) and the taxation of corporate earnings through individual stockholders independent of how and where they are reinvested. Lester C. Thurow, dean of MIT's Sloan School of Management, has suggested that a 14 percent VAT would raise enough revenue to replace the corporate and payroll taxes. Every 1 percent change in VAT would raise another $42 billion in revenue. VATs between 15 and 25 percent are common in western Europe. By eliminating the corporate income tax the earnings of companies can be allocated to individual shareowners who will have to treat it as income and pay taxes. The shareowners can decide the best way to invest their earnings. Both the VAT and the distribution of corporate earnings to shareowners can restore the health of the U.S. economy.[62]

One advantage of VAT over the corporate income tax is that it is free of loopholes and less subject to manipulation by the multinationals. The VAT is based on the difference between the selling price of a product and the price of components purchased from other suppliers. On imports the VAT could be collected and rebated on exports. It would not be necessary to price products to include corporate income taxes. With a VAT both U.S. and foreign-based multinationals would be placed on a level playing field. If the United States tries to target the foreign multinationals with minimum corporate taxes others are bound to retaliate against U.S. based multinationals. But with a VAT the U.S. economy can come out ahead as noted by David Wyss, an economist: "Other countries have a VAT, and if you're out of step with your trading partner you're at a disadvantage". Also the VAT should help the U.S. economy by reducing the imports and increasing exports and reducing the trade deficit.[63]

For the U.S. economy the revenue generated from VAT could be used to balance the budget and channel the nation's savings into the public infrastructure. The corporate income tax is a giant buffer to cover the mistakes and inefficiencies of the upper class and to transfer risk to the general public. By replacing corporate income tax with a VAT the spending of the nation's savings is transferred from the shepherds' private control to the public domain. President Reagan, as a spokesman for the shepherds, had said VAT "gives the government a chance to blindfold the people and grow in stature and size". True to his class, President Reagan preferred the shepherds to the national economy growing in stature and size.[64]

By eliminating corporate income tax and allocating the earnings of corporations to individual stockholders the stranglehold of institutional monopoly on the U.S. economy will be released. If the stockholders have to pay taxes on the earnings they will decide wisely where to invest their earnings. American shareholders may also decide they have had enough of consumer products and might prefer to spend their money on education or recreation.

Getting the sheep to pay monopoly prices for goods and services is only half the game plan. The other half is taxation and waste so that the distribution of savings coincide with the interstices of the American class system.

CHAPTER 7

TAXATION AND WASTE

There's no such thing as a free lunch.–**Milton Friedman**[1]

The real certainties of this world are death and tax avoidance.–**George Cooper**[2]

The purse of the people is the real seat of sensibility. Let it be drawn upon largely, and they will listen to truths which could not excite them through another organ.
–Thomas Jefferson[3]

The organized grassroots in this country, when it comes to taxes, is the business community.
–A Washington Corporate Lobbyist[4]

Under the heading, "Tax Aide's Clothes Line", *Congressional Quarterly* reported:

> A top aide to Ways and Means Chairman Dan Rostenkowski has earned almost $100,000 over the past five years by selling clothing to women, including lobbyists with business before her powerful boss' committee. As Rostenkowski's administrative assistant and long-time scheduler, Virginia C. Fletcher helps control access to the Illinois Democrat. Questioned by *Congressional Quarterly*, Rostenkowski said through a spokesman that Fletcher had agreed last year to give up the

sideline after the Congressman told her it "could be viewed as exploiting your relationship with me." House records show that in the later half of the year before, Rostenkowski increased Fletcher's salary from the annual equivalent of roughly $70,000 to about $90,000—which would offset the clothing-sales income she would forgo. Rostenkowski's spokesman said the raise had nothing to do with Fletcher agreeing to abandon her clothes selling operation.[5]

As this story illustrates, tax lobbyists and tax lobbying are an accepted way of life in the United States. Between the stated objectives of the tax system and the reality falls the shadow of tax lobbying and waste which are part of the structure of generating revenue and spending in the United States.

Adam Smith defined the need for and the general principles of taxation in 1776. He limited the activities of the state to making provision for common defense, the administration of justice and necessary public works. Taxes should be certain, convenient and economical to assess and collect. For a fair standard he advocated a proportionate income tax: "The subjects of every state ought to contribute towards the support of the government, as nearly as possible, in proportion to their respective abilities, that is, in proportion to the revenue which they respectively enjoy under the protection of the state". However, these principles were for a free market economy based on classical economics.[6]

America, however, has never had a free market economy based on a democratic form of government. From the beginning it was based on the economic class system requiring that all savings for the nation end up with the shepherds. Before the Civil War, federal government revenues relied on tariffs and the sale of public lands. The first federal income tax was enacted because of the Civil War expenditures that targeted the wealthy with incomes exceeding $10,000. The rest of the population was spared because they were at a basic replacement level. However, this law was repealed in 1872 and the upper class challenged the constitutionality of the income tax. It took a Supreme Court ruling and a constitutional amendment before an income tax on the wealthy could be established in 1913. With World War II and increased expenditures income tax became a major source of revenue for the federal government. Income tax revenue increased from $1 billion to $90 billion between 1939 and 1970 and constituted about 45 percent of the federal government's tax receipt in 1970.[7]

Income tax before World War II was applied only to the wealthy (seven percent tax for incomes exceeding $100,000) and the income disparity of the different classes was starkly evident. The shepherds decided for the sake of appearances first to increase incomes for everybody, especially with inflation, and then take it back in the form of income and payroll taxes. This way the disparity between pre-tax incomes would be reduced and everyone could pretend to be middle class and conceal the existence of the American class system. To make the working and the middle classes pay income tax, it had to be progressive in appearance so that the rich paid higher rates. But the taxes of the shepherds were reduced through the backdoor with loopholes and tax preferences built into the structure. In 1966, as an example, the top marginal income tax rate was 70 percent while the effective income tax rate on the richest one percent was 16.4 percent.[8]

The appearance of a progressive tax to cloud the class system is what a system of payroll deductions and loopholes achieved. Even an effective flat rate tax is insufficient to meet the goals of the shepherds. A hidden system of taxation and waste is required for this apart from institutional monopoly control of prices.

Visible Taxes and Loopholes

The overall effect of the visible part of the tax structure can be understood by differentiating between regressive and progressive taxes and different types of incomes and deductions. Payroll and sales taxes are generally regressive, the former because there is a maximum income level after which the social security tax is not collected. The tax rate then goes down as income increases. Sales taxes are regressive because the upper classes spend a smaller proportion of their income on basic necessities. A 1973–74 study showed that the working, middle and upper classes spent 80 percent, 48 percent and 38 percent of their net income after taxes on food, energy, shelter and health care. For the working class the sales tax was a greater burden because they spent 80 percent of their income on basic necessities compared to the upper class which spent only 38 percent.[9]

The income taxes are structured to give the appearance of progressivity, the tax rate increasing with income. But this is distorted with varying rates for different kinds of income and deductions. Income from municipal bonds and health care benefits provided by the employers are not taxed. A reduced rate is provided for capital gains income. Disproportionate subsidies for the middle and upper classes are provided with deductions from income for mortgage interest payments, property and state taxes, and charitable contributions.

Social security deductions from payrolls are the most regressive of the visible taxes. It amounts to a flat tax of almost 15 percent (taking the employer's contribution into account) on the first $53,400 in wage income as of 1991. With social security taxes going up and the income tax rates declining, George Mitchell, the Maine Democratic Senator, complained in 1987, "There has been a shift of about $80 billion in annual revenue collections from the progressive income tax to the regressive payroll tax". The payroll deduction on a $40,000 annual income from 1980 to 1988 doubled from $1,500 to nearly $3,000 and the portion of annual federal tax receipts represented by social security rose from 31 to 36 percent.[10]

Social security taxes are targeted at the sheep as these do not apply to dividends, interest or capital gains and because of the limit on the wage income. Senator Daniel Patrick Moynihan proposed in December 1989 to roll back social security taxes and charged that "no other democratic country takes as large a portion of its revenue from working people at the lower end of the spectrum and as little from persons who have property or higher incomes". With only 50 percent of the benefits being taxable this provides an annual windfall of $6 billion in reduced taxes for the top 18 percent of retirees.[11]

The purpose of social security taxes is also questionable. The Supreme Court *(Fleming v. Nester)* ruled in 1960 that workers did not have any accrued rights associated with social security. There is no separate fund for social security. It is a giant Ponzi scheme where the future generations promise to pay the current generations and Congress can change the rules at any time. As funds collected for social security can be used for other purposes, the whole scheme is an accounting gimmick. The social security structure serves two purposes: first, it adds a premium to the minimum wage, creating a permanent underclass; and second, it gives the appearance of the sheep earning more than their actual wages, thus reducing class disparities.[12]

In addition to social security tax deduction a payroll deduction for medical health insurance is likely. Medical health insurance is generally divided into the visible portion which is a payroll deduction and the hidden part which is a subsidy paid directly by the corporation or employer. As the system stands the payroll deduction for health insurance is even more regressive than social security deductions. A 1992 study found that four-fifths of companies required the employees to pay an average of $107 a month for family health coverage. The payroll deduction being independent of income the burden falls heaviest on the lower income employees. When a payroll tax of two percent for health coverage was suggested as part of health insurance reform, Henry Aaron, a Brookings Institution economist, noted, "It's going to cause a lot of income redistribution, not just among classes but also among regions, industries, companies, in patterns that do not make sense to many people".[13]

Although payroll taxes are admittedly regressive the income tax structure claims to be progressive. In 1992 the bottom rate on income was 15 percent while the top rate was 31 percent. In theory, therefore, the rich were paying taxes at twice the rate of the poor. But many among the middle class had to pay 28 percent rates on part of their incomes. That meant the spread between the middle class and the upper class was three percent. This did not take into account special income tax treatment for municipal bonds interest and capital gains and a system of deductions to remove the progressivity of the income tax.[14]

Exemption of municipal bonds interest from federal income tax cancels out the progressivity of the federal income tax and is one of the most carefully guarded rights of the upper class, presumably granted by the Constitution itself. Despite the Sixteenth Amendment to the Constitution, which gave Congress an all-encompassing power to tax income "from whatever source derived, " the upper class has decided to give the benefit of the doubt to this exemption. Representative Ogden L. Mills, a Republican from New York, noted in 1923:

> Tax-exempt securities constitute, in my judgment, the greatest evil in the whole field of taxation—an evil so far-reaching in its consequences, both social and economic, as to be deserving of the most serious and immediate attention on the part of the people of the country. Of one thing I am perfectly sure: a progressive income tax at high rates and tax-exempt securities cannot exist side by side. Tax-exempt securities must inevitably destroy the progressive income tax, and I am by no means sure that the evil has not already reached such proportions as to make any possible action too late to save our present federal income tax.

Andrew Mellon, Treasury Secretary, commented on the power of the upper class in 1924: "It is incredible that a system of taxation which permits a man with an income of $1 million a year to pay not one cent to the support of his government should remain unaltered".[15]

More recently in 1969, John Tunney, a Democratic Senator from California, said: "The tax exempt bonds that are owned by individuals are concentrated in the hands of the wealthiest 2 percent of population . . . It will be possible for a select few

to receive vast amounts of tax-free income, while persons
with incomes of one-hundredth the size will be taxed at
effective rates of 20 to 30 percent". According to Federal
Reserve Board data in 1989 there were more than $625
billion outstanding in municipal securities. Overall, 31.8
million individuals and families with incomes below $10,000
collected interest totaling $15.4 billion and had to pay taxes
on the income. At the same time 809,000 individuals and
families with incomes over $200,000 picked up $14 billion in
tax-free interest.[16]

Special capital gains tax rates favor the upper class. Capital
gain rates apply to income from the sale of stocks, bonds,
commodities and other assets. According to IRS statistics
capital gains reported totaled $150.2 billion in 1989. Of that
sum $108.2 billion were reported by the top 1 percent of all
tax filers; that is, the trustees. The remaining $42 billion in
capital gains income were reported by another six percent of
the filers, the gatekeepers. Capital gains tax rates are merely
a loophole to contain the progressivity of the income tax.[17]

Apart from special tax rates for municipal securities and
capital gains, other loopholes allow deductions from income
before taxes are applied. These include deductions for mortgage interest and property taxes, charitable contributions, state
and local income tax deductions. The upper class takes advantage of these deductions which also help cement the relationship between the upper and the middle classes so that they
combine to support the prevailing tax structure.

The current income tax structure allows homeowners to
deduct from their income interest on mortgage up to $1 mil-
lion. The average mortgage in the United States was only
$104,000 in 1992. This deduction allows the upper class to
deduct mortgage interest on their principal residence and
vacation homes. According to the calculation of the Joint
Committee on Taxation, the upper class takes 60 percent of
the total mortgage interest deductions while the middle class
gets the rest. This is also true of local property tax deduction.
As the middle class constitutes 40 percent of the population
while the upper class is only 10 percent, the subsidy from this

deduction is loaded in favor of the latter. The working and underclass do not get these deductions because they are renters and do not itemize deductions.[18]

Deductions for state and local income taxes, including personal property taxes, are even more lopsided. More than 90 percent of these deductions are claimed by the upper class. State sales and excise taxes are regressive as well given the larger share of income spent on basic necessities by the working and middle classes.[19]

About 90 percent of the deductions for charitable contributions go to the upper class. Approximately $90 billion was donated to charities in 1988. There is no law to regulate how much can be spent on expenses and overhead by a charitable organization. In July 1987 the *Virginian Pilot* reported a scandal, where six heart disease and cancer charities raised $34 million but less than 10 percent of the funds—$3.3 million—went for research and patient treatment. As presidential candidate H. Ross Perot said about charities, "The whole trick (to judging deserving charities) is to figure out which deliver results, which have leadership and which are using the money for the people who need it, as opposed to chewing it up in overhead and making it disappear in enormous amounts wasted".[20]

In many cases charitable organizations and tax exempt foundations are the fronts for peddling political influence and self-dealing and are becoming more popular with the politicians. Representative Les Aspen of Wisconsin, chairman of the House Armed Services Committee, founded his own think tank, named after himself and financed by "charitable" contributions from defense manufacturers. Senator Jake Garn of Utah, ranking Republican on the senate Banking Committee, did the same by financing his foundation by tax deductible donations from banks and financial institutions. According to a *National Journal* survey 51 senators and 146 House members were founders, officers or directors of tax-exempt organizations that produce research and propaganda. Charitable contributions serve to reduce the progressivity of the income tax and increase the political leverage of the upper class.[21]

When all federal, state and local taxes are combined, 50 percent of the total taxes, that is personal income taxes and corporate profit taxes, are supposed to be progressive while the rest, including indirect sales, excise, property and payroll tax, are regressive. The net result is that overall tax burden works out to be a flat tax of 25 percent of total family income. According to economist Joseph A. Pechman, "because the degree of progressivity or regressivity is relatively very small under any of incidence assumptions, it is clear that the tax system has very little effect on the distribution of income". Studies for the year 1970, 1980 and 1985 show that the variation in the effective tax rate for the underclass with incomes less than $10,000 or the upper class incomes exceeding $100,000 was less than 2 percentage points.[22]

The New York Times reported in 1992 that the tax changes of the eighties changed nothing. Eugene Steuerle, a former Treasury official under President Reagan, noted, "Highly visible taxes were cut, but less visible taxes went up". The tax burden for all classes over the last three decades has been the same. Why then go through the charade of a complicated tax collection and enforcement system to attain such a simple end result? The answer lies in the "fairness" issue. There is no other way to hide the fact that a family below poverty line and a millionaire pay the same flat tax rate of 25 percent. But these are only visible taxes. A system of hidden taxes and waste are necessary for the transfer of the nation's savings to upper class control.[23]

Hidden Taxes and Waste

The key to understanding and estimating hidden taxes and waste is in the saying, "There is no free lunch". All goods and services have to be paid for one way or another. This includes free television, a 100 page newspaper for a quarter and junk mail. All defense gizmos, including missiles, planes and ships, have to be paid for by the general population. The advances in health care, where millions are spent to give a newborn baby a heart transplant, are borne by the consumers. Even million dollar jury awards against corporations for negligence and product liability are passed on to the public. If public transportation and mass transit are to be designed to accommodate the handicapped, the transit users have to pay the additional costs. In short, there is no escape. The question is which class bears the cross and who receives the major benefit.

One form of hidden tax and waste is the expenditure for advertising, sales promotion and planned product obsolescence. For this the quality of the product or the receptivity of the consumer to the advertising message are unimportant. Tightly intermeshed with advertising is the strategy of planned obsolescence. Advertising tells consumers that what they have is obsolete and invites comparisons to encourage conspicuous consumption. James M. Roche, chairman of General Motors, noted, "Planned obsolescence, in my opinion, is another word for progress". The sheep pay for the propaganda in increased prices even as they are being told they are getting something for nothing.[24]

In 1990 almost $32 billion was spent on newspaper advertising alone. The average newspaper had 66 pages, of which 65 percent, or 43 pages, were kept for advertising. Of the remaining 23 pages 18 were "fluff" and only five pages hard news. "Fluff" is the gray area between real news and advertisements, and required by advertisers to provide the stimulus for buying. With only five out of an average 66 pages of hard news the newspapers are sinking under the weight of "revenue related reading matter". The *Los Angeles Times* averages 123 pages daily and 512 pages on Sunday. In all probability, the reader must plow through masses of pages of no interest, with little news related to his own community and then pay to have it hauled away as garbage. It has been estimated that 11 percent of all landfills in America consist of old newspapers. There is an additional $8 billion annual expenditure for magazines. The paper requirement for magazines, newspapers and direct mail required the destruction of one million acres of forest annually.[25]

Television advertising expenses were estimated at about $28 billion in 1992, which came to about $300 a year for each television household. In return the sheep get a narrow spectrum of views repeated over and again. The greatest damage done by television advertising is the limits on competition through the Federal Communications Commission which requires a license for operating a T.V. station and stifles pay T.V. and Cable T.V. services. As television is paid for by the public through purchase of advertised products it has led to deadening uniformity with limited choice, low cost, low quality programs that could be produced cheaply to serve as fillers between advertisements. For $300 a year, every household could get programming tailored to its own needs.[26]

Direct mail, or "junk mail", absorbs another $24 billion a year. This does not take into account the subsidy provided by the Post Office through the first class mail monopoly. Third-class mail is now a nearly four million-ton colossus that accounts for 39 percent of all U.S. postal volume. This amounts to about 637 pieces of mail per household per year and it has been estimated by *Time* magazine that over the course of a lifetime, the average American will devote eight full months to sifting through mail solicitations. To pay for this waste the post office charges 32 cents for a first class stamp, about half of which is for subsidies to businesses for direct mail and other services such as keeping track of address changes and forwarding mail. Each penny in the first class stamp brings in $850 million for the postal service, bringing the annual postal subsidy to $13 billion. Essentially the postal service creates a two percent sales tax because the average check paid through the mail is about $15.00.[27]

The total advertising volume for all media was $130 billion in 1990. According to one estimate heavily advertised industries charge prices that are 15 percent higher (like a sales tax) than under truly free enterprise. In addition to advertising, credit, obsolescence, Senator Hart (D. Ind.) has estimated that almost one in every three cents spent is stripped from the consumer by what amounts to fraudulent means, including overpricing, substandard goods and surcharges. Even if only $1,000 per household spent annually for media advertising and added to the price of goods were saved, it would amount to annual savings of around $100 billion a year.[28]

Military spending represents perhaps the largest waste of manpower and resources and burden on the U.S. economy. From World War II to 1988 more was spent on military than the estimated value of all country's tangible assets except for land. In 1992 the stock of military "machinery" weapons was valued at 40 percent of all industrial equipment and more than a third of U.S. engineers and scientists work for the military. President Reagan alone spent $2 trillion on defense in eight years and the current military spending is in the ballpark of $300 billion annually.[29]

Defense spending is the least productive segment of the economy since weapons contribute virtually nothing to the fabrication of other goods. The defense establishments now employ more than half of the best research minds, which do not contribute to the strengthening of the economy. The hundreds of billions spent for military purposes are a misallocation of resources because they are permanently lost to society.[30]

For the shepherds military spending is the most profitable and least troublesome because most of the costs and risks are assumed by the sheep through the government. A Brookings Institution study estimated that virtually all large military contracts had cost over-runs of 300 to 700 percent. Small items too are not exempt from larceny: the military has paid $51 for light bulbs that cost ninety cents, $640 for toilet seats that cost $12 and $7,600 for coffee makers.[31]

The per capita spending of $1,000 for military purposes, and that too with borrowed funds, is not only wasteful but also a major cause of the decay and decline of the U.S. economy.For the working class, who do not have much wealth to defend, this amounts to exploitation which denies the basics. A conservative annual savings of $150 billion can be achieved by cutting the defense spending in half and eliminating waste.[32]

The medical industrial complex is another area of rampant theft from the public treasury through Medicare and Medicaid while 40 million Americans go without basic medical care. It is organized as a publicly subsidized private enterprise whose purpose is to give superprofits for the shepherds. Dr. Bernard Winters points out:

> Just as our defense budget has little to do with actually defending the United States, so our health budget has little to do with maintaining the health of the American people. It is a costly wasteful mechanism for funneling money to a sprawling medical industry that encompasses not only physicians and hospitals but equipment manufacturers, pharmaceutical corporations, banks and insurance companies. The impulse that drives this industry is the same that drives every industry—the maximization of profit.[33]

For the shepherds and the middle class most of the health care is paid for by the corporations, who treat it as a business expense. The corporations pass on the costs to the general public as increased prices. The result is that the general public pays for the gold plated health care for the haves while the havenots make do with occasional health care. If the system was not rigged and health care premiums were counted as income for all recipients the haves would have had to pay another $40 billion in taxes while the general public would get a price break exceeding $100 billion.[34]

The shepherds are not keen on providing health care to the working class during their working life. However, the system gladly provides the best health care in the world for the old and the underclass as long as it is paid for by Medicare or Medicaid. This provides ample opportunity to raid the public treasury because the government foots 41 percent of the bills for the health industry. The shepherds are willing and able to spend hundreds of thousands to take care of "crack babies" as long as they are covered by Medicaid. Americans spend half their lifetime medical costs during the last 12 months of their life because they are paid for by Medicare. As a result the

Ehrenreichs observe in their comprehensive study of American health empires, "From an economic point of view, hospitals are on their way to being little more than conduits, places where consumers' and taxpayer money is funneled into private profits".[35]

The average income for physicians in 1991 was $170,600, ranging from $229,800 for specialists in radiology to $111,500 for general physicians with family practice. The *Wall Street Journal* reported that the United States had the highest priced drugs in the world with a sampling of common medications having on the average prices 280 percent of those in Mexico. *Fortune* magazine reported U.S. medical spending increased from 7.3 percent of the GNP in 1970 to 13.4 percent in 1992, which amounted to around $800 billion dollars. Thus almost half the medical costs could have resulted in savings of $400 billion annually without affecting the quality and the quantity of health care.[36]

A good example of how the medical-industrial complex operates is the cancer tax. Tobacco is a $44 billion-a-year industry with a sales promotion and advertising budget of $1.7 billion. It has been estimated that this habit kills 434,000 people annually, more than eight times the car accident deaths, and results in health costs for smoking-related illness of $65 billion a year. In addition, $1 billion in subsidies have been provided to tobacco growers. Together this amounts to an annual wastage of $100 billion in the nation's resources, which works out to about $1,000 per household. As the working class are more susceptible to the appeals of drug pushing, they pay a disproportionate share of the cancer tax. The suggestion that a tax of $2 per cigarette pack, just as in Canada, could reduce smoking and raise $30 billion for health costs has not found favor with the shepherds. A ban on all tobacco advertising is considered an interference with free speech. Killing half a million Americans annually is a small price to pay for the health of the American class system.[37]

The tort tax is another sleight of hand. The *Economist* explained the need for the burgeoning numbers of lawyers and litigation:

> There are, in essence, two ways to get rich. You can either invest in some productive activity and so create new wealth, or you can try to get a share of somebody else's existing wealth. Transfer-seeking, which is what the second activity is called, differs from productive investment in that it does not create wealth. At best it redistributes it; at worst it destroys it. For if everybody indulged in transfer-seeking, just as if everyone took to thieving, all would end up impoverished. Of course, transfer-seeking can be perfectly legal—provided that legislators and courts agree to it.[38]

There were 756,000 lawyers in the country in 1990; that is more than 300 lawyers per 100,000 of population. Japan has only 12 and Germany 82 lawyers per 100,000. Further, 42 percent of the members of the House of Representatives and 61 percent of the Senate are lawyers. Stephen P. Magee, an economics professor, notes, "When lawyers artificially stimulate the demand for legal services through politics, we cannot rely on the usual market forces of supply and demand to control their numbers".[39]

Lawyers get the opportunity of enriching themselves by setting husband against wife, parents against children, doctors against patient, schools against students, employers against employees, neighbor against neighbor; in short, any situation where two parties are involved. The inherent vagueness of law makes it necessary to engage a lawyer. The Supreme Court has ruled that "evidence of intent" to discriminate is necessary in job bias suits. *Forbes* magazine notes that, "The Civil Rights Act of 1991 promises to generate countless lawsuits against employers". With billions of dollars involved, including the life, liberty and property of the citizens, opportunities for intimidation and exploitation are only limited by the imagination of the lawyers.[40]

According to Ralph Warner, co-founder of Nolo Press, a legal publisher, "The prime beneficiaries of the legal system are lawyers, not victims and not society as a whole". The lawyers are on the lookout for deep pockets. Most of the activity involves insurance companies who can pass on costs to the general public in higher premiums, or giant corporations who can pass on costs as higher prices or in raids on the public treasury which can raise funds through taxation. To maximize the revenue the system calls for jury trials, contingency fees and punitive damages and encourages the "I'll sue" mentality.[41]

The insurance industry and the lawyers operate hand in glove to prevent no-fault insurance for automobile accidents and encourage litigation. A 1991 study of auto injury claims in Hawaii by the Insurance Research Council reports that medical treatment for a typical neck sprain from whiplash comes to about $1,300 if handled without a lawyer, on a no-fault basis. The cost of treating the same injury if a part of a tort claim comes to about $8,000. Million dollar verdicts in malpractice litigation—one of every five jury awards in 1984—raise the average and with it insurance premiums. As a result obstetricians and surgeons are walking away from their practices rather than pay insurance premiums of up to $50,000 a year. A 1989 American Medical Association Study estimated that for every $1 they spend on insurance premiums, doctors spend $2.70 performing largely unnecessary tests and beefing up record keeping to avoid litigation. This suggests that excluding premium costs of $5 to $6 billion, the indirect tort tax related to medical malpractice liability alone costs the economy about $15 billion a year.[42]

Product-liability claims is the preferred route to go after giant corporations. Dow Chemicals gets hit with some 2,000 new product-liability claims in the United States every year, but only 20 such claims are filed against it in the rest of the world. The claims are "used to extort money" because it takes a lot of courage to go to trial on punitive-damages claims because of the unpredictability of the juries. *Forbes* reports that lawyers prospect for personal injury cases against several utility companies and electrical transmission equipment manufacturers alleging brain damage, cancer and leukemia caused by electric and magnetic fields. They go for drug companies manufacturing Halcion and Prozac alleging behavioral side effects resulting in paranoia, suicide and murder.[43]

Law firms in 1991 grossed more than $100 billion, a Commerce Department report estimated, not including what companies spend on their own legal departments—and what they must pay to resolve legal suits. The average partner profit for the largest law firms was $406,000 in 1992. More than 95 percent of contingent fee cases are settled with a payment. Nevertheless, contingent fees routinely are charged in the absence of real risk, often leading to rates of $1,000 and occasionally as high as $20,000 per hour for plaintiffs' attorneys. *Forbes* estimates that legal fees grew from 0.9 percent of the GDP in 1972 to 1.7 percent of the GDP in 1990 to an annual cost of $184 billion in 1992. If the growth in litigation could be eliminated it could result in annual savings of $100 billion per year. Passed on to the sheep, the tort tax amounts to $1,000 per household per year, the income being transferred to the shepherds.[44]

The transportation tax is the worst offender among the hidden taxes, being very regressive and squeezing the sheep where it hurts the most, since it is a basic necessity like food and shelter. The practical alternative of public transportation has been eliminated for most Americans to make room for transportation tax. Americans are forced to depend on an automobile if they are to work and earn a living. With an average rush hour occupancy of 1.1 persons per car it forces every working individual to divert resources to owning and operating a car. Every individual has to carry with him a 2,000 to 4,000 pound car with the accompanying energy and resource inefficiencies. One mass-transit railway car can do the work of fifty automobiles, and railroads consume one-sixth the energy of trucks to transport goods.[45]

These efficiencies, however, created undesirable competition for the automobile and oil industries and have engendered the forces to destroy public transportation during the last 50 years. The fate of Los Angeles is a case in point. In

1935 the interurban rail system covered a 75 mile radius with 3,000 electric transit cars and carried 80 million people a year. Using dummy corporations, General Motors and Standard Oil of California purchased the system, tore down the power transmission lines, scrapped its electric cars and placed diesel buses on Los Angeles streets. By 1955, 88 percent of the nation's electric-streetcar network had been eliminated followed by a cutback in city and suburban bus services, forcing the people to rely on private automobiles. In 1949, General Motors was found guilty of conspiracy but fined a pittance of $5,000 for engaging in these activities.[46]

The demise of public transportation was helped with a multibillion dollar highway program to subsidize the automobile industry and the cheapest gasoline in the world. As a result the communities were spread out with more than 60 percent of the land in most cities taken up by the movement, storage and servicing of vehicles. Once the communities were spread out the shepherds could be sure that public transportation would never again challenge their monopoly. With the loss of control over oil prices in the 1970s and the decline of the U.S. automobile industry in the 1980s, the U.S. economy was stuck with the inefficiency and waste of the transportation system along with the social costs. Now the United States has to live with air pollution and the deaths of 45,000 people annually in highway accidents and hundreds of thousands   injured and maimed.[47]

Once the American consumer was anchored to the automobile, the shepherds began squeezing him for every cent he had to stay mobile. According to an American Automobile Association survey the average U.S. motorist who drove 15,000 miles a year forked out more than $5,804 in 1993 to own and operate a car. Of this, more than $1,000 per car is for insurance alone. The tort law system compels drivers to purchase "third party" insurance as a buffer against lawsuits rather than to compensate them for their own accident-related losses. This obliges working class people to cover the claims of the upper class. As an increasing number of the working class cannot afford insurance, they are forced into "outlaw" status of driving without insurance. A no-fault system of insurance alone would provide savings of $300 per car annually.[48]

The viability of public transportation has been eroded over the years, with regulations demanding exorbitant capital and operating costs. Public buses have to be equipped with wheelchair lifts while subway stations must have elevators or ramps to accommodate the disabled. As Edward I. Koch, the mayor of New York City, claimed, it would be cheaper for the city to pay cab fare for every disabled New Yorker than to make the subway system accessible. The mayor did not realize that the rules were not to help the disabled but to eliminate public transportation as a viable alternative to the automobile.[49]

The federal deficit is the most regressive and damaging way of fleecing the sheep. Normally balancing the budget is part of the checks and balances process because it forces evaluation of the allocation of resources and makes the sheep aware of what is being charged to them. Deficit financing is literally a license to steal, because it lets the upper class manipulate accounting procedures and taxes to transfer funds to themselves which are then lent back to the government to earn interest. In the bargain the sheep "feel good" because their taxes haven't changed. By the time the day of reckoning comes, the operators have long retired, shifting the burden to future generations.

This is what happened during the Reagan–Bush presidencies. From 1980 to 1992 the federal deficit increased from less than $1 trillion to more than $4 trillion. By 1992 almost half a trillion was owed to foreigners while the rest of the money was owed to the upper class. The upper class reduced corporate taxes through accounting gimmicks and personal income taxes with tax reform. William Greider in his 1987 study of the Federal Reserve wrote: "The 1981 tax legislation proved to be regressive in a more fundamental way, hardly noted at the time. It became the pretext for a vast redistribution of incomes, flowing upwards on the income ladder, through another powerful channel—interest rates". Columnist

George Will reluctantly came to the same conclusion: "To pay the interest component of the 1988 budget will require a sum ($210 billion) equal to almost half of all the personal income-tax receipts. This represents, as Sen. Pat Moynihan has said, a transfer of wealth from labor to capital unprecedented in American history". When all is said and done the shepherds still need an ideology for damage control.[50]

Ideology and Answers

The net effect of the visible taxes, hidden taxes and waste can be seen from the distribution and level of savings in the U.S. economy. Historical data from the Federal Reserve Board indicate that the savings generated by class mirror approximately the distribution of wealth. The savings of the U.S. economy are distributed according to the game plan of the American class system.[51]

An explanation for the difference in the savings rate of 8 percent for the U.S. economy compared to 16 percent for Japan and 12 percent for Germany may lie in the wastefulness of the American class system. Compared to other countries the U.S. economy has built-in inefficiencies and waste and misallocation of resources. Before considering solutions to the economic mess, it would be worthwhile to bring down the protective ideological walls.[52]

The ideology of the American class system regarding taxes, savings and investments was summed up by Andrew Mellon in 1923: "The prosperity of the middle and lower classes depends on the good fortune and light taxes of the rich". This assumes that if taxes on capital income are low, the upper class will invest in new productive facilities, creating new jobs.

Economists Robert E. Lipsey and Irving B. Kravis examined the role of savings and capital formation in economic growth: "We suspect that the differences in taxation are not likely to explain the differences in savings rates". It was difficult, they said, to find any evidence linking tax rates on capital to subsequent rates of savings, investment or economic growth. The relationship was typically stronger between economic growth in one period and capital formation in the following. Mellon had said it backwards. A full employment economy with widely distributed incomes creates the effective demand that leads to increased investment in factories and jobs. Capital will not build new factories to make goods that no one can afford to buy, especially when there is a worldwide surplus capacity of productive facilities.[53]

For 12 years the Reagan–Bush administration raised the slogan "no new taxes" and went on a transfer-and-lend binge unmatched in the history of the United States. By cutting taxes and using borrowed funds they cut the links between spending and taxes and removed all checks and balances built into the system. All borrowing and spending is not alike. Borrowing for productive facilities or human capital investment may be justified because of the dividends expected in the future. But borrowing for defense spending violates all accepted principles. The U.S. economy has reached a critical stage because of the buildup of the federal debt and interest payments. There is no way the interest on transfers in the past can be paid by taxing current income. The way out lies in balancing the budget by cutting waste and recovering the past transfers from the shepherds.

One way of reducing waste, as noted earlier, is to replace the federal payroll and income taxes with a flat tax. Even Milton Friedman notes:

> The personal income tax would come far closer to achieving its objectives if we substituted a flat rate on income above personal exemption for the present loopholes and deductions that enable so many persons to avoid paying their fair share of the taxes and that requires so many more to take tax considerations into account in their every economic decision.

The key to a flat tax is the selection of a standard deduction large enough so that accompanied by the state and local sales taxes and the corporate value added taxes the result is the historical flat tax rate of 25 percent in the U.S. economy. All deductions for mortgage interest, charitable gifts and other loopholes would be eliminated. This would allow a simple and efficient method of collecting the visible tax rate which has existed for decades. As an example, W. Kurt Hauser, a board member of the Hoover Institution, noted that with a standard deduction of $16,000 indexed to inflation and a flat rate of 20 percent, tax collections around the historical rate of 19.5 percent of the GDP can be maintained.[54]

A flat tax would improve efficiency and cut down wastage by reducing tax avoidance and by eliminating the effort required to comply with a complicated tax code. According to recent IRS estimates, cheating cuts federal income tax revenue by 25 percent a year. About half the total tax gap involved corporations, partnerships, landlords and other businesses. Poor compliance rates were particularly disturbing because income from interest, dividends, businesses and capital gains are predominantly enjoyed by the better-off. With the elimination of deductions and a flat tax rate opportunities and motivation for tax avoidance would be eliminated.[55]

The federal income tax code takes up more than 5,000 pages. According to Citizens for an Alternative Tax System, the cost to the economy of the current tax system is six billion hours and $600 billion annually, which is 10 percent of the GDP of $6 trillion. A flat tax code, as the authors of a study "Low Tax, Simple Tax, Flat Tax" Robert Hall and Alvin Rabuska envision, would entail a postcard-size tax form. The capital and labor resources can be then directed to more productive activities.[56]

Two problems the flat tax cannot resolve is the interest payment on the federal deficit and checks on defense spending. The income tax can only tax new income and prevent a regressive transfer of wealth from the sheep to the shepherds. But it is ineffective in confronting past transfers. One way of restoring sanity is to have a federal tax on wealth. It would be similar to the local property taxes, only the tax would not be levied on the value of the property but on the equity in the property and other components of wealth and have a standard deduction indexed to inflation. This will exempt the middle class from the tax. As the wealth tax would apply to wealth already accumulated it would have less of an effect on the motivation to accumulate wealth out of current income. Such a tax has been suggested by James E. Meade in his book *Efficiency, Equality and the Ownership of Property*, and has been applied in other free market countries of western Europe.[57]

The level of wealth tax should be set so that the tax receipts equal the sum of the interest paid on the federal debt and defense spending. This will cancel the regressive flow of income from the sheep to the shepherds in the form of interest. As between 60 and 70 percent of the nation's wealth is owned by the upper class it is only fair they pay for its defense. If the upper class has to pay for defense spending with a wealth tax they will critically evaluate the preparedness required for national security. A wealth tax is the only way to balance the budget without destroying the long-term stability of the U.S. economy.

Implementing these reforms is a different kettle of fish in an economy and government controlled by the shepherds. The problems would not have occurred if the government was democratic with a free market economy. To understand tax reform it is essential to gauge the stranglehold of the shepherds over American democracy.

CHAPTER 8

MOCK DEMOCRACY

Silence of the lambs.–**Anonymous**

Till there be property there can be no government, the very end of which is to secure wealth, and to defend the rich from the poor.–**Adam Smith**[1]

The great functions of state should be reserved to the rich, the well born and the able.–**John Adams**[2]

The legitimate object of government, is to do for a community of people, whatever they need to have done, but cannot do, at all, or cannot, so well do, for themselves—in their separ-ate, and individual capacities.–**Abraham Lincoln**[3]

No candidate be deemed fit for the office of the presidency unless he could prove a net worth of $100,000 (1787).
                                          –**Charles Pinckney**[4]

Politics is the world's second oldest profession, closely related to the first.–**President Jimmy Carter**[5]

Under the heading "Japan Buys A Used President" *The New York Times* reported on November 6, 1989:

> Just two weeks ago, Mr. Reagan turned up in Tokyo waving and smiling, literally bowing for dollars. It is sad and disturbing to witness with what insouciance he now sells the stature

which his country afforded him to any country which can afford him. It demeans us all to see him so available, so eager to please for a price, to become "Rent-a-Ron", the performing presidential seal . . . Ron and Nancy, went to Japan, where our former leader prayed out loud (at so many dollars a prayer) that the Sony Corporation, which has purchased Columbia Pictures, would "bring back decency and good taste to American movies".

Other Japanese firms and the Japanese Government itself are pouring millions into the Reagan Library. Why is America's favorite napper so big in Nippon? Why is Ronald Reagan so adored in a country where most people don't understand what he's saying? Do the Japanese millyenaires have some hidden agenda? Is it possible that Mr. Reagan is being set up to run for Emperor? . . . Would you buy a used President from those car salesmen? May I offer a modest proposal? Japan has a noble tradition of honoring its leading citizens by designating them as national treasures. Ronald Reagan has clearly demonstrated that he cares about amassing one. The next time he dons his Max Factor and whips out his index cards to remind himself of what it is he's being paid to care so passionately about, the next time he tries to sell you something, anything—a corporation, a candidate or a country—answer him in the language he's sure to appreciate: Just say Noh".[6]

As this episode illustrates, even a former U.S. president is blind to the country's interest and sees no conflict in becoming a foreign lobbyist less than a year after vacating the White House. In fact Ronald Reagan's actions are a telling indictment of the concept of democracy in America. If democracy means a government of, by and for the people, then count America out. Ever since the Constitution came into force, the United States has always had a government of, by and for the shepherds, with a facade of elections.

In a society where wealth and property are controlled by the class system, a government is necessary to protect the interests of the haves. John Locke wrote in 1689: "The great and chief end . . . of Men's uniting into Commonwealths, and putting themselves under Government, is the preservation of their Property". The founding fathers were clear about their objectives, remembering Adam Smith's dictum of 1776 that government was necessary to secure wealth and defend the rich from the poor.[7]

Since the founding fathers had just come through a war of independence with the slogan "no taxation without represent-ation" they also knew the importance of appearances and elections where most of the white population could vote without property qualifications. Periodic popular elections ratify the rule of the shepherds and stabilize the system by avoiding the appearance of coercion or personal or class dictatorship. It also reduces the dangers of military rule or takeovers. Most political thinkers at the time of the Constitution recognized the possibility that the propertyless majority might, once it had the vote, attempt to turn nominal democracy into real power and threaten the security of the minority property holders. The shepherds had to devise a system of checks and balances, the purpose of which was to make it as diffi-cult as possible to change the prevailing system of property relations.[8]

The Constitution was devised in a way that, once ratified, it would prove extremely difficult to amend. A pyramid struc-ture of governance with the legislative, executive and judicial branches ensuring an equilibrium, and power decentralized between the center and the states, ensured upper class do-mination while preserving the notions of democracy.

Pyramid Structure

The Founding Fathers understood the dilemmas of demo-cracy while framing the Constitution in 1787. James Madison warned that protection against majority oppression "is the real objective to which our inquiries are directed". They knew that with universal suffrage, the havenots might try to pillage the property of the middle and upper classes and the Constitution needed to guard against this danger.[9]

Alexander Hamilton outlined the principles of American democracy in the *Federalist* No. 35:

> It is said to be necessary, that all classes of citizens should have some of their own number in the representative body, in order that their feelings and interests may be better understood and attended to. But we have seen that this will never happen under any arrangement that leaves the votes of the people free. Where this is the case, the representative body, with too few exceptions to have any influence on the spirit of the government, will be composed of land holders, merchants, and men of the learned professions. But where is the danger that the interests and feelings of the different classes of citizens will not be understood or attended to by these three descriptions of men?

To provide universal suffrage and yet ensure a government of the shepherds, the pyramid structure was written into the Constitution.[10]

At the base of the pyramid of American democracy is the House of Representatives with 435 elected members allocated to the states based on population. This means that with universal suffrage and the principle of one-man-one-vote the House could theoretically mirror the entire population by representing all the classes in the right proportion. The lower chamber was supposed to give the appearance of democracy in operation. Even in 1787 the principle of proportional representation was not strictly adhered to because the blacks who were not considered citizens and could not vote were still counted as three-fifths of a person for the purpose of representation in the House. The intent of the founding fathers was to provide leverage for property even in the lower House.[11]

The reality of representation in the lower House is different. In 1984, according to conservative estimates based on Congress Financial Disclosure statements, more than 53 members owned assets exceeding one million dollars. At that time, according to a Federal Reserve Board Survey, a net asset value exceeding approximately $200,000 placed a person in the upper class. Thus most members of Congress can claim membership in the upper class. With House salaries of $125,100 a year since 1991, benefits and expense budgets, most members have successful entrepreneurial and professional careers and are older white men, native born of native parents, Protestant with privileged backgrounds. A majority of the House members were lawyers or with business or banking backgrounds. The House of Representatives is packed with members of the upper class as Hamilton predicted more than two centuries ago.[12]

By itself the House of Representatives is powerless in acting against the upper class. Its purpose is to mirror the virtual representation of the people. As blacks are a visible minority who cannot be hidden, a House of Representatives with very few blacks would reveal the hollow core of American democracy. Elizabeth McCaughey noted in the *Wall Street Journal*, "For the political process to be seen as legitimate, people of all races must win office". After the 1990 census, the Justice Department ordered North Carolina with its 22 percent black population to make two of its twelve congressional seats safe for black candidates. As a result the state legislature created a safe 12th District for blacks which snakes for 160 miles through 12 counties and is barely wider than a highway in places. Although the Supreme Court struck down this "racial gerrymandering" Justice Souter clearly deemed the plan as harmless so long as it achieved proportional representation of the races statewide. The discussion and debates at the base of the pyramid do not alarm the shepherds because the outcome has no practical effect in mock democracy.[13]

In the Senate, which has two elected members from each state independent of population, the principle of one man one vote breaks down. As both the House of Representatives and the Senate have to agree before a bill becomes law, the will of the majority can be set aside by the Senate. The election for a Senator occurs over a whole state instead of a congressional district and is more expensive, requiring the financial backing of the shepherds with their corporate organizations and tax deductible contributions. Even if a candidate is not a member of the upper class at the beginning of the election process he will be one by the time he is elected. Moreover, to be elected as a Senator individuals need experience as a member of the House of Representatives, or a state governor or in some other capacity and is well tested to ensure that he shares the objectives of the shepherds and defends the status quo. The Senate makes sure that no bill clears the legislative branch without the specific approval of the upper class. Providing stability and continuity is the fact that the senators are elected for six-year periods and the elections are staggered. The power within the Senate is determined by committee memberships and appointments are based on seniority.[14]

A typical senator is an atypical American. With rare exceptions they are from the upper class. That is why less than five percent of the general population have any significant chance of ever serving in the Senate. In 1992 the Congressional newspaper *Roll Call* reported 28 millionaires, or almost a third of the Senate, by conservative estimates. The IRS put 1.3 million people in 1989 with net worth exceeding $1 million, barely one percent of the U.S. households. This means the system is set up in a way that only the shepherds gain entry to the Senate and appropriately filter ideas that survive the legislative process.[15]

Before a bill which passes the lower House and flows through the Senate filtering system becomes law, it must obtain the signature of the President, who is the head of the executive branch of the government. The President, with his cabinet and the executive branch, is the putative final guardian of mock democracy. He can veto a bill passed by Congress unless both the Houses muster a two-thirds majority and override him.

The control of the presidency is crucial to the shepherds. This they do by various means. At the Constitutional Convention in 1787, Charles Pinckney proposed a property qualification of $100,000 for the presidency, which would amount to around $10 million at present value. Though the requirement was not written into the Constitution it has been seemingly followed in practice. The election of a President is based on a system of electoral votes where the winner takes all the electoral votes in each individual state. The national campaign for the presidency is so long and expensive that the candidates have literally to beg for funds even if he is a member of the upper class. For the shepherds the best presidential candidate is one who was not born into the upper class but fully identifies with their goals and aspirations. This masks the reality of a government run for the benefit of the shepherds and controlled by them.[16]

The President is the head of the executive branch but has to function through a Cabinet and executive administration. To keep tabs on the President and have him on a tight leash the Cabinet and the executive branch are filled with upper class representatives. This makes the government, especially the executive branch, identify the upper class interest with the national interest. Studies have shown that between 1933 and 1980 nearly two-thirds of the Cabinet and major diplomatic appointees were linked to the corporate world or sizable family fortunes. It is common practice for Cabinet members to return to the corporate world on leaving public office or become lobbyists for big business. Many cycle themselves between government and corporations. Alexander Haig was at several times a general, Chief of Staff in the White House, a corporate president, and Secretary of State.[17]

President Clinton and his Cabinet are good examples of the upper class control of the executive branch. Mr. Clinton himself was the ideal presidential candidate. He was not born into the upper class though he has reportedly amassed assets of $863,000 which means he became part of the upper class before being elected President. He has more millionaires among his top advisors than either Ronald Reagan or George Bush did. Among them figure Treasury Secretary Lloyd Bentsen, worth at least $5.9 million, and Secretary of State Warren Christopher, who is worth at least $4.2 million. To top these fortunes were Wall Street investment bankers Robert Rubin and Roger Altman, each worth tens of millions of dollars. The U.S. government and the economy is as usual in good hands and there is little danger that the annual interest payments of over $200 billion to the upper class will be checked or the federal budget balanced. The American class system is always the victor, irrespective of whether the President comes through the Democratic or the Republican party.[18]

American Presidents of either party are good salesmen for the class system ideology of the "free enterprise system". President Carter described himself "an engineer, a planner and a businessman" who understood the value of "minimal intrusion of government in our free economic system". One description of President Ford could apply to most presidents:

> [He] follows the judgment of the major international oil companies on oil problems in the same way that he amiably heeds the advice of other big businesses on the problems that interest them . . . He is . . . a solid believer in the business ideology of rugged individualism, free markets and price competition . . . virtues that exist more clearly in his mind than they do in the practices of the international oil industry.

Presidents treat the interests of the upper class as being synonymous with the nation's well-being. Overseas investments of giant corporations are described as "United States investments abroad", part of "America's interests in the world", to be defended at all costs.[19]

The third branch of the government is the federal judiciary headed by the Supreme Court. However, the federal judges are appointed by the President and subject to confirmation by the Senate, which is an upper class stronghold. As the federal judges are appointed for life and can only be removed from office for misconduct through impeachment by the Senate, the federal judiciary applies a conservative influence creating precedents which can last for generations. By using the President's appointive power the upper class controls the "character" of the judges in terms of their socioeconomic status, their training, and their beliefs. To help the President avoid "mistakes" in the appointment process is the Committee of the Federal Judiciary of the American Bar Association.

Studies of the 11-member ABA committee show that they are from the upper class and associated with large law firms and giant corporations.[20]

The Supreme Court and the federal judiciary have the crucial power of reviewing the constitutionality of actions taken by the other two branches. As Chief Justice Hughes remarked, "We are under a Constitution but the Constitution is what the judges say it is". To make sure that the judges say the right things they are drawn from privileged backgrounds. The class biases of the judiciary were noted by Justice Miller, a Lincoln appointee:

> It is vain to contend with judges who have been at the bar, the advocates for forty years of railroad companies, and all the forms of associated capital, when they are called upon to decide cases where such interests are in contest. All their training, all their feelings are from the start in favor of those who need no such influence.

President Reagan took special care in making more than half of the 744 federal judgeship appointments during his term. He selected rich conservatives in their thirties and forties who will shape the laws of the land into the second and third decades of the next century. Eighty-one percent of Reagan's appointees had incomes of more than $200,000 and 23 percent admitted to being millionaires.[21]

Through most of its history the Supreme Court has shown "a definite partiality for the rich". When Congress outlawed child labor, the court found it to be an unconstitutional usurpation of the reserved powers of the states under the Tenth Amendment. In *Plessy v. Ferguson* (1896) the Supreme Court decreed segregation for blacks the law of the land by enunciating the "separate but equal" doctrine in public facilities. When the Great Depression followed the monopolization phase of the U.S. economy Justice Brandeis expressed the position of the sheep in the American class system:

> There will come a revolt of the people against the capitalists, unless the aspirations of the people are given some adequate legal expression . . . Whatever and however strong our

convictions against the extension of governmental function may be, we shall inevitably be swept further toward socialism unless we can curb the excess of our financial magnates.[22]

The binding reality of the federal judiciary is that interpretation is an enormously flexible process. The Justices, once appointed, possess a great deal of latitude to turn their personal preferences into opinion. The Presidents in making appointments are keenly aware of the judiciary's great power to interpret the law. With the Reagan–Bush appointments the federal judiciary is securely in the hands of the shepherds for at least another generation.

The upper class secures domination of the government by dividing responsibilities between the federal and state governments. Programs such as defense are the responsibility of the federal government while education and social welfare are allocated to the states. By transferring responsibility to states without allocating the necessary funds, programs for investment in physical infrastructure and human capital can be restricted. The budgets have to be balanced in the states and investment is restricted unless the taxes are approved by the voters. On the other hand the federal budget can fund defense and welfare for the upper class with deficit spending without asking for a tax increase, at least in the short run.[23]

The upper class controls the state governments by playing one state against the others for maximum advantage to the corporations. The state administration is weakened and the hands of the governor tied by creating multilayered bureaucracies at the state, county and city level. The multiplicity of elected officers for the administrative agencies thwarts coordination and robs state governments of effectiveness. By decentralizing authority to an extreme level the state administrations have made extensive concessions to the demands of narrow interests and public authority has been parcelled out to private groups. The shepherds dominate the state governments and control the policies at the local level.[24]

The role of government was supposed to be a system of checks and balances because society was a balance of classes with the independent middle class occupying the pivotal position. But in the American system the upper class dominates all three branches of government and the checks work only in one direction, that is against democracy, the majority and the middle class. The middle class itself is employed by the big corporations and remains under the thumb of the upper class with no independent role other than selling their votes.[25]

The system of government has been structured so that none of the branches can operate without the cooperation of the other two. All three branches are stacked with upper class members with personal incomes in the top one percent slot. As a last resort the upper class can paralyze the functioning of the government. If a program is marked for destruction, it will first be attacked in the public attitude area where the upper class controls the opinion molding industries. Failing there, they will direct their energies to preventing a majority for the measures in either House of Congress using to their advantage the committee system, the rules of parliamentary delay and filibuster and lobbying pressure. If a bill survives all this to reach the President's desk a veto can kill it. In the event Congress overrides the presidential veto the issue can be transferred to the judiciary for appropriate interpretation by the property-minded Supreme Court. If the Supreme Court somehow falters, the shepherds can concentrate on weakening the administrative will, machinery and its personnel or simply fund the right persons in the next election. In short, the battle for an affirmative democratic program is like an action in which the sheep, in order to win, have to take every one of a succession of fortified places, while the shepherds have only to win and hold one, even if they lose the rest. This is the essence of the pyramid structure and class control in practice.[26]

Class Control

The key to ensuring acceptable outcomes in a mock democracy is carefully pre-selecting the choices before the electorate. One strategy is to have primaries to select the names of those who will be on the actual election ballot. By making the primary as expensive as the actual election itself, candidates not favored by the upper class can be eliminated. Another strategy is to limit the choices to two individuals with a two-party monopoly. Now the upper class wins no matter which candidate is victorious. Elections in a mock democracy are based on the "forced choice, false choice" principle which ensures governing rights for the shepherds.

The electoral game was run for decades by party professionals and political machines where power was concentrated tightly. The result was a government which kept the middle class contented without threatening the status quo. Over the last three decades the influence and role of party organizations has declined because of new developments in primary elections, campaign financing and television communications. Now most states have adopted the direct primary where candidates can independently pursue the nomination without first getting approval of the party organization. The party resources have weakened because campaign finance laws allocate election funds to candidates directly instead of to parties. Television allows each candidate to reach the voters in their homes without the party machine's assistance to canvas the neighborhood. As a result participation in primary contests requires rich backers or personal wealth to pay for individualized staff and costly media campaigns with campaign management firms, private pollsters and media experts.[27]

Property qualifications have been revived in an underhand manner. To overcome the primary hurdle the candidate has to belong to the upper class with independent resources or be a frontman for the shepherds by supporting their objectives in return for campaign contributions. With television elections, issues and commitments to voters become dispensable. Election outcomes are instead determined by image manipulation of candidates with spot-advertisements. The survivors of the primary process will inevitably be two candidates who are well financed and who meet the shepherds' qualification requirements. The discussion of issues is limited to areas such as family values, education, and crime prevention which are a local responsibility and only need token effort at the federal level. In the actual election, the process is repeated again along with the expenses. No matter how the voters react the shepherds come out winners.[28]

The corporations as well as the unions know that both the Republican and Democratic parties represent the upper class: "Top executives may still be Republican, but they are no longer partisan . . . Most of them have come to think it does not usually make all that much difference which party wins, and indeed that business and the country fare better under the Democrats". Rawleigh Warner Jr., chairman of Mobil, observed: "I would have to say that in the last ten to fifteen years, business has fared equally well, if not better, under Democratic administrations as under Republican administrations". Other top executives echo Warner's sentiments. Labor leaders like William Winpisinger, president of the International Association of Machinists, understand the game: "We don't have a two-party system in this country. We have the Demopublicans. It's one party of the corporate class, with two wings—the Democrats and Republicans".[29]

Mock democracy limits the choice to an either-or proposition discouraging the growth of a third party. All 50 states have laws making difficult third party access to the ballot by requiring a large numbers of signatures on nominating petitions submitted by minor parties. Pennsylvania requires signatures of 36,000 registered voters within a three week period from third party candidates for statewide offices.

Between 1980 and 1984 the requirements were made more rigorous in the states of Indiana and North Dakota, which quadrupled the number of signatures required, and Alabama went from none to 11,000. Other hurdles set up for minor parties included limitations on when and where petitions may be circulated and who may sign them. In Texas, registered voters who did not vote in the preceding presidential primary and could recall their eight digit voter identification number could sign petitions. An independent candidate in Louisiana must pay a $5,000 filing fee while Florida requires a minor party to pay ten cents for every signature submitted. More than $750,000 would be needed in filing fees by a third party to get all state ballots in one national election. Hostile officials often throw out petitions on trivial and false technicalities. The result is that the voters can rarely exercise their right to choose between more than two predetermined candidates.[30]

The Federal Election Campaign Act of 1974 has been set up to stack the deck against smaller parties. More than $110 million was granted in equal measure to the two major parties, including matching funds for primary campaigns and millions of dollars for national conventions. For third party candidates, public assistance is only payable after an election, if they received more than five percent of the vote, which is only possible in the case of billionaire candidates like Ross Perot. The intent is to set up a classic Catch-22 situation: "you don't get the money unless you get the five percent vote; and you don't get five percent unless you get the money". To check third parties and individual candidates from slipping through the dragnet a Federal Election Commission composed of three Democratic and three Republican commissioners checks their activities and files lawsuits against them. The impression is created that the Democratic and Republican parties are the two recognized parties under the U.S. Constitution. A 1977 survey found half the nation's 13-year-olds believed third parties were illegal. The objectives of the shepherds have been achieved.[31]

The system of single-member district elections with the winner take all eliminates minor parties. Thus a party that polls a plurality of the vote wins 100 per cent of the district representation while smaller parties receive no representation regardless of their vote. This is in contrast to a system of proportional representation in many western democracies, which provides legislative seats in accordance with the percentage of vote. The American system deprives the minor parties of representation and votes too because many citizens do not want to waste votes for a party that has no chance of a legislative presence. In effect the election system keeps out third parties.[32]

The election process is manipulated by gerrymandering to guarantee a preferred political outcome. This has historically been used to deny representation to blacks and other minorities. A report on Jackson, Mississippi, notes:

> While blacks make up 47 percent of the population of this Mississippi capital city, no black has been elected to city office here since 1912 . . . Since 1960, white suburbs have been annexed three times, each time substantially diluting black voting strength just as it appeared blacks were about to become a majority. And each election, like this one, has been characterized by racial block voting and increasingly apathetic black voters. "Many Blacks in Jackson have just given up" state legislator Henry Kirksey said.

The New York City Council split 500,000 working class black voters in Queens into three predominantly white districts, making them a numerical minority in all three. Although blacks and Latinos constitute 50 percent of New York's population, they are only represented by eight representatives of a 43-member council. The result is that though blacks are nearly 12 percent of the population, they compose slightly more than one percent of the elected and appointed officials in the country, according to Jesse Jackson.[33]

Even with a narrow prestructured choice in elections it is necessary to keep the voting among the working class and underclass to a minimum. Restrictions on the right to vote based on race, age, sex, property ownership and religion have been used at one time or another. The gradual elimination of the restrictions—the property qualifications were relaxed in the beginning of the 19th century; the 15th amendment (1870) allowed black males to vote; the 19th amendment (1920) gave women the right to vote; the 24th amendment (1964) forbade the poll tax; the 26th amendment (1971) allowed 18-20 year olds to vote—did not lead to universal suffrage.

In spite of the Civil Rights Acts of 1957 and 1960, the Voting Rights Acts of 1965, 1970, 1975 and 1985 the haves vote at twice the rate of the havenots says a 1984 report. This happens as administrative barriers largely remain in place of legal restrictions.[34]

Mock democracy encourages civil rights and voting acts for photo opportunities while administrative controls restrict voting for the working class. "There is still only one registration office in most counties; it is still usually open only during working hours; and it is likely to be administered by political appointees hostile to minority groups and the poor". According to one voter registration organizer, "In Mississippi a person has to sign up both at a town courthouse and then at the county courthouse. This can mean driving 90 miles in some cases". By closing down all but one of 13 polling places in a Texas county minority voter turnout was reduced from 2,300 to 300. It is the same in the North because more than half the major registration suits filed during the 1984 campaign were taken against election officials in the Northern states.[35]

The Reagan administration was outright hostile to the working and underclass voters, threatening to cut off federal aid in attempts to have state and local agencies deny space in their buildings for registration booths. They urged states to prohibit registration drives at food lines and arrested voting rights activists who tried to register people in welfare offices. In 1984 the government issued an advisory opinion that federal employees whose unions had endorsed a candidate would not engage in voter registration. In 1986 the Alabama state legislature passed a "reidentification" law requiring counties with a concentration of working class voters to register at inconvenient hours in obscure locations, with hostile officials presiding over the process. Since many working class blacks were without transportation and depended on whites for jobs the result was a predictable decrease in black registration.[36]

In mock democracy it is futile for the working and under classes to vote because no positive outcome can be expected. Elections only affect the distribution of wealth between the upper and middle class. The working class is destined to live at a basic replacement level no matter which party wins. If a Democratic Party candidate tries to get elected with a special assist from the black voters the Republicans cancel that with working class white supremacist votes. As there are twice as many white working class voters as black ones, it does not pay to be closely identified with the black voters. Black voters being stereotyped with the underclass, even some white middle class voters who do not directly compete with the blacks recoil from a party identified with blacks.

Voting among the havenots is based on alienation and blame game along racial lines. Votes are cast not to gain something but to distance themselves from the underclass. It was for this in 1988 George Bush used "Willie Horton" in the television spots image game. His objective was to connect all criminals with blacks, then associate all blacks with the Democrats, giving the impression that they were the party of the "untouchables". As the Democrats did not dispel this association Bush was elected by a larger number of white supremacist working class votes. Clinton avoided the pitfalls of the 1988 campaign by dealing with several blacks instead of just Jesse Jackson and attacked sister Souljah for her racist remarks, thus preventing an ironclad identification with blacks.[37]

Mock democracy does not offer the voters a real choice, because Republicans or Democrats, both represent the shepherds against the interests of the sheep. If the Republicans are identified with management the Democrats are associated with middle class union workers. Working class blacks are placed in the Democratic camp while working class whites distance themselves by joining the Republican camp. Both the Democrats and the Republicans are financed by upper class special interest groups. The rules are consistently determined by the dictates of the American class system.[38]

The Republicans have been traditionally identified with big business and the upper class. The Democrats countered this with backing from the unions and the middle classes which could depend on the troops to deliver the votes on election day. Because of inherent advantages in the system of primaries where the voter turnout was skewed in favor of the upper class, the Republicans were at a slight disadvantage in Congress but could hold their own.[39]

With the increasing role of television and the decline of the party organizations the fundraising abilities of the Republicans put it in a commanding position. From 1978 to 1982 Republican Party (GOP) fundraising increased its share three to five times the Democratic share. The total cost of House and Senate races grew from $197 million to $343 million, an increase of 74 percent during the same period. The GOP could take advantage of the expensive technology of politics, including television, polling, computerized information bases and targeted direct mail, changing the rules of the game. They devised a new strategy to obtain the votes of the sheep based on the principles of alienation and powerlessness and using the techniques of media manipulation.[40]

Television campaigning does not allow targeting of the message according to the audience. The universality of access makes every political message a potential liability. An attempt to appeal specifically to middle class union members is likely to alienate as many votes among working class consumers and upper class business owners worried about inflation. The strategy for television elections is based on confusion and cynicism among the electorate. GOP consultant Douglas Bailey told the *Washington Post*, "Campaigns are not for educating, they're for linking up with the public mood". According to Bailey, "Pollsters are so good that it is possible to know at every minute what people think". There is no point discussing the issues, the trick is to tell the people what they want to hear.[41]

Television screens are so cluttered with advertisements that it is difficult to catch the voter's attention and then count on him to remember and act on the message. Provocative negative attacks are more exciting. Media consultant Greg Schneider explained, "It is immeasurably easier to make your opponent unacceptable than to make yourself acceptable". The Republican Party has taken every opportunity to connect the Democrats with extreme forces within society that are said to threaten the electorate, such as gays and lesbians, communists, criminals and blacks who prefer to stay on welfare. George Bush held attention in 1988 with his "Willie Horton" message and Senator Jesse Helms won reelection in North Carolina with a "white hands" commercial depicting white hands replaced by black hands to attack quotas for affirmative action.[42]

The game was relatively new, invented by the Republicans and they took advantage of the show before the electorate caught on. It took the Democrats more than a decade to react and come up with a counter strategy. But it became an established fact that money was the only game in town and the fuel for mock democracy.[43]

The Democrats represent the middle class, the unions, the blacks, the Jews and other minorities. What they lacked in funds was made up by the party organization and union supporters who could deliver votes on election day. However, during the last few decades the unions have been losing power. As the unions look after their members at the expense of the working class, they are encountering hostility from the latter as well as the upper class which employs them. The unions have been giving the Democratic Party a bad name for more than a decade and cannot match the fund donations of the corporations and the upper class. With the maturity of television elections the unions have become a liability for the Democratic Party.[44]

The Democrats carried out a series of political reforms in the 1970s that weakened the role of the working class and gave more power to middle class voters. The requirements that states adopt open primaries strengthened the hands of the middle class because voting in primaries is limited and skewed in favor of the middle class. The Democratic Party lost some working class support and later the middle class because of their stand on court-ordered busing.[45]

With television elections the Democrats could not tailor their message to the blacks and Jews individually. If Jesse Jackson was given a prominent spot at the Democratic convention to attract the black vote it would reduce support from the Jews who disliked his proximity to the Moslems and Palestinians. A close identification with blacks was detrimental because most white middle class voters wanted to maintain their distance from the "underclass". Frank Mankiewicz, the Democratic pollster, noted why Democrats are labeled as liberals by the Republicans: "Liberalism is read as code word for helping blacks. The battle over liberalism is a racist argument".[46]

The reality of media elections dawned on the Democrats during the last decade. They realized the middle class was dead because it could not match the campaign contribution of the upper class, who provide 90 percent of campaign contributions. The Democratic Party had a contribution base of roughly 100,000 people compared to the Republican Party's 750,000 contributors in 1989. The average age of Democratic Party contributors is 70 which means that they contribute out of habit. The only important function of the Democratic National Committee is to hold a national convention every four years and nominate someone for President as determined in the primaries.[47]

The new Democratic party knows that survival depends on selling out to the upper class. Every state has a money network assembled around individual politicians. New Jersey has a Bill Bradley network, Texas has a Lloyd Bensten network and Virginia a Chuck Robb network. Democratic Congressional leaders have adjusted to the new reality. Mike McCurry explained, "The congressional party is the only lifeline we've got to money and legitimacy. The DNC—the party as a party—does not have an independent base it can rely on". When DNC Chairman Ron Brown was stepping on the toes of the Congressional Democratic leadership by opposing the Republican proposal to cut the capital gains tax or suggesting a cut in the regressive social security tax he was publicly rebuked. As McCurry noted, "a DNC chairman who gets a little too far out front can get slapped around".[48]

It is clear why the Democrats never did anything in the 1980s to confront the self dealing and lending of the shepherds while the federal debt grew by approximately three trillion dollars. There is no more a pretense of democracy. The United States government has become a plutocracy.[49]

The expenses of indulging in mock democracy call for channeling funds through the corporations. William Winpisinger, president of the International Association of Machinists and Aerospace Workers, explained the logic of campaign contributions in the spring of 1981:

> The Reagan tax plan clearly demonstrates to Corporate America that the rate of return—in the form of tax subsidies and other benefits—on its relatively modest investment in campaign contributions and lobbying expenses is far greater than any they can obtain by exercising their entrepreneurial skills in the market place.

Congressional candidates feel obliged to vote as their political action committee (PAC) contributors want: "Campaign money becomes an overriding factor. Constant trips to raise money eat you up and get in the way of talking about issues and meeting voters. It poses a problem for many candidates. They are tempted to compromise their positions in return for PAC money".[50]

From 1976 to 1980 the number of PACs sponsored by the corporations and trade associations grew from 450 with $6.7 million in contributions to 1,885 with $67.7 million in contributions. Within four years the campaign contributions mushroomed by 900 percent. Election expenditures from local ballot issues to the presidential elections doubled from 1976 to $1.8 billion in 1984. The PACs outspent the political parties with their matching federal funds. Both parties received approximately equal amounts. To hedge their bets, some big donors sometimes made contributions to both candidates. The Wall Street Journal reported that in 1992 special interests gave $205 million to campaigns and the money was split more or less evenly between Democrats and Republicans. The study by the nonpartisan Center for Responsive Politics found that business interests pumped in $158 million while the labor unions gave $28.6 million. In the same issue a Wall Street Journal /NBC News poll found that 49 percent of voters surveyed believe the political system was stacked against people like them.[51]

A favored method of channeling funds to individual members of Congress is speaking fees. Dan Rostenkowski, the Illinois Democrat and committee chairman who is a guardian of America's tax system, is also the record holder for speaking honoraria. From 1980 through 1990 over a period of 11 years he garnered $1.7 million in speaking fees from businesses and organizations with an interest in tax legislation. He could keep a percentage and the rest had to be donated to charity. In 1991 the lawmakers' salaries were increased to $125,100 a year and they were prohibited from accepting fees for speeches. However, there was an escape clause, the personal congressional foundation or related tax exempt organization.[52]

As a consequence both the parties have been corralled by the shepherds and practically gagged. According to Charles R. Babcock of the *Washington Post* more than 70 percent of each major party's contributions now come from corporations. Robert Shrum, a campaign consultant, has noted how new ideas are discreetly buried: "It costs so much to get elected and reelected, that the system inhibits anyone from taking positions that will be too controversial and will make it more difficult to raise money". Mock democracy has reached its ultimate stage where it becomes a plutocracy. The only defense before the sheep is stop going to the polls. Eventually it will become clear to all that the U.S. government is not a people's government and the propaganda balloon will burst. But before that happens the plutocratic system of government will destroy the U.S. economy. For this reason it is necessary to look for answers beyond the straitjacket of mock democracy.[53]

Ideology and Answers

The basic premise of the class system ideology is that America represents the greatest functioning democracy. However, according to the *Wall Street Journal*, until the dawn of the civil rights era, "people" meant almost always the whites. Throughout American history the "people" referred to less than 50 percent of the whites comprising the middle and the upper classes. During the last decade "people" have come to mean only 10 percent of the population constituting the upper class. But impressions count. After the 1990 census, in answer to the Voting Rights Act of 1965, the Justice Department ordered the creation of more than 50 congressional districts to guarantee representation in Congress for blacks and other minorities. The visibility of blacks in Congress, it was hoped, would give the impression of a functioning democracy with representation for all classes of the population without altering the reality of mock democracy. Unfortunately the Supreme Court took the gerrymandering of districts too literally and struck down the harmless deception. The reality of racism in politics is represented more accurately by the "Willie Horton" campaign in 1988 and the "Sister Souljah" incident in 1992 rather than the gerrymandering of congressional districts for blacks. More than the role of blacks and minorities the elimination of a majority of the whites from the democratic process should be the focus of concern.[54]

Another ideological claim is that money and PAC contributions are not a major influence on elections. It is said that all the diverse and numerous PACs cancel one another out. This may be sometimes true because a weak labor PAC may conflict with a strong corporation PAC, but more often corporate PACs move in the same direction with cumulative impact. It has been argued that money is not all that important because well financed candidates have sometimes lost elections. The state of the economy and incumbency are said to be more crucial. The reality is that PAC donations are targeted to the incumbents, ensuring their election. Class ideology claims that by making the PACs pay for election expenses the taxpayer is getting a free ride. As Bob Dole asked in the *Wall street Journal*, "Why dip into the taxpayers' pockets to pay for politicians?" He didn't mention the annual federal subsidy of $200 million going to one of his major contributors, ADM, the big agribusiness firm from Kansas. The reality of tax deductible contributions is that the corporations and the upper class are being subsidized by the sheep for self-interested political expression.[55]

Low voter turnouts in elections is passed off as a "politics of happiness". The people are indifferent about voting because they are fairly content with the current state of things. The "politics of happiness" is more likely to be a cover for the politics of alienation and discouragement. Anthony Downs noted in his essay "An Economic Theory of Democracy" that as citizens become better educated and less bound by habits of family and party tradition they perceive clearly that political participation, even just going to the polls and voting, offers such a diffuse and uncertain return that a "rational economic man will decide: Why bother?" When cost has been erected as a permanent barrier to democratic expression, mock democracy becomes a contest for organized economic interests with minimal citizen participation. Roughly half of adult America stays home despite the expense and showmanship of presidential elections. In other elections the electorate base is limited to less than a third of the eligible voters. Important senators and representatives are returned to office in off-year elections by votes of small minorities, often as little as 15 or 20 percent of their constituents. Mock democracy has not surprisingly lost accountability to the governed because there is no reliable linkage between citizens and those who hold power. America has evolved into a government with taxation but without representation.[56]

Congressional Digest summarized the need for election and campaign finance reform. America has reached a point where money has replaced votes in determining elections and this is a major factor in the steady decline in voter turnout over the last two decades. Officeholders are being forced to spend too much time raising money for re-election instead of performing their duties and representing their constituents. The PACs are increasingly dictating the campaign rhetoric and positions of the representatives to accommodate the interests of the upper class. The current laws are riddled with loopholes, making meaningful controls impossible. As the system is set up to favor incumbents, any changes or reform are unlikely.[57]

If at any time in the future the American government is to be restored to the people, votes must replace money. The best way of doing this is to remove the tax deductibility of campaign contributions for individuals and corporations. More than 90 percent of the current campaign contributions come from the upper class, who pass on the costs to the public by reducing their own taxes or charging higher prices. In 1976, the Supreme Court ruled in *Buckley v. Valeo* that statutory limitations on campaign expenditures constituted a restriction on a candidate's First Amendment right of free speech. It did not say that tax deductions for campaign expenditures were required by the Constitution. As this is an issue which gets to the heart of the American class system, it will be shielded even from discussions.[58]

Once campaign contributions and lobbying activity for tax purposes is denied deductibility, contributions made by corporations on behalf of the employees would have to be declared as income. This will make the enforceability of campaign contribution limits easier and plug the loopholes in the law that encourage "bundling" and "soft money". Both parties use "bundling" and "soft money" to get around spending limits and federal election laws. The *Wall Street Journal* says that for the two-year period ending with 1992 the soft money collections of the Republicans were $32.4 million compared to $29.9 million for the Democrats. Counting all contributions over the two-year period, the Republicans gathered $117.8 million, while the Democrats collected $95.7 million.[59]

Some kind of public financing of television elections is needed if votes are to replace money. A framework for public financing is in place for presidential general elections. This system can be extended to congressional and lesser races. Some combination of "threshold" fund-raising requirements and matching funds could be used in primaries to keep them within manageable limits. Television and radio time can be guaranteed to the candidates before elections for debates and political speeches. The increase in tax collections by limiting deductibility of campaign contributions would probably be enough to pay for the public financing of elections. Reduction in political payoffs and transfers from the Treasury would be net benefits to the American people.[60]

Once votes replace money in elections the system can be modified to facilitate participation in elections. The "motor-voter" bill was a move in the right direction, though restricted in its provisions by pressure from the Republicans. The elections should be held on the weekends instead of Tuesdays to allow working class participation. Owing to the Presidents' pivotal role in the American system of government, a direct election of the President would limit the leverage of the upper class. In the current system of presidential elections through an electoral college, where the winner takes all the votes in a state, a President can be elected with a minority of the popular vote.[61]

Another area which needs reform is the revolving door between public service and private lobbying when administrations change hands. *Time* magazine titled a report, "Peddling Power For Profit," showing how Richard Darman, the former Budget Director, and James Baker, the former Secretary of State, were recruited by the Carlyle Group, a growing Washington investment firm. It noted that the group seemed like a Republican administration in exile. Starting with $5 million in capital in 1987 the company now controls 10 companies in 35 countries with about $5 billion in revenues a year. There is no attempt at hiding the goings on when even the President of the United States sets a precedent selling out to the Japanese. Controls are needed to prevent beneficiaries on the federal government payroll from engaging in lobbying, say for five years after leaving the government, and working as consultants for foreign governments.[62]

Most of these reforms have been suggested and debated in Congress and by presidential candidates like Ross Perot. But eliminating the deductibility of campaign contributions and lobbying constitute the core of the issue and will seldom be discussed. The American class system will not easily release its stranglehold on mock democracy. The Founding Fathers of the Constitution knew that politicians were crooked and the name of the game was conflicting interests. The only hope was that a free press would reveal the lying, cheating and stealing and protect American democracy from the class system. However, the American class system has debased press freedom.

CHAPTER 9

PRESS FREEDOM

*One of the tendencies of democracy to be guarded against is the temptation to allow the problem of persuasion to overshadow the problem of knowledge.–***Plato**[1]

*The most disturbing problem in American politics is the gap between rhetoric and reality.–***British Journalist**[2]

*The ruling ideas of each age have been the ideas of the ruling class.–***Karl Marx**[3]

*A third element composed of a political mind and a civic heart to resolve the difficulties of the administration and the administered is a free press.–***Karl Marx**[4]

Television tends to be two dimensional. Anyone who depends on it entirely for his news is not doing his job as a citizen.
–Dan Rather[5]

In his book, *The Camera Never Blinks*, Dan Rather commented on the salary of Barbara Walters in 1976, "If anyone comes close to being worth a million she may. But in my own view no one in this business is, no matter what or how many shows they do, unless they find a cure for cancer on the side". Later he commented on the relative stability of news ratings,

203

"Unlike entertainment shows, news ratings are not volatile. Among the networks it is understood that it may require four to five years to change ratings". If rating did not result in million dollar salaries another possibility was whoredom:

> Having isolated television as the primary enemy, Nixon and Agnew and their people scouted tirelessly for whores among the press. They always kept an eye out for those who, by their definition, were conservative, middle American, silent majority types. What time and Watergate proved was that they sought anyone who would slant the news in their favor. They would take advantage of their beliefs or prejudices, use them, and then do whatever was necessary to keep them as their allies. If you look hard enough, you will find a few as they did.

He also understood the power of the presidency:

> There is little real awareness in this country of the breadth and depth of a President's public relations and propaganda apparatus. Within the White House itself if he chooses to do so—and President Nixon did—he has the power to mount a campaign to wipe out anyone or anything. There are tremendous resources to be summoned.[6]

Forbes reported that Dan Rather had compensation around $4 million in 1992 and most of the news correspondents on all three networks had salaries exceeding $1 million. Why are newscasters paid these amounts when the United States President earns $200,000 annually? It is the consumers who pay through higher prices for advertising and television. Why in a free market economy does the public have to pay more than a million dollars for six minutes of anchor airtime presence a day? The answer lies in what President Johnson remarked about the role of the press, that he would rather have the press inside his tent pissing out than the other way around. The American class system tries to gag the press by making it turn a blind eye to the evil around it.[7]

The shepherds recognize that to control the U.S. economy and government the press has to mirror the upper class interests. This is achieved with ownership of the media through the large corporations. By the 1980s most of the American media—newspapers, magazines, radio, television, books and movies—were controlled by 50 giant corporations interlocked in common financial interest with other industries and financial institutions.[8]

Coordination and control of the media is achieved through mass advertising. Consumers are charged a markup for advertising and marketing when they make purchases. The print and electronic media are then paid by the corporations to spread the advertising messages mixed with news and entertainment. All concerned understand that the media operations and paychecks are provided by the advertisements and commercials.[9]

Media manipulation and control introduces self-censorship and news management. This may lead to the media avoiding some subjects or pursuing others for upper-class benefit. The greatest danger with a class-controlled press is that it eliminates the checks and balances essential for the operation of a democracy. By denying the existence of the American class system public awareness may be delayed until it is too late.[10]

Media Monopoly

The appearance of a free press was abandoned during the 1980s and the mass media became concentrated components of corporate America. The objective was to obtain horizontal and vertical integration of the media components not only in America but worldwide. Rupert Murdoch owns major newspapers in Australia, England, Chicago and New York, a European cable network, and is part-owner of a chain of television stations in the United States, including 20th Century Fox. The Tribune Company owns the *Chicago Tribune* and the *New York Daily News* among the newspapers, television stations in Los Angeles, Atlanta and New Orleans, five radio stations and 15 cable television systems and the Chicago Cubs. It seems that only a handful of media oligopolies will survive. In 1993 The New York Times Co. took over the *Boston Globe* in a billion dollar deal when it already owned the *International Herald Tribune* (with the *Washington Post*) and more than 30 regional newspapers, five TV stations, radio stations in New York City and several magazines. Charles Perlik, president of the Newspaper Guild, noted: "The news industry has always been a business, run by businessmen—and an occasional businesswoman. Today it is in danger of being run—and overrun by financiers".[11]

Eighty percent of the so-called independent television stations are affiliates of the three major networks, ABC, CBS and NBC. Practically all their shows are supplied by the networks except for local news programs. Within a space of nine months in 1986 ABC was bought by Capital Cities, a media conglomerate, NBC by General Electric, the tenth largest industrial firm in the world, and CBS by Laurence Tisch, one of its board members, to prevent a hostile takeover by Ted Turner. Television is a natural monopoly business because of government regulation and licensing requirements. With takeovers by conglomerates the media monopoly is extended across individual media boundaries.[12]

The newspaper ownership pattern is similar to that of television with two-thirds of the 1,700 dailies controlling 80 percent of circulation owned by chains like Gannett and Knight-Ridder. This constitutes a monopoly press because less than four percent of American cities have competing newspapers under separate ownership. Most of these dailies rely on the wire services and big circulation papers for stories, special features and syndicated columnists. Coverage of national and local affairs is usually scant and superficial. The ideological perspective and editorial policy is usually in defense of the status quo. Like the local television stations the local newspapers are in the business of collecting and distributing local advertisements.[13]

Mass advertising produces a monopoly economy and monopolylike media. Media owners enjoy monopoly profits and stability in their businesses. Newspapers, magazines and broadcasters collect $5 from their advertisers for every $1 obtained from their audiences, which also helps insulate the media from the pressure of the readers. The support from advertisers is like an advertising sales tax on consumers, collected automatically by the large corporations and flowing into the coffers of the media monopolies. Giant firms have now joined hands with giant advertising clients in an incestuous giantism where the largest sellers of ads are also the largest buyers of ads. This provides stability for the advertisers and the media monopolies by limiting entry and price competition in their own markets and allowing them to charge monopoly prices and earn monopoly profits.[14]

A fine example of this is the *Washington Post* which was founded in 1877 when the city had a population of 130,000 and five daily newspapers. By 1970 the city had a population of 2.8 million with three dailies, the *Post* having a circulation of 500,000, the *Star* about 300,000 and the *Daily News* about 200,000. The fixed cost of gathering news and advertisements, printing and distribution is roughly the same for all three papers. The competitive price for an advertisement is based on the price per household reached. Owing to economies of scale the advertisements flow to the newspaper with the largest circulation; the smaller newspapers have to operate at a loss and soon go out of business. As a result the *Washington Daily News* suspended operations in 1972 and the *Star* followed in 1981. Once the *Washington Post* became the only paper in town its circulation increased to 700,000 and its advertisement rates went up 58 percent within two years. Not only does mass advertising lead to a monopoly in daily newspapers but also increases advertisement prices, which are ultimately borne by the consumers.[15]

Before the age of mass advertising, newspapers had to satisfy the personal wishes of a significant portion of its readers and have vigorous and direct news coverage. In a memo to his editors E. W. Scripps, the founder of the first modern newspaper chain, noted around 1920:

> A newspaper . . . must at all times antagonize the selfish interests of that very class which furnishes the larger part of a newspaper's income . . . The press in this country is now

and always has been so thoroughly dominated by the wealthy few of the country that it cannot be depended upon to give the great mass of the people the correct information concerning political, economical and social subjects which it is necessary that the mass of people shall have in order that they shall vote and in all ways act in the best way to protect themselves from the brutal force and chicanery of the ruling and employing classes . . . I have only one principle and that is represented by an effort to make it harder for the rich to grow richer and easier for the poor to keep from growing poorer.[16]

With mass advertising the newspapers' objective is to maximize circulation which, in turn, maximizes advertising revenues. For this the papers need readers of all political persuasion and tailor their editorial policy to appeal to large advertisers by omitting liberal views that might question the role of big business. Newspapers' editorial policies have become conservative and news is reported "objectively" without value judgments. The doctrine of objectivity tells reporters to avoid expressing their personal values in stories, stick to the facts as far as possible and have each fact certified by a suitable authority with opinions acceptable to advertisers. American news under this doctrine, especially by the process of systematic omission, has become increasingly conservative, slanted and devoid of meaning. The media practice safe journalism by sticking to politically neutral subjects like crime and natural disasters and avoiding intelligent examination of events.[17]

The media reinforce the illusion of engaging in a value-free enterprise though both news and advertising are selective and ideology tested. Everything is projected as value-free and equally significant. If the differences between alternatives and their importance has not been clarified the readers have no reasonable basis for choosing the best course of action for themselves. The suppression of controversy and blunting of distinctions in viewpoints damage the political process. The readership collectively withdraws from controversy and status quo is maintained.[18]

Mass advertising has made television into a "a license to print money" with numbing repetition of commercials and uniformity in the news, entertainment and filler programs. In 1989 almost 20 percent of newscast time was reserved for commercials and every 30 seconds of network news time sold to commercials brought in $50,000 a week. As the choice available to the viewers is limited to three channels which are literally interchangeable, an audience is guaranteed to all channels. The only condition is that programming should not be boring or offensive and should stick to light, noncontroversial and nonpolitical subjects. If a company is large enough to afford television commercials it is guaranteed shelf space in retail stores which is a necessary condition for sales. The result, as the Supreme Court has noted, is that mass advertising restrains competition by preventing new products from new companies from reaching the public. Industries use advertising to maintain their power in the economy.[19]

For the television industry mass advertising guarantees revenues of approximately $25 billion annually which comes to about $250 per household. This steady flow of funds provides stability to the industry and monopoly profits for the station owners. The revenues generated are sufficient to ensure that the national network anchors become members of the upper class while even local station journalists enjoy solid middle class life-styles. These are essential requirements for the mass media to spread the myth of a free market democracy while at the same time make monopoly profits.[20]

The salaries of newscasters and national network journalists in the mid-1980s apart from the three anchors Dan Rather, Tom Brokaw and Peter Jennings, crossed the $1 million mark. This means that even second tier journalists like Sam Donaldson, Diane Sawyer, Connie Chung and members of the *60 Minutes* team were receiving these salaries when the budgets for the news divisions were being slashed. Surely improvement in news coverage was not the goal because news division budget cuts would have the contrary effect. Doubling the anchor's salary to $2 million while paring the budget by 10 percent resulting in an estimated savings of $30 million makes sense. The company achieved savings while focus of the public was directed at the anchor's salary. Dan Rather put his courage on display in the editorial pages of *The New York Times,* which is read by the elite, but otherwise kept quiet to protect his self-interest. Former CBS News president Ed Joyce had this explanation in 1989:

> You simply cannot pay a large stable of news stars these million-dollar salaries in the diminished economy that now exists in television without it coming from somewhere. My concern is that it is happening at the expense of the basic responsibility of network news organizations to maintain bureaus overseas, to maintain bureaus domestically, and to cover the news coherently and responsibly.[21]

The reality of television news is that it is produced for the convenience of the advertisers. More important than the content of the news is that the newscasts on the different networks be synchronized so that when the viewers switch channels they cannot escape the commercials. Whether they remember the advertisements or if it has any influence is unimportant so long as the rules of accounting and ratings are consistent for all three networks.

Dan Rather learnt the ground rules of network news in a confrontation with George Bush. Relying on his multimillion dollar contract with CBS, Rather deserted a CBS news set in Miami in September 1987 for a station break of six minutes. In a live interview on the *CBS Evening News* on January 25, 1988, Rather intended to ask tough questions to Bush about the then Vice-President's evasive and unsatisfactory answers on the Iran-Contra scandle. Bush diverted his attack by a pointed reference to the anchorman's desertion of the CBS news set. Later it emerged that the Bush political advisor Roger Ailes had planned the attack. Rather learnt from "the great TV shout-out" that the television news game operates for mutual benefit and public confrontation is like washing dirty laundry in public. Dan Rather later claimed, "I tried to do my job as a reporter. The job of a reporter is to ask questions and to keep on asking questions . . ." He did not say that a million dollar reporter knows which questions to ask and when to shut up.[22]

Star status and million dollar salaries are a small price to pay for inclusion of these point men in the upper class. If members of the government and the media work and play together then there is less chance of unwanted surprises on both sides. The ABC White House correspondent plays tennis with the President. A media dinner party at the home of Albert R. Hunt, bureau chief of the *Wall Street Journal*, and his wife, Judy Woodruff of *The MacNeil/Lehrer News Hour*, is attended by the President and the First Lady. Andrea Mitchell, who covers Congress for NBC, is the live-in companion of Alan Greenspan, chairman of the Federal Reserve Board. By being a member of the upper class Dan Rather can report on the *CBS Evening News* the amount of federal deficit without mentioning that it is money lent to the government by the upper class or how the money was obtained.[23]

The Washington Center for Politics and Journalism was created in 1989 to formalize the relationship between political elites and journalists. The membership includes media heavyweights like ABC, CBS, NBC, *Newsweek* and *Time*, the *Wall Street Journal* and the *Washington Post,* while the politicians are represented by the Republican and Democratic party chairmen, prominent members of Congress and professional campaign consultants. The center teaches young journalists the rules for covering politics along with the code of conduct and mutual expectations. The American class system is strong and confident enough to ritualize its relationship with the media. A *Los Angeles Times* survey found that 67 percent of the public thinks the press did not do enough to keep the government honest. Most people believe that reporting on public figures is too soft and that the media are in bed with the leadership in Washington.[24]

The print media understand and encourage the relationship with the American class system. *The New York Times* correspondent Thomas L. Friedman, who covers State Department, plays tennis with the Secretary of State. Rita Beamish of the Associated Press jogs with the President. The reporters and editors at the *Washington Post* are mostly college graduates from Ivy League universities, some having graduate degrees in law, economics and journalism. Their culture and income is securely middle class or upper class. Their voice and political perspective match their upscale readership. These are the ways the media reflect the views and ideology of the American class system.[25]

The stereotype of the journalists as a radical and antibusiness group does not stand up to scrutiny. A study by Stephen Hess of Washington correspondents showed that 58 percent considered themselves "middle of the road" or politically "conservative". "In the past," Hess wrote, "the Washington press corps was liberal . . . a stereotype of the news corps that is no longer accurate". The media personnel know where their interests lie and which areas to pursue and which areas to avoid. The Investigative Reporters and Editors Organization has 1,110 members, of which only six have the corporate beat. William F. May, chairman of American Can Company, admitted the bias in favor of business, "There is a tendency for business to stand on tippy toes and communicate only the favorable. We need to present more unvarnished information".[26]

One way of making the media mirror the thinking of the shepherds is having them rely on the Washington think tanks for ideas and analysis of issues. The think tanks determine conventional wisdom and decide what is important and relevant and what ought to be omitted. The reporters and television news programs use this canned expert opinion to add credibility to their shows. David Ignatius, a former editor of the *Washington Post*, wrote: "It often seems that these large and well endowed organizations exist for the sole purpose of providing articles for opinion sections and op-ed pages". He declared, "I will confess here to a dangerous vice, I like think tanks, and mainly for one simple reason; their members know how to play the game, that is, they know how to be provocative, they can write quickly under deadline pressure and they don't mind being heavily edited". Think tanks favored by the media include the American Enterprise Institute, the Brookings

Institution, the Center for Strategic and International Studies and the Heritage Foundation. Most of these organizations are financed by tax-deductible contributions from major banks and corporations to serve the interest of the shepherds. By using the think tanks the media enhance their own standing with the upper class and the ostensible objectivity is supposed to be its contribution to the democratic process.[27]

While identifying with the upper class agenda, the media value the middle class whom the advertisers desire mainly for their purchasing power. Dave Laventhol, president of Times Mirror, noted, "The daily newspaper . . . is published for people who read and for people who consume . . . It's largely a middle class publication". But the media also know that the paymasters are the upper class who contribute the advertisements. So long as the media are in a monopoly market the middle class consumers have no choice but to watch network television and buy newspapers if they want any news or entertainment at all. There is no incentive for the media to take the side of the middle class in conflict with the upper class. They avoid the politics of governing decisions even if it matters most to the citizens and move their spotlights away from the culture of lawlessness practiced by the upper class in government and in the economy.[28]

The print media can afford to ignore the working class because they are functionally illiterate and are glued to television. Though newspapers have the power to highlight exploitation and working class slavery they look the other way because there is no economic advantage or political leverage to be gained from it. The print media are free to take advantage of the working class without having to operate responsibly. So far as the electronic media is concerned the working class audience is guaranteed because news and entertainment are free. Sex and violence give a guaranteed third of viewership and Nielsen rating necessary for advertising funding. The programming itself is devoid of significance or responsibility. Professor Robert M. Entman says the media business has no economic incentive to take responsibility for democracy—and faces economic risks if it tries to. If the media take on civic obligations and change the character of journalism there is a risk of upsetting the mass market for advertisers which is the basis of their commercial existence. In essence the set-up both for print and electronic media is tuned to the vibes of the American class system.[29]

Manipulation and Censorship

Media manipulation and censorship are central to the smooth functioning of the class system and control of the economy and the government. Management of the news has been developed to an art form. The rules of engagement are clearly understood by the newsmakers and the news reporters. Individual wrong-doing may be exposed but the system is never to be questioned. This sets limits on criticism of foreign policy and business. Even if the media coverage is slanted or incomplete it must show deference to the needs of the class system. If in the process democracy is trampled and violated that is to be regretted but it cannot be helped.

Dan Rather explains the management of presidential news conferences in *The Camera Never Blinks*. Out of say 200 people at a news conference most are White House staffers, technicians and reporters with passes and merely observers with no expectation of asking questions. There may be 35 reporters who regularly travel with the President and who represent the White House Press Corps and may ask questions. The seating is stage-managed, with the regulars having marked seats in the first three or four rows. Beyond that the seating is available on a first-come first-served basis. If a reporter does not play the game by the rules his marked seat can be given to someone else and he can fight it out with the troops.[30]

The fixed seating allows the President to identify on his chart the location of important reporters. He knows when to call on reporters with planted questions. Or if the going gets tough, which reporters can be counted on to ask distracting questions with no bearing on current events. The President dreads follow-up questions on avoidable topics. His prerogative to pick and choose journalists of his liking gives him an escape route. He can make or break gargantuan egos and million-dollar salaries by playing favorites with the networks and the news media and keep them in line. When Dan Rather was starting out as a White House reporter the Nixon staffers tried to plant questions with him. He had reservations about participating in a rigged game, but his million dollar compensation package later smoothed the way.[31]

Government manipulation of the Press is a continuing enterprise. The White House, the State Department and other agencies constantly release self-serving reports and statements to the media which are uncritically transmitted to the public as information obtained from independent sources. The public is fed misleading data and pertinent information may be omitted. Helen Thomas, the UPI representative of the White House press corp, complained:

> They [the administration] pick the story every day. They pick the one that will almost invariably wind up on the nightly news, and that's the one they answer questions on or give access to information about. [On] a lot of events, we're absolutely blacked out, and if you don't like it, too bad. The whole attitude is: We will tell you what we think you should know.[32]

An example of how the President can play favorites with the media to obtain the kind of coverage he wants was "the book project" at *Newsweek* in 1988. It called for an inside account of the 1988 presidential election by the writers and reporters of *Newsweek*. There was agreement that the reporters would get access to internal strategy sessions of the various campaigns but not write about them until after the election. It is clear that if a candidate is engaged in a particularly dirty or illegal campaign he is not going to let the reporters know about it under any circumstances. But in the case of candidate George Bush it gave him the opportunity to terminate access to *Newsweek* if they displeased him in any way.[33]

On the day George Bush was to launch his race for the White House, *Newsweek* came out with a cover describing him as a "wimp," which could doom his candidacy if it stuck in the public mind. An angry Bush retaliated by barring the "book project" staff from his campaign. Bill Turque, a member of *Newsweek*'s book project team, recalled, "Right after that, they [the Bush campaign] just put the lid on the project. They were furious. Bush was furious". *Newsweek* faced a major investment in a book project which would get an inside look only at the losing campaigns. When James Baker left his post as Treasury Secretary in mid-1988 to run the Bush campaign *Newsweek* tried to mend fences, but that was not to be until two months before the election with a meeting between The Washington Post Company chairman, Katherine Graham, and *Newsweek* Washington bureau chief Evan Thomas on one side, and Bush and Baker on the other. Turque noted, "A lot of color and texture was permanently lost to us. We were making the best of a bad situation".[34]

After this the *Washington Post* and *Newsweek* became "soft" on the Bush campaign. When Bush engaged in nasty, negative television commercials of the "Willie Horton" variety, *Newsweek* avoided singling him out for criticism as even *Time*, a more conservative magazine, had done. *Newsweek* like most of the media simply chastised both candidates in equal measure for their negative advertisements though Bush was more vicious and effective in misleading the public. In several pre-election issues *Newsweek* rated television campaign advertisements like movies with one to three stars for production values and slickness. These were not evaluated for distortion or unfairness. In a post-election article entitled "How the Media Blew It" *Newsweek* criticized the press handling of the campaigns for tolerating sound bites over issues, excluding probing articles, and sitting mute as the candidates ducked live questioning so that their answers would not disrupt the prepared advance script. Bush and Baker used the book project to maneuver *Newsweek* into a compromising position and created enough fear within the magazine to ensure that amends were made for past misdeeds.[35]

Foreign policy is one area where the media unquestioningly sells the government position, which is the upper class standpoint, to the public. Public opinion on foreign policy is shaped through the executive branch, foreign policy discussion associations and the mass media. In 1986 the Reagan administration admitted generating misinformation against the Libyan leader Colonel Muammar Quaddafi, hoping to overthrow him. This was not surprising, as most American presidents and top government officials have no trouble obtaining press cooperation by killing "sensitive" stories and planting favorable ones. Patriotism in the guise of national security provides a no-lose situation. The press knew about the U-2 spy plane flights over Soviet territory; the planned invasion of Cuba at the Bay of Pigs; the distortion in facts about the Tonkin Bay incidents in Vietnam and the prolonged secret bombing of Cambodia. The press, it seems, is accountable to the upper class but not to democracy or the people. In 1983 the White House refused reporters to cover the invasion of Granada, removing all pretense of news reporting, a process it repeated in the Gulf War.[36]

A telling example of the media's role in U.S. foreign policy was Panama's comic "declaration of war" against the United States in December 1989. ABC News' Sam Donaldson declared, "If they declare war on us, we can declare war on them and then we can send in troops with impunity". The Office of Legal Counsel even created a legal framework for the invasion of Panama because the President and Attorney-General had "inherent Constitutional power" to violate international law whenever they identified serious threat to U.S. domestic security from "international terrorist groups or narcotics traffickers". Ted Koppel of *Nightline* rationalized the invasion: "Noriega's reputation as a brutal drug dealing bully who reveled in his public contempt for the U.S. all but begged for strong retribution". The media virtually ignored Panamanian civilian casualties. After the fighting was over human rights groups estimated 2,000 civilians killed. The U.S. military offered an estimate of 23 American servicemen dead with 315 Panamanian soldiers and 202 Panamanian civilians. The media know it is politically safe to strike a jingoistic "Oliver North Can Do" stance in any foreign conflict and minimize American casualties.[37]

The financial and political interests of the corporation or owners take precedence over the editorial content of the publication. Sometimes, when the situation gets out of hand and to prevent future occurrence, it becomes necessary to remind the professionals of this. The *Wall Street Journal* reported in August 1982 the firing of Earl Golz, a reporter with 13 years' experience with the *Dallas Morning News,* along with his editor Wayne Epperson, for writing a story considered offensive by Abilene National Bank of Dallas. Golz reported that the bank had serious loan problems and could fail as Penn Square National had done a few days ago. Golz and his editor were removed from the paper after a complaint by the bank chairman. Less than two weeks later the bank failed, confirming the Golz story when federal examiners revealed insufficient capital. Although the bank chairman who had denied the allegations was fired, the reporter and editor were not rehired. Publicity to this episode ensured that the message of self-censorship beyond the official requirements for job security was well received.[38]

When the interests of a giant corporation are threatened by the activities of another, the interlocking class interest can be counted on to end hostilities even if the public interest suffers. Gerard Colby Zilg, a former congressional aide, spent five years writing a book, *Du Pont: Behind the Nylon Curtain,* which was published by Prentice Hall in 1974 and quickly sold its first edition. It obtained rave reviews from *Publishers Weekly* and *New York Times Book Review* and Prentice Hall signed an agreement that made it a Fortune Book Club selection. But Du Pont did not like the book and complained to the Fortune Book Club (which was owned by Time Inc.) and Prentice Hall, resulting in cancellation of the agreement, and Prentice Hall ceased promoting the book.

Cancellation of the book contract was caused by a threat from Du Pont to withdraw its advertising from Time Inc. if Zilg's book was offered for sale. Richard H. Rea, a representative of Du

Pont, in a memorandum related his conversation with William Daly, General Counsel for Prentice Hall: "Daly related that BOMC (Book of the Month Club) as of last Thursday (August 1) had notified Prentice Hall that, after further pressure from Du Pont, they were canceling their agreement. Daly said the pressure consisted of threats of litigation and cancellation of all of Du Pont advertising in *Time*, *Life* and *Fortune*". Zilg sued Prentice Hall and Du Pont for conspiracy to suppress his book but won his suit against Prentice Hall only after four years. It was understood that silencing an individual was preferable to a battle between giants.[39]

Owners use the media to further their interests. In Delaware the Du Ponts owned the dominant newspapers and regularly censored news stories or changed emphasis in display for stories affecting family interests. Their bossing was so crude and blatant that a distinguished editor resigned rather than comply with the orders. When General Electric bought stations KOA AM—FM, and TV, General Electric was constantly promoted in the programming. In the years after World War II, most newspapers rejected advertisements from Consumers Union to protect their advertisers because its magazine, *Consumer Reports*, tested and reported, sometimes negatively, brands advertised in newspapers.[40]

Big corporations and advertisers believe they have the right and duty to control the programming spaced between advertisements. The programming reinforces the myth of the wonderful American way of life. The taboo against criticizing the American class system is almost as sacrosanct within mainstream journalism and broadcast programming in the United States as criticism of Communism in the former Soviet Union. Beyond criticism the programming must obtain the blessings of the sponsoring organization. Prospective shows are usually discussed with major advertisers, who look at plans and pilot projects and suggest, approve or reject changes.[41]

In 1965 the Federal Communications Commission (FCC) investigated the control of noncommercial content of television and radio by advertisers. Albert N. Halverstadt, spokesman for Procter and Gamble, testified that programs sponsored by the company had to meet established directives and standards of "decency and common sense . . . I do not think it constitutes control". The memorandum of instruction to the advertising agency for television programs noted:

> Where it seems fitting, the characters in Procter & Gamble dramas should reflect recognition and acceptance of the world situation in their thoughts and actions, although in dealing with war, our writers should minimize the "horror" aspects. The writers should be guided by the fact that any scene that contributes negatively to public morale is not acceptable. Men in uniform shall not be cast as heavy villains or portrayed as engaging in any criminal activity.[42]

Procter & Gamble wanted special care in the depiction of business and business people on television programs:

> There will be no material on any of our programs which could in any way further the concept of business as cold, ruthless, and lacking all sentiment or spiritual motivation. If a businessman is cast in the role of villain, it must be made clear that he is not typical but is as much despised by his fellow businessmen as he is by other members of society. Special attention shall be given to any mention, however innocuous, of the grocery and drug business as well as any other group of customers of the company. This includes industrial users of the company's products, such as bakeries, restaurants, and laundries.

The company view of morality and patriotism were applicable to both entertainment programs in which Procter & Gamble commercials appeared and to news and public affairs documentaries. Thus corporate and upper class ideology is built into entertainment and documentary programming though the viewers are unaware of the filtering process.[43]

Procter & Gamble was not alone in demanding control over the programming. A vice-president of Whitehall Laboratories, an advertiser of headache tablets, told the FCC that the company demanded of networks that "if a scene depicted somebody committing suicide by taking a bottle of tablets, we would not want this to be on the air". A vice-president of Prudential Insurance Company noted the importance of sustaining a positive image of business and finance on the air. A program on the Bank Holiday during the Depression was rejected because "it cast a little doubt on all financial institutions". The prevailing consensus was stated by a Procter & Gamble vice-president for advertising in 1979: "We're in programming first to assure a good environment for our advertising".[44]

The television industry claims the networks give the people what they want. But in reality the people get what the advertisers desire. The president of Bell & Howell Company told the FCC the standards applied by most advertisers which he described, disapprovingly: "One should not associate with controversy; one should always reach for the highest ratings; one should never forget that there is safety in numbers; one should always remember that comedy, adventure and escapism provide the atmosphere for selling". Serious programs are to be avoided because they remind the audience that complex human problems cannot be solved by switching over to a new deodorant. The manager of corporate communications for General Electric noted, "We insist on a program environment that reinforces our corporate message". Du Pont told the FCC that the corporation has found that "lighter, happier" programs improve the effectiveness of commercials.[45]

Before television emerged, successful magazines were 65 percent advertisements and designed for advertising rather than editorial matter. Conde Nast, the creator of *Vogue, Glamour* and *House & Garden* among other magazines, regarded his mission "to bait the editorial pages in such a way to lift out of all the millions of Americans just the hundred thousand cultivated persons who can buy these quality goods". In 1962 Paul Willis, president of the Grocery Manufacturers' Association, boasted of his success with national magazines to improve coverage of the food industry: "We suggested to the publishers that the day was here when the editorial department might better understand their interdependent relationships . . .

as their operations may effect the advertiser—their bread and butter". As a result favorable food articles appeared in *Reader's Digest, Good Housekeeping, and Ladies' Home Journal* among others, according to *Advertising Age*. In 1972 Richard Shortway, the new publisher of *Vogue*, made his own candid statement: "The cold, hard facts of magazine publishing mean that those who advertise get editorial coverage".[46]

Corporations have learnt they can pressure media empires through their magazine publications. The New York Times Company is one such media conglomerate owning magazines, books, and broadcasting arms as well as newspapers. *The New York Times* published a series of articles on medical malpractice in 1976 which angered the medical industry, including pharmaceutical firms. Although *The New York Times* did not carry much medical advertising, many magazines, including *Modern Medicine,* published by the parent company were vulnerable to attack. When the pharmaceutical firms threatened to withdraw 260 pages of advertisement from *Modern Medicine,* costing half a million dollars, the Times group sold its medical magazines to Harcourt Brace Jovanovich. As the Times company continues with its media expansion it will probably be more careful in adhering to the norms of the class system.[47]

Another example of bringing erring media members in line was the case of Reader's Digest Association, which owns the *Reader's Digest* magazine and Funk & Wagnalls book publishing. A book criticizing the advertising industry, titled *The Permissible Lie*, was to be published by Funk & Wagnalls in 1968. Realizing the threat from the loss of $50 million a year in advertising revenues generated by *Reader's Digest*, the parent company ordered the book subsidiary to cancel it a month before publication date. Censoring and suppression of information offensive to advertisers is a common experience in the media industry.[48]

The weakest link in the chain of American newspapers is their inability to resist the demands of advertisers even when they prove contrary to public interest. Newspaper advertising is controlled by industries providing the basic necessities food, transportation and clothing. Consumers need reliable information about comparative shopping and benefit from typical family shopping list surveys in major supermarkets. But the grocery store advertisers dislike these survey stories and these have practically disappeared from American papers when they were the most needed. Most papers refused to carry reports even when the market basket surveys were conducted by university researchers. In 1980 the *Washington Star* announced a five-part series on the merits of shopping coupons but discontinued it after the first story to avoid loosing coupon advertisers.[49]

Nowadays not even book and movie reviews can be trusted because of the incestuous media relationship and pressure from the advertisers. In 1987 a senior vice-president of MGM was disturbed by too many negative reviews of movies and warned newspaper executives that the $500 million worth of movie ads:

> cannot be taken for granted and you've got to get this word to your editorial counterparts . . . Today the daily newspaper does not always create a climate that is supportive and favorable to the motion picture industry . . . gratuitous and hateful reviews threaten to cause the romance between the newspapers and the motion picture industry to wither on the vine.

It appears that the golden rule "let the buyer beware" has to be used even for the news and nothing can be taken at face value.[50]

Perhaps the most shameful advertisement-induced censorship and corruption of news contributing to millions of deaths is the coverup in the link between tobacco and heart-lung diseases by the American news media. In 1953, the American Medical Association stopped accepting tobacco advertising in its journals, including the *Journal* of the AMA. The media has noted tobacco-linked disease as the biggest single killer in the United States, resulting in more than 300,000 casualties annually. Cigarette advertisements were banned from television in 1970. Seven years after the ban R.C. Smith of *Columbia Journalism Review* noted in a study: "In magazines that accept cigarette advertising I was unable to find a single article, in several years of publication that would have given readers any clear notion of the nature and extent of the medical and social havoc wreaked by the cigarette smoking habit". What has happened with tobacco advertising is typical of the media industry. Tobacco is the most heavily advertised product in America with spending exceeding a billion dollars. Smoking generates hundreds of billions of dollars for the health industry. Therefore, with its partisan silence the media are doing their part in the perpetuation of the American class system.[51]

Ideology and Answers

Total control of the media by the shepherds through monopoly ownership and advertising spending reinforces the dominant ideology. This is done by the appropriate selection and editing of stories, editorials and op-ed pieces. The impression is created that America is a classless society with most people belonging to the middle class. If the underclass does not fit into the pattern it is because of personal choices and moral deficiencies.

The media justify the status quo and reinforce the rationale for class differences by reporting about crime and drugs. *The New York Times* did a "special report" titled; "Selling Crack/ The Myth of Wealth". The theme of the story is that drug pushing is no road to success and young people deceive themselves by believing "the persistent myths about opportunities". It implies that members of the underclass face two clear choices. One provides a solid job, steady advancement through training, the security of long-term benefit packages, retirement pensions and other middle class perks. The second is a season of glitter, followed by jail, death or both. Without specifically referring to the underclass or the inner-city ghetto, but with references to faking, bluffing and self-deception the story suggests that stupidity and gullibility may be responsible for the choices made and the drug crisis. Only in passing does the "special report" note the fact that "jobs for uneducated, unskilled workers (are) hard to find". The middle class read-ers are given to understand what they believe to begin with, that opportunities are available to most people but some choose the path of crime and drugs because of a lack of middle class values.[52]

The central themes of the mythology of classlessnes—mobility, individual responsibility and choice—are repeated endlessly. As a homage to the advertisers the *Times* editorial-ized against those who complained about conspicuous con-sumption and denounced birthday party extravaganzas mounted by one or another tycoon. It suggested that moralizing may result from envy and repeated the class system rationale:

> Even moralists may acknowledge that there's a silver lining in modern plutocratic parties. Kings once invited lords to their extravaganzas. Now the principle is not nobility but mobility. Malcolm Forbes did not invite Henry Kissinger, child of Fuerth, Germany, or Walter Cronkite, child of St. Joseph, Mo., be-cause of their lineage. The parties of August may have glit-tered tastelessly, but at least in terms of personal achievement, they were open to the public.[53]

The *Times* conceives itself as the voice of affluence, reflect-ing the expensive goods and services advertised. Affluence is taken as a sign of superiority emanating from intelligence, taste, public spirit and responsibility. In contrast the working class and the havenots find themselves outside the mainstream as a result of weak minds and shaky morals. An excerpt from an article in *The Public Interest* by Isabel V. Sawhill spells out the meaning of responsibility:

> Laws and mores may vary with time and place, but in America today certain norms are widely held. First, children are expected to study hard and complete at least high school. Second, young people are expected to refrain from conceiving children until they have personal and financial resources to support them; this usually means delaying the child bearing until they have completed school and can draw on a regular salary. Third, adults are expected to obey the laws.

These are social obligations. Those who fulfill them are unlikely to be chronically poor. If they are poor despite having abided by the rules, society is much more likely to come to their rescue. This is and (with the possible exception of the 1960's) always has been the nature of the social contract. The problem is too many people who are not fulfilling their end of the bargain: these people constitute the underclass. Have such people failed society, or has society failed them?

This is the standard class system ideology of blaming the victim and attack as the best form of defense.[54]

Media ideology promotes the politics and image of the corporate and private interests. Ideology image advertisements are a half-billion-dollar-a-year enterprise the purpose of which was described by the head of a large advertising agency: "It presents the corporation as hero, a responsible citizen, a force for good, presenting information on the work the company is doing in community relations, assisting the less fortunate, minimizing pollution, controlling drugs, ameliorating poverty". Flaws in the public, tax-supported sector of American life can be pursued and exposed in depth while flaws uncovered in the private corporate sector are to be toned down. Items like welfare cheating and labor feather bedding are to be amplified and repeated but corporate convictions for cheating on defense contracts are to be treated with caution. The impression is that public sector activities are essentially flawed and should be limited while private enterprises provide greater efficiency and are to be encouraged.[55]

According to a recent Roper survey, 64 percent of Americans get most of their information from television. Yet network news is skewed and limited and anchors themselves admit the newscasts are not intended to inform the public. The facts are shockingly lacking in historical, geographical or ideological context. Followup is tardy. Though much news goes unreported the three networks cover the same stories at the same time. Public is deluded it is being informed, when all they have learned is a random assortment of facts. All three networks routinely dedicate 15 percent of their evening news to human interest stories such as square dancers, ghost towns or adorable gorillas. It seems these "sayonara" pieces are designed to soothe the audience and ready them for the advertising messages.[56]

The need for political correctness has made news official, establishmentarian, and meaningless. News reporting chooses the safe way by quoting official figures in a public relations setting with a high degree of imprecise and self-serving declarations. Physical crime, natural disasters and accidents are politically safe and reported regardless of their relevance to the viewers. To maintain maximum attention among disparate consumers and avoid social or political controversy, television presentations are concentrated on sex and violence. Sex has to be used obliquely but violence is politically safe because fighting crime by eliminating robbers, criminals and foreign enemies is acceptable. The media claims that sex and violence on television do not change human behavior. Recently television has agreed to rate programs for violence so that the parents can help children choose the program they want to watch. The media concede that the sheep's clothing of sex, violence or a trusted personality is needed to encase the wolf of the sales pitch and is essential for survival.[57]

A 1991 report sponsored by the Kettering Foundation concluded that many citizens "feel locked out" of the political process. The citizens attacked the news media for joining the elite political class. News coverage of political campaigns was obsessed with triviality, negativism and a lack of comprehensible explanations of the nation's choices. The government/ business/media in their collective judgment determine "politically correct" thinking and restrict the range of free expression by creating subtle taboos against unapproved points of view. Ellen Hume, executive director of the Harvard University's Shorenstein Barone Center on the Press, Politics and Public Policy, sees a broader problem:

> The Press has become more the keeper of the status quo than the challenger from the outside, partly because the reporters tend to be much better paid than they used to be, and they

hobnob with the policy makers they're allegedly monitoring. Our inability to unravel and explain the importance of the Iran-Contra abuses, the Housing and Urban Development influence-buying schemes and the savings and loan excesses is a scandal in itself.[58]

Media conglomerates over the last two decades have monopolized the industry and attend to quarterly profits and the bottom line instead of meeting the needs of a well-informed public. Investigative journalism is not seen as cost-effective because of the muscle of the advertisers and the potential of libel suits, which can lead to enormous expenses. Yet the need for straightforward and comprehensive information has never been greater for the country. It is not enough for the media to repeat the benefits of apple pie, motherhood and the flag. What can be done to make the media responsible to the people instead of being town criers for the shepherds?[59]

One suggestion is to limit severely cross-ownership of the media. In theory competition in the media could be restored with television, newspapers, magazines, books and movies competing with one other. But the conglomeration of the media has proceeded unchecked for decades and has almost reached its monopoly state. Instead of competing with cable television or pay television, the television networks are buying their own cable channels. Recently Capital Cities / ABC Inc. announced a deal with Continental Cablevision, the nation's third-largest cable operator, for the introduction of the new ABC owned cable channel with an agreement not to seek financial compensation for carrying ABC stations. The trend of monopoly in the American economy and the media is irreversible. Other solutions are needed to restore press freedom.[60]

Mass advertising is the engine that drives much of the media into giantism, toward monopoly and socially insignificant editorial content, and limits entry by new media entrepreneurs. In a monopoly economy the amount of advertising is not determined by the needs of advertising, but by the opportunities for advertising. The opportunities for advertising have expanded with subsidies. One way of limiting opportunities for advertising in television is to prevent interruption of programs and restricting commercials at the beginning. In a free society there is no justification in force-feeding the public with propaganda and then making them pay for it through higher prices for consumer goods. Advertising opportunities in the print media can be reduced by eliminating subsidies for newsprint and postage and imposing taxes to reduce wastage and conserve resources. In a true free market economy the consumer should have the choice of paying for what he wants instead of being charged $1,000 per household annually and given supposedly free doses of television, radio and junk mail and healthy helpings of newspapers and magazines. Once the media have to provide the public what they are willing to pay for, press freedom and freedom of choice for the public will be restored.[61]

Another effective way of limiting advertisements by need instead of by opportunity is by eliminating the deductibility of advertising expenditure. This will reduce the automatic picking of consumer pockets with money wasted in advertising and upper class lunches. *Advertising Age* reported, "The future of advertising deductibility looked pretty bleak after last week's American Advertising Federation government affairs conference, where congressional leaders warned the industry to prepare for the legislative battle of its life". It predicted that in 1993 proposals to reduce or eliminate advertising deductibility for alcohol, tobacco and drugs were a virtual certainty. Senator Dole noted that limiting deductibility for advertising, "will be very tempting" to the Clinton administration and Congress as they search for new revenue sources. What is less appreciated is that eliminating advertising deductibility could remove the media from the clutches of the American class system and restore press freedom and responsibility.[62]

Press freedom is part of the mosaic of checks and balances necessary for a truly democratic society. The operation of the American class system has debased press freedom. But then no institution or policy is immune from the system. As with freedom, the class system handles war and peace, life and death with the same selfish unconcern.

CHAPTER 10

WAR AND PEACE

Mutually Assured Destruction—An eye for an eye and a tooth for a tooth makes the whole world blind.–**M.K. Gandhi**

The Sovereign, for example, with all the officers both of justice and war who serve upon him, the whole army and navy are unproductive workers.–**Adam Smith**[1]

War is an extension of politics by other means.
                                                    –**Clausewitz**[2]

Rich man's war and poor man's fight.
                    –**Civil War Confederate Soldier**

To understand this world you must know that the military establishments of the United States and the Soviet Union have united against the civilians of both countries.
                    –**A high official (State Department)**[3]

In 1988 George Bush defended the patriotic credentials of his running mate James Danforth Quayle, who had evaded the Vietnam War by joining the Indiana National Guard a week before he became eligible for draft on graduation. Addressing ex-servicemen in Chicago, he said about Quayle, "He did not go to Canada, he did not burn his draft card and he damned sure didn't burn the American flag". Dan Quayle's joining the National Guard was a familiar form of draft dodging. The president of the National Guard Association in 1970 said 90 percent of those joining did so because they did not wish to fight in Vietnam—though they did not want to take the more drastic step of going to Canada either. Dan Quayle's example confirmed the suspicion, supported by statistics, that class connections could get one out of serving in Vietnam. Mostly white, middle class and well educated, the National Guard in the War had 28,000 more university educated men than in all active forces combined, and until 1971 there was a waiting list to get in.[4]

However, the same George Bush changed his tune during the 1992 election campaign. On the Larry King show Bush said Bill Clinton should "level with the American people on the draft, on whether he went to Moscow, how many demonstrations he led against his country from a foreign soil". Clinton never denied his opposition to the fighting in Vietnam. While in England, he said, he "helped to put together a teach-in at the University of London" and also joined a group of American antiwar protesters outside the U.S. Embassy in London. But Bush continued with his calumnies and innuendoes on the show, "I don't want to tell you what I really think, because I don't have the facts . . . but to go to Moscow one year after Russia crushed Czechoslovakia, not remember who you saw . . . I really think the answer is, level with the American people".[5]

Clinton had not done anything different from what Dan Quayle did. Using the George Bush test, "He did not go to Canada, he did not burn his draft card and he damned sure didn't burn the American flag". Bill Clinton was a working class boy who learnt the upper class tricks, used them to his advantage and avoided being suckered into martyrdom in Vietnam. Bush did not discuss the class basis of most wars, that wars are fought to meet upper class objectives by sacrificing the working class youth.

Of the two kinds of wars, offensive and defensive, it is easier getting the people to fight and die in the latter because the masses feel they could loose their freedom and lives if they didn't defend themselves. However, in offensive wars, the populace wants to know the reason for it and want to be sure it is worth dying for.

Though the working class are expected to fight and die in wars the primary objective of the upper class is to concentrate on the opportunities for class dominance of the U.S. economy and risk-free profits. Defense spending was traditionally checked by the need to raise revenue through taxation. The checks of a balanced budget were removed in the 1980s so that the upper class could raid the public treasury. A Cold War ideology was devised to cover the tracks.

The mechanism and results of the policy of Mutually Assured Destruction in the Cold War has become clear by hindsight. The destruction of the Soviet Union in the arms race is obvious. What is still not appreciated is that the U.S. economy also was destroyed by the same process.

Working Class Fighters

The American class system has always admitted special privileges for the shepherds. During the Civil War, the North allowed the wealthy to exempt themselves from draft by hiring a substitute or paying a "commutation fee" of $300 which was almost a working man's annual salary. In the South the large planters saved themselves by the provision of exempting one white man on every plantation with 20 or more slaves. Many of those who deserted the Confederate armies agreed with a Mississippi farmer who went AWOL (Absent Without Official Leave) because he "did not propose to fight for the rich men while they were at home having a good time". With exemptions for the shepherds, morale suffers and the fighters take on the characteristics of a mercenary group. A captured Confederate soldier, asked why he, a nonslaveholder, was fighting a war to uphold slavery, replied, "I'm fighting because you're down here". For the soldier the war was self-defense and not a fight to protect slavery. A draft is inevitably more successful when the goal is self defense.[6]

During World War II, manpower needs were extensive and exemptions, including student deferments, were sharply restricted to those studying engineering, science or medicine. By the end of the war 70 percent of eligible males from ages 18 to 38 had served in the armed forces. In 1951 Congress extended the draft beyond the end of the Korean War. As the late fifties were peaceful years, the middle class youth did not question the rationale of the Cold War. At that time only 12 percent escaped both the draft or some form of military service, while 24 percent were declared unfit for service. The Cold War rhetoric provided the danger of nuclear annihilation and emphasized the need for self preservation by performing draft duty.[7]

The Vietnam War brought the class aspects of wars to the fore. The war was not defensive because American lives or the American way of life was not even remotely threatened by the Vietnamese. It was started as a "might is right" war to show the world the shepherds in America intended to dictate the ground rules and impose their class system. The stated objectives changed with circumstances. Initially America was defending Asia against the Communists, then it had to prove the credibility of its power lest others developed similar revolutionary ideas, and finally, after 50,000 Americans had been killed, to prove that they had not died in vain. The real purpose of the Vietnam War was to create a climate in Asia receptive to the shepherds' investment plans. This was not questioned so long as America was winning; the war looked to be a short one. But once the stink of war invaded the drawing room on television every night and its end nowhere in sight, the cannon fodder started getting restive.[8]

The manpower requirements for the Vietnam War were initially low. Though a universal draft was in place, the requirements were met by recruitment from the working class. The middle class was silenced with liberal exemptions for higher education, critical skills and alternative service in the National Guard. The upper class had suitable escape routes woven into the system. As a last resort their children could always claim to have gay inclinations to beat the draft and later change their minds. But usually such harsh claims were unnecessary because of their economic security and priority status in educational, employment and alternative service institutions.

Of the 27 million men who came of draft age between 1964, when America formally entered the Vietnam War and 1973 when the Viet Cong took over Saigon, about 16 million, that is 60 percent, escaped military service. Only about three percent of the 16 million, that is 570,000, were draft dodgers. Most of those who escaped the war because of official deferrals, exemptions and disqualifications based on mental or physical handicap were from middle class families.[9]

William Broyles, who served as a Second Lieutenant in Vietnam, recounted the experience in his book, *Brothers in Arms*:

> I have fifty-eight men. Only twenty have high school diplomas. About ten of them are over twenty-one. Reading through their record books almost made me cry. Over and over they read—address of father: unknown; education: one or two years of high school; occupation: laborer, pecan sheller, gas station attendant, Job Corps. Kids with no place to go. No place but here.

General S.L.A. Marshall wrote about the composition of the front lines: "In the average rifle company the strength was 50% composed of Negroes, Southwestern Mexicans, Puerto Ricans, Guamanians, Nisei and so on". A Chicago-based wartime study noted, "Youths from neighborhoods with low educational levels [were] four times as likely to die in Vietnam as youths from better educated neighborhoods". A northern Wisconsin Congressman found that 100 of those inducted from his district and who had missed out on deferments came from families with annual incomes below $5,000.[10]

In contrast James Fallows polled his Harvard class and found only two out of the 1,200 classmates had served in Vietnam and those who went were seen as "suckers". As early as 1972, social commentators with upper class backgrounds remarked that they "had never known a single family that had lost a son in Vietnam, or indeed, one with a son wounded, missing in action, or held prisoner of war". The Johnson administration made sure that through undergraduate and graduate school deferments, sons of the rich and powerful who could articulate their objections to the war were exempt from the draft.[11]

Gordon Dillow, an Army sergeant in Vietnam and later a newspaper columnist, related the draft dodging game in this way: "[We] were losers in the great American pastime: avoiding Vietnam . . . By 1971, anybody who was smart or wealthy or educated, and who couldn't manage to beat the draft in one way or another, simply wasn't trying very hard". James Fallows, a Harvard senior in good health, explained in a magazine article how he beat the draft. Before his physical examination he was carefully coached on how to obtain a physical deferment. A doctor told him his "normal weight was close to the cut-off point for an 'underweight' disqualification" and he could drive the point home by faking a fainting spell. At the physical checking he insisted on a second weighing when the first did not give the desired result and told the doctor, untruthfully, that lately he had contemplated suicide. The physician understood him and wrote "unqualified" on his folder. There were boys just out of high school taking their physicals along with him who were completely uninformed. Fallows wrote, "It had clearly never occurred to them, that there might be a way around the draft. They walked through the examination lines like so many cattle off to slaughter".[12]

There was a small army of "draft counselors" including attorneys, doctors, dentists and psychiatrists who specialized in draft avoidance and provided expert guidance to the middle class for a fee. They were usually to be found in university settings. Panels of draft attorneys prepared appeals of draft board decisions for fees ranging from $200 to $1000. The head of the Los Angeles panel told reporters, "Any kid with money can absolutely stay out of the army—with 100% certainty".[13]

Other options open to sons of upper middle class families with connections were duty with the National Guard and the reserves. It has been noted that, "Reservists and guardsmen were better connected, better educated, more affluent, and whiter than their peers in the active forces", and the minorities knew better than to apply. Dan Quayle's induction into the National Guard has been well documented in the press. Quayle graduated from DePauw University with mediocre grades in 1969 and had a student deferment from his draft board. Meanwhile he had had his physical examination and was on the way to being drafted. To prevent the inevitable he applied for a spot in the National Guard, but there was a waiting list and he would have been long drafted if he had waited his turn. Fortunately, a spot for Quayle was found with a telephone call to a senior employee at one of the family's newspapers who was a retired major general in the guard. Quayle survived to be the Vice-President because on paper he "served his country". He repaid the class system by becoming a "chicken hawk", who cawed loudly in support of the war while fluttering far from the theater of combat.[14]

The upper and middle classes knew their options in the rigged draft dodging game. The haves and havenots work with different assumptions. Joining the armed forces was the only option for the working class even if the draft was abolished. They did not question the rules. But for the haves a universal draft was only acceptable with suitable escape clauses at every step.

Officials made pious rationalizations and pronouncements to defend the myth of classlessness. Because the education system is an open one, high school graduates could be in college if they chose—and might be tomorrow. As the education system is meritocratic high school students in college are there by virtue of merit while those who weren't in college were probably lazy and stupid and could be properly regraded as moral inferiors. Public testimony and statements by the Selective Service head, General Lewis B. Hershey, were intended to emphasize this: "The psychology of granting wide choice under pressure to take action is the American or indirect way of achieving what is done by direction in foreign countries where choice is not permitted". It is also the best way, because "an individual generally applies himself better to something he has decided to do rather than something he has been told to do".[15]

During the beginning of the Vietnam War, the shepherds could start an offensive war with a universal draft and still give the impression of classlessness. As the manpower commitment increased the revamped Military Service Act of 1967 abolished graduate study deferments. This was a fatal mistake because it forced a greater number of middle class youth into the military (283,586 in 1969) who started questioning the rationale for the war. Antiwar protests accelerated, President Johnson decided not to seek re-election, the universal draft was exposed for its unfairness and the ideology of the war came down like a house of cards. Had the middle class been left alone the working class youth could have continued fighting and dying in Vietnam indefinitely with probably a different outcome to the war. As President, Nixon began looking for a face-saving retreat. He could not abolish the draft at this juncture because it would expose the class structure of American society. Therefore, a draft lottery was introduced in 1970: a number from 1 to 366 was randomly assigned to each day of the year and men were picked for military service based on their birthdays. This was an attempt to respond to the fairness issue and buy time for bringing the war to an honorable end.[16]

In reality the war was fought for the upper class interests by working class youth. Some 76 percent of the 2,150,000 servicemen sent to Vietnam from 1973 came from working class backgrounds. Roughly 25 percent were from families below the poverty line. Studies of Vietnam casualties show that whereas only 14.9 percent of high school students came from poor families, nearly twice as many, 27.2 percent of the war casualties, were from among the poor. Among the privates, who were most likely to be draftees, 35.2 percent were from poor families. Stewart Alsop in *Newsweek* bluntly said the Selective Service System "is quite clearly based on class discrimination". This was not much different than the casualties in the Korean war as reported by Mayer and Hoult for

Detroit, "The lower the relative economic standing of a man's home area, or the greater the number of nonwhites in his area, the more likely it was that he would be a war casualty".[17]

The process by which class stratification was achieved in the armed forces has been identified. The Selective Service System was set up to protect the privileged classes from the ravages of wars fought in their interests. More than just enforcing existing regulations, draft board members were empowered to decide on deferments. Most draft board members were middle class and white with only 6.6 percent from manual occupations in the metropolitan areas of the United States. Board members' judgments reportedly were based on such values as "thrift, education, morality, nativism, etc." Even when some middle class youth ended up in uniform, those from professional, technical or other middle class backgrounds were assigned administrative and noncombat posts. Behind the facade of classlessness, the class system was entrenched in the selection, administration and combat set-up of the armed forces.[18]

Two months after his inauguration, President Nixon appointed a commission "to develop a comprehensive plan for eliminating conscription and moving towards an all-volunteer armed force". He had clearly understood the problem at hand. The Vietnam War and any future wars were likely to be offensive in nature, fought to protect the interests of the upper class. He wanted to protect the right and ability of presidents to engage in wars of their choosing without double guessing about motives by the sheep. The class composition of the armed forces would anyway remain the same with a volunteer force and could be fine tuned with benefit packages and recruitment standards. The freedom of action in military matters had to take precedence over concealing the class nature of the armed forces. At the first available opportunity close to the end of the Vietnam War the draft was ended on June 30, 1973, and the era of an all-volunteer armed force came into effect.[19]

There was wide support for an all-volunteer armed force, ranging from liberals such as Galbraith to conservatives like Barry Goldwater. This, it was agreed, was one measure that would bury class distinctions which were threatening to tear this nation apart. The military had initial reservations and at the end of 1973 the army conceded it had met only 89 percent of its 1973 recruiting goal. But this was to be sorted out with television advertising which abandoned patriotic pleas in favor of immediate economic advantages and subsequent advancement. However, concerns were expressed about the social composition of the military and Congress directed the Defense Department to submit annual reports on population representation in the armed forces. Senator Ernest Hollings noted:

> The decision of 1973 [to end the draft] insured that our nation's defense burden would rest for the most part with the poor, the black, and the disadvantaged for years to come. And without a cross-section of representation, we have no cross-section of support. There is not an equal call on all Americans to defend our security.

But then without a cross-section of support there would be no cross-sectional objections, either, to military adventures overseas.[20]

By 1980, blacks as the most visible indicator constituted more than 22 percent of active duty recruits, far more than their 13.6 percent share of the 18 to 21-year-old population. For the army alone the percentage of blacks was 29.7 percent. The all volunteer force replaced a system of forced conscription that was biased against the poor with one of "economic conscription" in which those who enlisted were those whom society had presented no viable alternatives. There were apprehensions that equity-based calls in the armed forces might arouse the public with calls for greater equity in American society. There was the question of credibility overseas as well, where the combat units were seen to be drawn overwhelmingly from the racial minorities. Alarm bells started ringing in Congress, that appearances did count and something ought to be done to give the impression of greater cross-sectional representation.[21]

Accordingly military pay was improved along with G.I. Bill benefits and other changes were made to attract more whites. The military entrance test was refined along with standards for enlistment to limit the number of blacks. The higher standards in effect by 1987 disqualified more than 70 percent of black males from enlisting, compared with only 30 percent of nonblacks. By 1987 the percentage of blacks in the army was reduced by six percent to 23.5 percent and in the armed forces overall by three percent, to 19.7 percent. Another way of attracting whites was to provide opportunities for women in the services. As women earn less than the males in the private sector, they would find military service more attractive, especially in the reserve components of the Air Force and the Air National Guard. Most of the enlistment by 1987 was still from the working class because the maximum family income in 1979 dollar value was close to $27,400. The objective was to retain the class bias while giving the impression of a more representative force.[22]

With a volunteer armed force the most urgent need was to blur the class issues. The role of women in the military achieves this objective. Women accounted for less than 13 percent of active-duty recruits in 1987. The Defense Department planned to scrap most restrictions on women in aerial and naval combat and from serving on warships.[23]

The debate over gays has been used to disguise the class bias in the armed forces. It is not surprising that the Defense Department's anti-gay regulations coincided with the institution of the draft in the early 1940s. Anti-gay regulations provided the ultimate escape route for the upper class. There was no infallible test for "homosexual tendencies". The problem with anti-gay regulations was that working class draftees could take advantage of it. At the peak of the final European offensive against the Third Reich in 1945, Secretary of War Henry Stimson ordered a review of all gay discharges in the previous two years, with an eye toward reinducting gay men who had not committed any inservice homosexual acts. Because of the potential for abuse and the tendency of the military to ignore the regulation when convenient, gay activists in the early 1970s had to go to federal court to force the government to observe its own policies regrading the exclusion of gays.[24]

Anti-gay regulations continued even after the all-volunteer armed forces had been instituted. The disadvantages of military service are the dangers of becoming a casualty in active combat and the lack of sexual outlets during military service. The anti-gay regulations helped resolve both problems. Many military personnel, especially in the reserves, tried to escape mobilization during Operation Desert Storm by telling their reserve commanders they were gay. One of the purposes of encouraging women in the military is to provide companionship and draw men to the military. If the women refused to grant sexual favors they could be accused of being lesbians and discharged or transferred. The overall national objective of a balanced armed force is achieved by not discharging all gays from the military but by selectively enforcing the ban on homosexuals.[25]

It is not surprising that the working class provides the bulk of the manpower in the armed forces. The American class system ensures this by denying savings and meaningful alternatives to the havenots. This, however, is only half the story. The other and more important part is the deficit defense spending and waste on Cold Wars, the diversion of national resources from productive projects and military adventures overseas to spread the gospel of the American class system.

Military-Industrial Complex

The defense policy of the United Sates along with the military-industrial-political complex are molded to meet the shepherds' goals. Defense spending is encouraged because it leads to socialization of costs and privatization of profits. For the upper class it provides an ideal combination of limited risk with no competition and guaranteed profits.

In his farewell address, President Eisenhower noted the danger from a "conjunction of an immense military establishment and a large arms industry" and urged the nation to "guard against the acquisition of unwarranted influence, whether sought or unsought, by the military-industrial complex". It appears President Eisenhower's warning was disregarded because the fox had the responsibility of guarding the chicken coop. William Proxmire, the Democratic Senator from Wisconsin, noted, "My own experience in the Senate has shown me the painful inability of our democracy to resist the momentum of excessive spending and waste that accompanies our vast military establishment".[26]

The Defense Department spends billions of dollars annually on terms most favorable to the military contractors. Since capital equipment required to meet military specifications has no alternative use, its costs are included in the contract. The arms business is virtually risk-free but generous profit margins are still provided. There is no risk of price fluctuations or changes in demand. The contractor is protected on the investment made if a contract is canceled. The members of the upper class rotate between assignments within the defense establishment and the contracting companies. By being generous and cooperative with the contracting companies the government and employees guarantee lucrative employment and consulting positions for themselves after a change of administration or after retirement. There are numerous precedents and the practice of job exchanges between the department administration and contractors and conflict of interest is overlooked. For the upper class, defense contracting is a preferred alternative to any other kind of investment.[27]

The upper class prefers privatization and contracting of regular military operations. Private contractors maintain aircraft, fire rockets, build and maintain launching sites, organize and direct other contractors and even make major public decisions for the Defense Department. Because of the myth of separation of public and private entities the private contractor can determine with little interference executive pay, expense accounts, fringe benefits, campaign contributions and numerous other matters for the benefit of the upper class. They also encourage campaign contribution dependency from both parties, ensuring a continuous flow of defense spending dollars at all times.[28]

Coordination between the military-industrial complex and the politicians in Congress is achieved by manipulating the military facilities in their home states and districts and contributions by defense contractors' political action committees. The armed service committees have members whose interests are in accord with the military-industrial complex and are the focus of special attention from Pentagon officials and civilian personnel. The military-industrial complex can overcome any hesitation or rational thinking on the part of the politicians. If the carrot of the campaign contributions is not enough to achieve compliance the stick of closing bases and shutting defense establishments in the home state can force the politicians into line. The politicians are held hostage to the system. Senator Alan Cranston of California, who took President Eisenhower's warning to heart, had to support the B-2 bomber which provides substantial employment in his state. Thomas J. Downey, a Congressman from Long Island and a proponent of arms control, had to support the continuation of military aircraft production by Grumman Corporation in his own congressional district.[29]

The job creation capabilities of defense spending is a nonsequitur. Modern warfare is becoming more and more high-tech and less a matter of men and conventional weapons. Rockets and cruise missiles are replacing bombers and aircraft carriers. A much larger proportion of military outlays is for research and development, engineering, supervision and maintenance and less for mass-produced military hardware. This means that a given amount of military spending employs fewer persons than it used to. For this, military spending may be highly desirable for the upper class but has relatively little effect on creating employment for the sheep. Military spending does not improve the standard of living for the public or the productivity of the U.S. economy. If the defense funds were diverted to improving infrastructure, it would create more jobs and translate into higher standards of living for the people. Military expenditures do not have much value for increasing aggregate demand and employment and may even contribute substantially to increased unemployment.[30]

Defense spending and the military-industrial-political complex achieved a new meaning in the 1980s beyond President Eisenhower's predictions. In eight years the Reagan administration spent about two trillion dollars on defense, which was more than the combined expenditure of all the administrations from Truman to Carter. The expenditure was remarkable because it was made with federal deficits, thus snapping the link between tax revenues and spending and removing all checks on the avarice of the upper class. As most of the federal deficits were financed by the upper class, defense spending was a patriotic conduit for sucking funds from the public treasury and lending the money back to the government to earn interest. The shepherds had achieved the ultimate goal of defense spending, which is the annual tribute the sheep pay to the master as a price for being kept alive. Officially the United States was defending Japan and Germany, who had in return bought $600 billion in treasury securities out of a deficit of $4 trillion. Yet the defense spending game was continuing in 1993 because the U.S. economy was hooked on it like a narcotic and nobody had figured out how to deal with the withdrawal symptoms.[31]

The Cold War was invented to justify the irrationality and destructive goals of the shepherds. In 1949 Harvard economist Sumner Slichter explained the purpose of the Cold War: "[It] increases the demand for goods, helps sustain a high level of employment, accelerates technical progress and thus helps the country to raise its standard of living . . . so we may thank Russians for helping make capitalism in the United States work better than ever". A few months later *U.S. News & World Report* noted with equal candor: "Government planners figure they have the magic formula for almost endless good times . . . Cold War is the catalyst. Cold War is an automatic pump primer. Turn a spigot, the public clamors for more arms spending. Turn another, the clamor ceases . . . Cold War demands, if fully exploited, are almost limitless". From the beginning thoughtful politicians, men like Chester Bowles and Senator Fulbright, understood the Soviet threat was not military but economic, political and ideological.[32]

The Cold War sought to avoid a disarmament agreement and engage in technological competition with the Soviet Union which would continue endlessly until they destroyed themselves economically. There was no real threat from the USSR because the United States was always ahead. This was true of the atomic bomb, intercontinental ballistic missiles and nuclear submarines. As of 1988 the U.S. had built Cruise missiles while the Soviets had yet to develop one. The military-industrial complex created the myth of military inferiority to the Soviets and the vulnerability to attack to sustain defense spending. President Reagan's announced goal was "to close the gap with the Soviets, and ultimately reach the position of military superiority . . ." In a June 1986 press conference, he claimed that the United States was then militarily inferior to the Soviet Union. To raise the stakes in the Cold War game, Reagan started expenditures on the Strategic Defense Initiative, or Star Wars, though the scientific community claimed it was not a practical proposition.[33]

The Cold War was committed to the policy of "mutually assured destruction" (MAD). There was no incentive for either side to start a nuclear war with a surprise first strike because none could escape destruction. In reality the Cold War was for enforcing the American class system ideology worldwide and bankrupting the Soviet Union with an arms spending spree. By the end of the 1980s the latter objective was achieved with the breakup of the Soviet Union. The American class system ideology did not realize that the MAD policy assured the destruction of the U.S. economy as well. Senator Moynihan noted the affects of the Cold War on American institutions:

The law of nations, somewhere that got lost in the fog of the Cold War. It just got lost. We have become a national-security state, a country mobilized for war on a permanent basis, and we got into the business of saying everything is secret. Can we recover the memory of what we were before we became what we are now? Can we discover a sense of proportion in the national security state? The task of purging the Cold War from our institutions is enormous. It will require a sustained and determined effort.

It is difficult to reverse the inertia of the American class system and the Cold War ideology could be replaced by the need for establishing and defending a "New World Order". Probably the MAD policy has to run its course economically before sanity can be restored in the domestic economy.[34]

Another function of the military-industrial complex is creating and defending international slavery. The savings flow from the sheep to the shepherds in the American class system using the mechanism of institutional monopoly. These are then utilized partly in defense spending to create the might for international adventures and the rest is invested abroad for higher returns. As Victor Perlo has noted: "The decisive fact we must recognize is that imperialism is a system of super profit and plunder first and foremost of the working people in the home country". The costs of militarization and war are paid by the American people while investments abroad support ruling-class profits and property expansion. Investment by the shepherds abroad can take advantage of low wages, absence of social legislation or environmental controls to exploit the resources and people abroad even at the expense of high domestic unemployment. Military might provides the means for creating a climate overseas for American investment.[35]

The $12 billion to $16 billion annual foreign aid abroad is designed to protect the investments by arming and bribing military leaders in various countries so that they keep the impoverished populations in line. A slave economy abroad, for sake of efficiency, needs foreign slave drivers. For this most of the aid goes to shepherds in the other countries. President Ferdinand Marcos stole billions of dollars from the Philippine public treasury, much of it being American aid. Most of the U.S. economic "aid" comes with strings attached: the recipient nations must allow the multinationals to repatriate profits, protect their investments and privatize their economies by transferring mines, mills and utilities into the hands of the foreign investors. In return the host governments can terrorize or abuse their own people without fear of sanctions. Senator Frank Church noted the essence of foreign and military assistance in 1972, "a government may torture or terrorize its own population but—from the standpoint of our policy makers—as long as it remains anticommunist, provides 'stability', generally supports American foreign policy and is hospitable to American investment, it qualifies for purposes of aid, as a 'free country' ". He also pointed out that foreign aid is presently designed "to serve business interests at the expense of the American people".[36]

The military-industrial complex routinely engages in military adventurism. As real hot wars in the nuclear age are too dangerous military adventures serve the purpose of training exercises and field tests for equipment and most important as a display of might for both domestic and international audiences. Examples of military adventures include the Vietnam War, the Gulf War, the invasion of Grenada and Panama to kidnap General Manuel Noriega and many other behind the scenes operations in Afghanistan, Nicaragua and El Salvador.

Vice President Hubert Humphrey characterized Vietnam as a "glorious adventure". President Johnson told a cheering Junior Chamber of Commerce audience in 1966, "We own half the trucks in the world. We own almost half of the radios in the world. We own a third of all the electricity . . ." But the rest of the world wanted the same things. "Now I would like to see them enjoy the blessings that we enjoy. But don't you help them exchange places with us, because I don't want to be where they are". President Johnson converted an offensive war into a defensive war where the United States was protecting its standard of living from the rest of the world. The domino theory was as good an excuse as any to start a war half the way around the world. Henry Kissinger noted in 1970 on organizing a coup in Chile, "I don't see why we need to stand by and watch a country go communist because of the irresponsibility of its own people".[37]

The real reason of Vietnam War was displaying the might and invincibility of the American class system. The total firepower used by the U.S. in Vietnam "probably exceeded the amount used in all previous wars combined". On the enemy side casualties included 2.2 million Vietnamese, Cambodians and Laotians killed, 3.2 million more maimed or wounded,

14 million Indochinese left homeless or displaced and over 300,000 missing in Vietnam alone. The U.S. adventure also left Vietnam with an estimated 83,000 amputees, 40,000 blind or deaf and hundreds of thousands of orphans, prostitutes and drug addicts. Environmental damage caused by 18 million gallons of Agent Orange poisoned hundreds and thousands of acres and made two-fifths of Vietnam's land unusable for forestry or agriculture. What had the Vietnamese done to suffer the fate comparable to the holocaust? They were guinea pigs to show the world the might of America and happened to be at the wrong place at the wrong time.[38]

The Vietnam misadventure proved to be a turning point in American history. One lesson was that there are limits to might. Firepower and high technology are insufficient to change people's thinking. With 57,000 Americans killed and hundreds of thousands more wounded it is not practical to fight offensive wars with appeals to patriotism. In short, wars cannot achieve upper class goals with the middle class and working class doing the fighting and dying. The draft was abolished after the Vietnam War. The effects of the deficits and inflation on the domestic economy resulting from the war couldn't be avoided. The shepherds realized that Cold Wars were preferable to hot wars and more could be achieved by acknowledging the existence of the Chinese Communists and working with them rather than wishing them away.[39]

The Gulf War was another example of the operation of the American class system on a global scale. At the beginning of the crisis President Bush committed hundreds and thousands of American troops to the Saudi desert to defend "our way of life". When some Americans picked up the slogan "no blood for oil", Bush modified his reasoning and claimed, "oil is part of it, but it is not a main reason—a main reason we are there is to see that aggression is unrewarded". In reality the politics of oil have governed the history of the Middle East for more than half a century. The Middle East was carved into kingdoms separating the oil reserves from the population by the Western nations. As one example Kuwait had the oil while Iraq had the population though initially it was a single country. This was also true of Saudi Arabia and other oil kingdoms in the region.[40]

The old trick of divide and rule was used to steal oil from the Middle East. First Kuwait would sell oil to the western world. As Kuwait did not have a population base the oil revenues would be invested in the western economies while a major portion would be spent on purchasing advanced military armaments. This way it ended up as a barter between oil and military hardware. As the price of oil was governed by worldwide competition while the military hardware could only be obtained from America at monopoly prices it was an ideal barter arrangement for the western nations. A secret cable from the State Department dated July 5, 1979, directed to Middle East specialist April Glaspie explained the special relationship, "The basis of this relationship is our need for oil and the Saudi need for security . . . Oil for security is still the essence of the special relationship". To prevent the Iraqis from taking over Kuwait or the Egyptians and Jordanians taking over Saudi Arabia a straw devil was created in Israel. Most of the hostility and anger in the Middle East was directed at Israel instead of the Western nations. Indirectly Israel was providing the manpower resources to protect the oil reserves in the Middle East and America was willing to pay billions of dollars in foreign aid for this service.[41]

Saddam Hussein made clear his concern before the Gulf War by accusing Kuwait and the Emirates of overproduction of oil with the resulting decrease in the price and Iraqi revenue. He claimed that as part of a U.S. led conspiracy, the price of oil had dropped from $21 a barrel to $16 in the first half of 1990 costing Iraq $14 billion in revenue. The course of this "subversive policy", he charged, was to "secure the flow of oil . . . at the cheapest price". Saddam Hussein accused the Kuwaitis of exceeding oil production quotas and stealing oil from the rich Rumaillah field that mostly rested in Iraq but dipped slightly into Kuwait. He wanted relief on Iraq's war debt and guaranteed access to the sea. Instead of encouraging the Kuwaitis to settle the small differences amicably with Iraq, the United

States provided guarantees of protection against attack. Five days before the invasion, Kuwait's foreign minister told Jordan's King Hussein, "We cannot bargain over an inch of territory. It's against our Constitution. If Saddam comes across the border, let him come. The Americans will get him out".[42]

The invasion of Kuwait and the subsequent Gulf War changed the whole political scenario in the Middle East. For the first time the United States had to send its own troops to do the fighting and had to keep the Israelis out of the war even when they were the targets of Scud missiles. A new coalition had to be made with Egypt and Syria, which had been previously labeled a terrorist state. As price for Soviet cooperation in the U.N. Security Council Bush had to make a deal with Gorbachev whereby the United States could get Saddam Hussein out of Kuwait but not proceed to Baghdad. The United States incurred the hatred of the Arab world and the real strategy in the Middle East was revealed to the whole world.

The United States needs a settlement in the Middle East among Israel, Syria, Egypt and Jordan because Israel cannot protect American oil interests there. The next time populous countries like Egypt, Jordan, Yemen, Iraq or Iran go after the oil kingdoms, it will not be practical sending American troops. Yet President Bush was convinced of the demonstration value of the war. "When we win, and we will, we will have taught a dangerous dictator and any tyrant tempted to follow in his footsteps, that the U.S. has a new credibility and that what we say goes, and that there is no place for lawless aggression in the Persian Gulf".[43]

Saddam's first peace overture came the same day as the invasion, with subsequent peace feelers to Washington. Iraq was desperately seeking a rational accommodation with the United States. Even when a bombed and battered Iraq accepted a Soviet sponsored plan for abandoning Kuwait in late February, Bush went ahead with his final offensive. As a result the retreating Iraqi army was slaughtered but Saddam ignited the Kuwaiti oil wells stopping oil production for over a year. Also because of U.N. sanctions, Iraqi oil was kept off the world market resulting in increased oil price. The United States being a net importer of oil, the American consumer indirectly paid for the war with increased gasoline prices. Eventually America played the game by Saddam's rules, having to cut oil production and raise oil prices. If the United States had thought out its strategy to the end, keeping its own interests in mind by reining in Kuwait, the invasion could have been avoided or a peaceful Iraqi withdrawal effected.[44]

The lessons of the Gulf war are instructive. Saddam Hussein not only set the agenda for the war but also survived it. The war could have been avoided if the United States foreign policy had been governed by national interest. George Bush, it appears, was more keen on playing the class system games. First the American sheep paid for the death and destruction in the war with higher oil prices. The oil revenue was returned to the U.S. in payment for military hardware to the shepherds. The overall effect was the transfer of revenues from the sheep to the shepherds in the American class system. Bush's popularity for showmanship in the Gulf did not last and the damage done to the U.S. economy was the predominate factor in the election of 1992. Only time will tell the long-term loss of stability in the Middle East and the Arabs' hatred generated by the Gulf adventure.[45]

The irrational policies of the military-industrial-political complex and the misadventures abroad have consequences at home. As Adam Smith noted more than two centuries ago, most of the defense expenditures are a waste of national resources and unproductive. Because of the principle of mutually assured destruction the U.S. economy can self-destruct. A system of checks and balances can restore sanity by getting around the ideology.

Ideology and Answers

The class system ideology claims the United States is in the business of defending democracy and the rule of law abroad, but the reality is exactly the opposite. During the Vietnam

War, Henry Cabot Lodge, the U.S. ambassador to South Vietnam, admitted, "For years now in Southeast Asia, the only people who have been doing anything for the little man —to lift him up—have been the communists". After the war Premier Ky, the U.S.-backed ruler of South Vietnam, told reporters, "The communists were closer to the peoples' yearnings for social justice and an independent life than his own government". The ruling family of Kuwait were the first to abandon the country ahead of the Iraqi invasion, waiting in luxury hotels in Saudi Arabia for the war to end. Not even President Bush said the Gulf War was fought to bring democracy to Kuwait. Worldwide democracy and the "national interest" ideology has been used to station a half-million American military personnel in hundreds of military bases around the world, costing billions of dollars annually. With only five percent of the world's population, the United States expends a third of the world's military funds. These trends have had adverse effects on the U.S. economy, manpower resources and the entire infrastructure.[46]

The class system maintains that defense spending has put the United States in the forefront of advanced technology that can be used for civilian uses. The goals of defense research diverge from purely economic projects. In the defense sector, production at the cutting edge of technology has precedence over cost considerations. In the consumer economy all costs have to be justified by the benefits perceived by the consumers. As a result, the U.S. economy has lost competitiveness in the consumer sector and the defense establishment is unable to transfer their talent and knowhow to the competitive consumer economy.[47]

For four decades the shepherds have used the CIA to report that the Soviet economy was growing faster than that of the United States, resulting in a formidable industrial power, the second largest in the world. To divert economic resources for defense the CIA concocted a Soviet threat that not only matched the U.S. arsenal weapon for weapon but would soon be achieving superiority. As part of the military-industrial-political complex the CIA was performing its duty by propagandizing the sheep in the American class system. The Soviet threat in the Cold War was an excuse for spending trillions of dollars on defense during the Reagan administration alone. To make this defense spending palatable it was all borrowed to delay the day of reckoning. Wall Street Financier George Soros described the contradiction: "There are many examples in history where military power was sustained by exacting tributes, but there is no precedent for maintaining military hegemony on borrowed money". As the lenders of the funds are the shepherds, the sheep will have to keep paying taxes forever to pay the interest cost.[48]

The American class system first applied the philosophy of might is right internationally to create a habit of lawlessness. The precedents creep into domestic affairs. During the covert war against Nicaragua in 1983, CIA agents mined the harbors of that country contrary to international law. When Nicaragua made a formal complaint to the World Court the Reagan administration announced that the United States was above the law in "disputes with any Central American state or arising out of or related to events in Central America". When the World Court ruled in 1986 that the United States had "violated general principles of humanitarian law", Senator Moynihan noted that this was a singular event in American history. Yet the decision was ignored domestically.[49]

Defense spending and the policies of the military-industrial-political complex are part of a larger breakdown of a system of checks and balances in the U.S. economy. This can be set right with a wealth tax on the shepherds to balance the federal budget. This will put brakes on unnecessary defense spending and waste and force the upper class to do a true cost-benefit analysis before engaging in foreign and domestic adventures. Though the solution is evident the possibility of the shepherds implementing it before the U.S economy self destructs appear to be remote. Part of the problem is the pain of conversion from a Cold War economy to a global competitive economy. The task in the U.S. economy would probably not be easier than in the former Soviet Union. Mutually assured destruction was not just a theory but a self-fulfilling prophecy.

Defense spending makes for neglect of vital areas such as physical infrastructure and human capital. This results in a steady decline in productivity, loss of global competitiveness and reduction in the domestic standards of living. Equality of opportunity and education for all are the keys to change and national survival.

CHAPTER 11

EDUCATION AND EQUAL OPPORTUNITY

We hold these Truths to be self-evident that all men are created equal.–**Declaration of Independence**[1]

The best means of benefitting the community is to place within its reach the ladders upon which the aspiring can rise.
–**Andrew Carnegie**[2]

Circumstances make men just as much as men make circumstances.–**Karl Marx**[3]

I have a dream that my four children will one day live in a nation where they will not be judged by the color of their skin but by the content of their character.
–**Martin Luther King**[4]

The whole effort of nature is to get rid of [the poor] to clear the world of them and to make room for the better.
–**Herbert Spencer**[5]

In 1991 George Bush nominated Clarence Thomas to replace Thurgood Marshall on the U.S. Supreme Court. Thurgood Marshall was the first black appointed to the Supreme Court by President Johnson in the 1960s. Other than being the Reagan and Bush administration's "pet affirmative-action nigger" Clarence Thomas won little distinction as a federal judge and less as a legal scholar. However, he was touted by George Bush as the best man for the job. He had chosen Judge Thomas strictly on merit and he couldn't see "even an appearance of an inconsistency" with his previously stated quota policy. When asked if race was a factor whatsoever President Bush replied, "I don't see it at all. The fact that he's a minority, you've heard his testimony, the kind of life he's had, and I think that speaks eloquently for itself". Even Bush's staff members acknowledged that Thomas was nominated under a strict racial quota because the only serious candidates considered for the vacancy were black or hispanic. The president was not lying, because Thomas was confirmed with support from Republicans, Democrats and blacks. But it is important to understand how the apparent contradictions were resolved by the various players because they hold the key to the business of affirmative action, equal opportunity and education in the American class system.[6]

George Bush knew what he was talking about when he said Clarence Thomas was not a part of the racial quota policy, because Thomas was a token. As one, he was a perfect candidate given the color of his skin and his identification with the Reagan–Bush Republican conservative ideology against quotas. He had a white wife and said civil rights leaders just, "bitch, bitch, bitch, moan and whine". After placing Thomas as a token on the Supreme Court, Bush could conveniently forget about blacks in the federal judiciary because Thomas would represent them all. Out of the 115 Bush and Reagan appointments on Courts of Appeals in 12 years only two were black. This was in sharp contrast to the record of Jimmy Carter, who appointed nine black judges to the Courts of Appeals in four years, including the first African-American woman, Amalya L. Kearse. George Bush was certainly not kidding in saying he did not believe in quotas, though he did not have the gumption to state in public and in the media that tokenism was the official, legal and accepted affirmative action and equal opportunity policy of the United States.[7]

The Democrats had to go along with George Bush's game because they understand tokenism and have been part of the official Civil Rights policy from the 1960s. Clarence Thomas stated his Civil Rights priorities, "I am tired of the rhetoric—the rhetoric about quotas and about affirmative action. It is a supreme waste of time. It precludes more positive and enlightened discussion, and it is no longer relevant". Though Bush had threatened to veto the 1991 Civil Rights Bill as a quota bill, the Democrats could not oppose the Thomas nomination. With Clarence Thomas' looks and poverty-stricken background, it would have been suicidal for them to do so. Jim Cicconi, a former senior civil rights official, explained the Democratic dilemma: "It's going to be difficult for liberals on the Senate Judiciary Committee to go after Clarence Thomas for not being sufficiently sensitive to the interests of blacks and the disadvantaged, since he has been both and most of them have been neither". The Democrats had nothing to gain by rocking the "civil rights, affirmative action" boat as long as the blacks themselves did not oppose the nomination and did not want to be accused of a "high tech lynching for uppity blacks".[8]

Clarence Thomas understood the "token" game and was willing to cooperate with Bush because there are no alternatives for the blacks in America. If he refused to cooperate, Bush would have had no trouble finding substitutes. There was no point in giving up the chance personally, because "tokens" are not expected to solve the problems of the black community or the underclass. In a *Washington Post* interview he stressed the need for more black self-reliance, "I'll put the bottom line on you: I don't think we [black Americans] caused our problem, but we're damn sure going to have to solve it". Thomas decided to be the loyal Republican parrot for the Reagan–Bush team. By opposing affirmative action policies he could declare his parity with the whites though he was admitted to the Yale Law School under the school's affirmative action policy. Also he could get even with the NAACP which was dominated by mulattos, though it pretended to represent all blacks. Clarence Thomas was going to beat them at their own game of tokenism.[9]

The NAACP had been playing the "token" game since its inception in the 1950s with the Supreme Court's *Brown v. Board of Education*. Both the Democrats and the Republicans cooperated by allowing the NAACP to provide the tokens. The NAACP was funded by and existed at the mercy of the whites. Though the NAACP represented the blacks, it knew how far to push in the affirmative action game. The American class system will only allow tokenism and the NAACP has accepted the guidelines. In return the NAACP is allowed to collect a "token tax" from the large companies by selective enforcement of civil rights laws. Although Benjamin Hooks, executive director of the NAACP, boasted he could call George Bush at any time, he was not asked to provide the Republican token for the Supreme Court. As a result the NAACP opposed the Clarence Thomas nomination. But in the end Bush outmaneuvered the NAACP by using the divide and rule strategy between the blacks and the mulattos, because since the Civil War some mulattos have had their own churches and even separate cemeteries.[10]

Until about 50 years ago most of America practiced total segregation. Because of the changing global situation and the need to project an image of racial tolerance and diversity internationally, segregation was replaced by tokenism. But tokenism was different from the practice of equal opportunity or equal protection before the law. A framework for civil rights laws and their implementation had to evolve over time to meet the objectives of the American class system without destroying it. Segregation and controlled opportunity are basic requirements of the American class system.

Free education is supposed to guarantee equality of opportunity and life chances for all people. But in reality education is used as a filter to distribute limited rewards. Education, being a local responsibility, is usually financed by property taxes. This allows control of educational opportunities based on class lines.

Affirmative Action and Equal Opportunity

Since the Constitution came into force, the working class has had to work at a basic replacement level. With the abolition of black slavery the working class became mostly white by immigration from Europe, while the blacks were reduced to being the underclass. The underclass was a constant reminder to the working class that they had to work or starve. However, the white working class was part of the master race and could feel superior to the black untouchables and knew that they were not at the bottom of the ladder. This reality of the class system and segregation was formalized into law. In 1896 the Supreme Court recognized the doctrine of separate but equal accommodation for the races and held that, "legislation is powerless to eradicate racial instincts". The treatment of blacks as second class citizens continued till after World War II and the beginning of the Cold War.[11]

With Cold War, the treatment of blacks became a national security issue since it would be the test by which nonwhites living in the underdeveloped countries would choose between Communism and Capitalism. At stake were the one and half billion people, largely Negro and Orientals, who lived in the Far East, the Middle East and in Africa. They were watching to see if America practiced what it preached about equality and justice. The Soviet propaganda machine was having a field day over the integration battle in Little Rock with statements like: "The United States monopolies train the murderers of tomorrow in such barbarous actions as the recent outbreaks of racism in the United States. Racial discrimination is an integral part of the United States policy, and the white people in the United States want to annihilate the Negroes". *Time* magazine summed up the world situation:

> The American people as a whole are becoming more mature about civil rights, which is why more injustices appear in the newspapers . . . We need more than the military bases and missiles. Read the editorials out of India, Ghana, Kenya, Ceylon and Jakarta, and you will not find a sentence about

foreign aid, military bases or electrical appliances. The editorials are about first class citizenship and human dignity. Civil rights have become important to the world and to America . . . These are the things watched by the uncommitted nations—and we must gain the confidence and trust of these uncommitted nations or lose the world. It is as simple as that.[12]

Also very damaging to U.S. prestige was the treatment of nonwhite diplomats and other colored foreigners in restaurants, housing and public facilities. There was no way of winning the nonwhite people of the world without treating them as equals. With no other choice the American class system had to tackle the problem head-on. Racial discrimination and the underclass could not be eliminated because it would destroy the foundation of the class system. But if equal rights for all citizens became the law of the land then selective enforcement and tokenism could keep the system alive. This way racial harassment under media glare could be avoided while the discrimination could become class specific. The burden of proof for discrimination would shift to the accuser because the token establishes the rule that there is no discrimination.[13]

Tokenism became a master strategy for the class system to have and eat the cake. Most of the black leadership comprised the mulattos with education and professional skills to constitute the intellectual and political elite. Making them the tokens would give them a stake in the existing social order and transfer their loyalty to the shepherds. With the black leadership bought off and neutralized, most of the blacks were condemned to the ghetto existence, unable to escape or hide their color-based destiny. Any new and potentially independent leaders could be co-opted into the class system with flattery, jobs or other material favors. Noel Day, a young Boston Negro leader who ran for Congress in the 1964 election, comments on this tactic:

Although the system is rotten it is nevertheless marvelously complex. The co-opting begins at birth; the potential for co-option is built into the system . . . The Negro and most other minority groups have been taught to desire entrance in the mainstream, they have not been taught to look to themselves and develop any sense of pride or prestige within their group, they have been taught to aspire to become mainstream Americans. In the case of the Negro, to aspire to become white . . . One way of become white is by having a higher salary, or a title or a prestige position. [The system] has so many built-in checks and controls that come into operation—some of these are vitiating the energy of the freedom movement already. The official rhetoric has changed—in response to the dislocations and pressures we are witnessing an attempt at mass co-optation similar to the mass co-optation of the labor movement.[14]

In contrast to tokens, quotas for different races was an unacceptable policy because it would interfere with the class set-up. The absence of quotas gave the tokens the pride to claim that they held their positions on the basis of merit. Among the blacks 78 percent are the havenots while only 22 percent are middle class. Absorbing the middle class blacks was acceptable but applying quotas by class was not. A company could have the right percentage of blacks in the total work force but not in individual segments and management levels. This would allow keeping the blacks and minorities in low paying jobs and still claim the absence of discrimination. The myth of equal opportunity could be maintained because equality of condition can only be justified with the availability of skills and qualifications.[15]

Once the objectives of tokenism and the avoidance of quotas became clear it was necessary to create the appropriate legal framework with enforcement checks. The fine print was kept deliberately vague so that all parties could interpret these according to their own expectations, making the implementation of the laws unlikely if not impossible. For 10 years the Fair Employment Practices Committee created by President Truman in 1951 lay dormant with little powers. In 1961 President Kennedy issued an executive order signaling intent to tackle the federal equal employment opportunity question. The federal government assumed responsibility to "promote the full realization of equal employment opportunity" within its own departments and in all firms that performed work for the federal government. An Office of Federal Contract Compliance (OFCC) was established to carry out the executive order.[16]

On paper the OFCC had powers to enforce the executive order with sanctions and contract termination where discrimination was discovered. These sanctions were applicable to all businesses that sold or serviced products to the federal government and could require employers to take "affirmative action" to rectify past discrimination. In 1974 the sanctions could have been applied to 30 percent of the labor force, including university faculties. But as OFCC is an agency of the executive branch its powers are rarely used. The bureaucrats are subject to the dictates of the President and his appointees and even from pressure originating from individual members of Congress. The Defense Department knows that weapons procurement is more vital than enforcing equal opportunity. The OFCC was an ideal framework to enforce policies of tokenism without threatening contractors with quotas.[17]

In parallel with President Kennedy's executive order President Johnson got through Congress the Civil Rights Act of 1964. Its stated aim was to end discrimination in employment and forbade any employer to "limit, segregate, or classify his employees in any way which would deprive or tend to deprive any individual of employment opportunities or otherwise adversely affect his status as an employee because of such individual's race, color, religion, sex, or national origin". The only way to get this Act through Congress was to ensure it was not a quota bill. Senator Hubert Humphrey, who was a strong backer of the bill, promised on the floor of the Senate that he would eat the paper the bill was written on if it were ever used to require corrective hiring preferences. But to make things perfectly clear section 703 (j) of Title VII noted, "nothing contained in this title shall be interpreted to require any employer . . . to grant preferential treatment to any individual or to any group because of race, color, religion, sex or national origin of such individual or group on account of an imbalance . . ." Civil Rights legislation from day one has been "token" legislation and understood that way.[18]

The intent of legislation can be surmised from the enforcement provisions which were delegated to the newly created Equal Employment Opportunity Commission (EEOC). Congress gagged the EEOC by directing it to "endeavor to eliminate any discriminatory employment practice by informal methods of conference, conciliation, and persuasion". The EEOC could not impose sanctions, issue cease and desist orders, or even make public the fact that discrimination was being practiced. Only in 1972 did the EEOC gain congressional authorization to initiate court action to halt discriminatory practices.[19]

The showcase nature of the EEOC was clear from its orientation to follow procedures as contrasted with effective action. Before the EEOC could show interest it needed a sworn complaint from an individual. Then it had to proceed on a case-by-case basis, the time-consuming review process. The objective was to tie up the commission in bureaucratic knots where not much could be achieved. As of June 1975 the EEOC had an unprocessed backlog of 90,000 complaints to be investigated by 270 staff lawyers. There was no protection for the individual making the complaint, which exposed him to retaliation from the union or employer.[20]

Once the EEOC got authorization for starting court action to stop discrimination the problem of burden of proof surfaced. Eleanor Holmes Norton, President Carter's appointee as chairman of the EEOC, assumed that the burden of proof lay with the employers. The EEOC might sue individual employers unless they had a balanced workforce. It was hoped the employers would voluntarily balance their workforce, which was the code word for quotas, to avoid expensive litigation. This was contrary to the intent of the shepherds, who wanted a token in place to be proof that there was no discrimination and the burden of proof to the contrary rested on the accuser.

During the Reagan years the Supreme Court made the token policy official. The Supreme Court ruling of *Ward's Cove Packing v. Antonio* in 1989 noted that if a workforce was out of balance, it would be the responsibility of those claiming discrimination to show that a job standard was unfair. Later it ruled that white employees could challenge consent decrees that their employers had reached with the EEOC in court for reverse discrimination. In 1993 the Supreme Court ruled in a job-bias case that it was insufficient for an employee to prove that he had suffered discrimination and the employee had to prove that the employer had the intention to discriminate. The employee had to be a mind reader to win a case of job discrimination. Justice David H. Souter in a dissenting opinion said the majority had abandoned, "two decades of stable law" to reach a result that would be "unfair to plaintiffs, unworkable in practice, and inexplicable in forgiving employers who present false evidence in court".[21]

The pendulum had swung to the other extreme. Even the policy of selective enforcement of the tokenism law was being eliminated. Benjamin Hooks, executive director of the NAACP, called the Supreme Court's ruling, "a disaster for all those committed to equal employment opportunity". A *New York Times* editorial charged that "the Court majority displays an icy indifference . . . to the hopes of discrimination victims". *Business Week* warned that "the Court is moving down a treacherous road" and regretted its lack of support for "plans aimed at ending racial discrimination". The carefully created framework for tokenism was being upset by the Supreme Court.[22]

To restore the status quo Congress passed a new Civil Rights Bill in October 1990. The Bill reinstated the prohibition against job standards intended for elimination purposes. It restored the inviolability of court ordered affirmative action programs and allowed consent decree agreements by companies. The bill specifically absolved employers from having to hire under quotas. But George Bush vetoed the Bill and it fell short of a Senate override by one vote. Next year the language in the Bill was made more vague to make its enforceability more uncertain and George Bush signed it into law. Just before the election George Bush and the Republicans could claim to be supporters of civil rights. In reality the practice of tokenism continued. Chances of individual discrimination cases being pursued were remote because of the expenses and delay. Most of the employers could make deals with the NAACP and other organizations accepting tokens so long as the discrimination was not blatant. This way equal opportunity and affirmative action was handled in an orderly and "civilized" manner.[23]

Part of the tokenism strategy was to make the NAACP and similar white-funded organizations spokesmen for blacks. Although the NAACP concerned itself with the problems of 20 percent of the middle class blacks, in the public mind it represented all of them. The NAACP took credit for the passage of Civil Rights acts though they were not enforceable and wouldn't affect the lives of 80 percent of the blacks. According to the Census Bureau the gulf between working class and middle class blacks widened from 1967 to 1990 because most of the gains were made by the middle class, while almost 50 percent of black families were headed by single women.[24]

The NAACP modus operandi is to reach mutual accommodation agreements with major employers. For employers an agreement with the NAACP is like buying insurance to protect themselves against discrimination lawsuits. In return the NAACP can get funds and show progress in the areas of minority hiring, education and minority business contracts. General Motors has promised the NAACP to give $500,000 to five law schools to support minority students. Ford and Chrysler have signed similar agreements. In 1990, the General Electric Foundation announced a 10-year, $20 million program to train minorities for teaching careers in business, science and engineering. To help corporations find qualified minority suppliers the national Minority Supplier Development Council charges 3,000 public and corporate clients $30,000 a year for introductions. It also manages a fund to provide working capital for minority business to which Ford contributed $750,000 and Boeing gave $1 million.[25]

In the 1990s the NAACP has come under attack from all sides for its role in the tokenism game. Julian Bond, a long-time NAACP member, said Republicans had successfully portrayed leaders of civil rights groups as "another group of special pleaders who just want to line their pockets". Representative Lewis noted, "The NAACP is much more at home signing agreements with banks and restaurant chains and utilities than it is looking out for the rights of individual black Americans". A poll by the Detroit News showed that the new black generation wanted a more activist leadership from the NAACP and other traditional rights groups in fighting crime, developing businesses, attacking poverty and educating black children. In spite of past accomplishments they want more attention to grassroots concerns instead of those of the middle and upper middle classes. Michael Rapp, executive director of the Jewish Community Relations Council and a member of the local NAACP chapter's board, expressed dissatisfaction with the NAACP's focus: "I'm not sure what its mission is". The result of the new mood is that minorities are starting new organizations like IMPACT because people cannot do things through the NAACP. Overall there is little danger to the tokenism game because it is not possible to survive in the long term without the blessings of the shepherds.[26]

Table 1   Race composition by class (1988)

Race	Families Percent	Havenots	Haves	Median $ Net Worth
White	83	47%	53%	43,279
Black	11	78%	22%	4,169
Hispanic*	6	72%	28%	5,524
Total	100%	50%	50%	35,752

* Hispanic - any race.

As part of the strategy to fight discrimination with tokenism, the issue of race is muddled up with sex, religion, disability, age, etc. so that those claiming discrimination would end up fighting one other and confuse the polemics to the point of absurdity. The practice of race-based discrimination shows up in the makeup of the classes. As shown in table 1, 47 percent of whites, 78 percent of blacks and 72 percent of hispanics are in the "have not" category. Discrimination based on sex, religion and other factors are contrived because they are not practically enforceable for the purpose of the class system.[27]

The civil rights laws prohibit discrimination based on race, sex, religion and other factors, with vague enforcement procedures. The economic class system is based on the generation, inheritance and transmission of wealth, and the ability to reproduce is essential for successful discrimination strategies. Men and women alone cannot reproduce and have no separate existence from generation to generation. They come together in families, which is the social-unit basis of class inequality, not individual men, women and children. Discrimination based on sex is not practical. The number of men and women in each class will be approximately equal. As noted by Marlene Dixon, discrimination is primarily based on class and not sex: "Sisterhood temporarily disguised the fact that all women do not have the same interests, needs and desires. Working class women and middle class women . . . have more conflicting interests than could be overcome by their common experience based on sex discrimination".[28]

Upper class women have as much interest in maximizing their share of the national wealth as upper class men and they need each other if they are to transfer their wealth to future generations. Working class men are as much victims of wage slavery as working class women and are likely to transmit their class status to the children. Parkin has summarized the issue succinctly:

> If the wives and daughters of unskilled laborers have some things in common with the wives and daughters of wealthy landowners, there can be no doubt that the differences in their overall situations are far more striking and significant. Only if the disabilities attaching to female status were felt to be so great as to override difference of a class kind would it be realistic to regard sex as an important dimension of stratification.

The gender as a factor in discrimination is used to dilute the effects of race and class and create identity problems for black women who have to decide if they are black or women first.[29]

Religion is another smokescreen, and being in the mind can be easily hidden or changed as a matter of convenience. Discrimination on the lines of religion is not practical but the rhetoric of discrimination based on religion has its uses. When Bush and other politicians talk about eliminating discrimination in America they first attack anti-semitism. It is safe to divert attention to a problem which does not exist in the first place. For example it is not possible to tell the difference between a Jew and a Christian. If anti-semitism were an important issue the Jews would not have come to the United States. About half the present generation of Jews are married to Christians. Although Jews constitute two percent of the U.S. population, 10 percent of Senators claim to be Jews. In contrast blacks, who constitute 11 percent of the population, have only one Senator. Politicians attack anti-semitism and support the U.S. Holocaust Memorial Museum in Washington not because there is a problem of discrimination but probably to get favorable coverage in the Jewish controlled media and campaign contributions which are essential for elections.[30]

A similar attempt to confuse issues is to compare discrimination based on race with that based on sexual orientation. Gays and lesbians cannot reproduce. Left alone they will wipe themselves out gradually. Sexual orientation is in the mind and claims are unverifiable and serve no social purpose. Mary Frances Berry, a member of the Federal Commission on Civil Rights noted that being black in America was not the same as being gay: "When people try to equate the two, all they do is offend some black folks who recognize that it is not the same thing and might be willing to be supportive". Several blacks said that insult was added to injury when prominent blacks like the Rev. Jesse Jackson and civil rights groups like the NAACP compared the march for gay rights with that of the 1963 march on Washington led by Martin Luther King Jr.[31]

Another issue which has been tagged to the debate is equating racism with discrimination against the handicapped. The definition of disability is so broad that disabled legislation advocates claimed that there were 35 to 43 million disabled Americans, with disabilities that interfered with such daily activities as working or keeping a household. The purpose of the handicapped legislation appears to be not so much to assist the disabled but to impose a tax making mass transportation and public facilities less competitive than private alternatives. Disabilities broadly defined are spread randomly across class lines while discrimination based on racism has been generated specifically to stabilize the class system.[32]

The effect has been to dilute and overshadow the role of racism in creating and maintaining a permanent underclass. Kenneth Tollett, a Howard University professor, says, "A substantial sector of the black community is suffering because so much of the energy and driving force of the movement have been deflected toward hispanic Americans, middle class white women, homosexuals, the handicapped . . ." The best insurance for the large companies is to have their tokens in place for each category and make their contributions to the co-opting organizations. All television networks have their minority newscasters with million dollar salaries. The American Medical Association has a black spokesman for television. In 1993 the American Society of Newspaper Editors installed its first black president, William A. Hillard. Lee Stinnett, executive director of the trade association, noted, "A major reality here is that Bill is black, and that has a huge symbolic importance".[33]

To keep blacks divided the class system rewards and publicizes those blacks who publicly claim they are living proof there is no discrimination. Thomas Sowell says about affirmative action, "While doing little or nothing to advance the position of minorities and females, it creates the impression that hard-won achievements of these groups are conferred benefits. Especially in the case of blacks, this means perpetuating racism instead of allowing it to die a natural death . . ." Another black, Shelby Steele, argues, "When power itself grows out of suffering, blacks are encouraged to expand the boundaries of what qualifies as racial oppression, a situation that can lead us to paint our victimization in vivid colors even as we receive the benefits of preference". Clarence Thomas believes blacks should not expect preferential treatment and that civil rights groups should concentrate on black self-help rather than on blaming whites. In response, Benjamin Hooks, former head of the NAACP, called Mr. Sowell and Mr. Steele "a new breed of Uncle Tom. [They are] some of the biggest liars the world ever saw".[34]

Economic class determined who survived when the *Titanic* sank. Among the women, three percent of the first class passengers drowned, compared to 16 percent of the second and 45 percent of the third class passengers. All but one of the first class victims had refused to abandon ship when given the opportunity. Third class passengers, on the other hand, were ordered at gun-point to stay below the deck. The different fate of the *Titanic's* passengers is an example of the connection between class structure and life chances in the U.S. economy. This connection with class is clear in the criminal justice and health systems.[35]

The connection between crime and class is not accidental. A study by Professor M. Harvey Brenner of John Hopkins University indicated a direct connection between the rates of unemployment, crime and imprisonment. The working class and underclass were more likely to commit blue-collar crimes which are more severely punished than white collar ones. There is a possibility that class system pressures may be creating criminal activity among the havenots.[36]

Health care opportunities and mortality rates are closely linked to economic class. A government study reported that by 1986 members of the underclass had a death rate more than three times that of the people with middle class incomes. Although mortality also reflects deaths from violence, accidents and occupational injuries and diseases, death rates are generally considered to be important indicators of the overall health of the population. Dr. Marcia Angell, executive editor of the *New England Journal of Medicine*, noted, "socioeconomic (class) status is a powerful determinant of health. This gap in mortality between the relatively advantaged and the disadvantaged is very large—larger than the gap due to many other well known risk factors, including cigarette smoking".[37]

The cover for equal opportunity is the availability of free education for all. In reality educational opportunity is also closely linked with economic class.

Educational Opportunity

Officially, education is the door to equal opportunity. The educational system offers perfect equality of opportunity, and success in school depends solely on intelligence, effort and merit. According to the government:

> our system is designed to give young people the knowhow to help them to excel in their fields of endeavor as free individuals. We look for the creative spark in every child and try to teach our youngsters how to think independently, and how to work to develop their talents for a useful happy living in a way of life which they may choose for themselves.

Much of the rhetoric about America being a classless society is based on the assumption that the educational system, by providing all citizens with equal opportunity to receive a good education, has eliminated other class barriers.[38]

In reality free public schools and compulsory attendance laws are just covers to conceal the truth of opportunities determined by economic status. As neighborhoods are segregated by class and because school attendance is based on the neighborhood school principle, schools tend to be segregated by class as well. Even within each school students of different classes are tracked into different programs, resulting in different educational outcomes. College attendance is controlled more by class origins rather than test scores and ability. Students from the middle and upper classes are more likely to attend college and graduate with a degree compared to students with working class and underclass backgrounds. Recent studies have confirmed that the ability to learn and absorb what is taught in school is determined by family background and class origins.[39]

The importance of education as a national priority can be understood by the amount of spending and the source of funds. Spending on education is approximately $300 billion annually compared to $300 billion for defense, $130 billion for advertising, $800 billion for health care and $500 billion for automobile transportation.Education is financed mostly from local property taxes and state taxes compared with defense, which is financed out of the federal budget. This means that children in the different school districts will have resources depending on the class composition of the neighborhood.[40]

The class system denies jobs to the underclass, forces their women into single motherhood and prostitution but provides access to schools for their children. There cannot be any meaningful learning on an empty stomach. This means no learning is expected in urban ghetto schools which are filled by the underclass. It is cheaper to provide access to education for the underclass rather than meet their basic needs while it also creates a good impression worldwide. The funds spent on education are channeled to middle class teachers, administrators and social workers who become vocal supporters of the class system.

If education were what ghetto schools strove for, the resources would be allocated first for breakfast and lunch programs. Officially there is the National School Lunch Program and the Special Milk program to provide reduced-priced or free lunches for poor children. These are, however tokens for public relations. The federal government spent $4 billion for the national school lunch program and $677 million for school breakfast. These are administered by the local officials in the counties and school districts. As a result only two of the seven million poor children received the free or subsidized lunches to which they were entitled. Less of the school lunch and school milk money was spent on poor children. Almost

50 percent of elementary schools did not have lunch rooms. Not only were these children denied free lunches but also the schools did not get the subsidies which go with the lunches.[41]

The New York Times reported about a high school in Newark, New Jersey. Before the school started the student body was checked for weapons and police officers were on hand after school to discourage violence. Almost all the students were having to cope with caring for babies, dealing with incarcerated parents and surviving gang violence. On any given day about 20 percent are absent. Fifteen percent of the freshmen had already lost their mothers. One-third were repeating their freshmen year for personal and academic problems including incarceration. The school system has failed to meet virtually every minimum educational standard since the state began monitoring in the 1970s. According to state education officials money has been misspent, student proficiency is low and the truancy rate is as high as 49 per cent. The shepherds can shrug it off by saying the underclass failed to take advantage of the opportunity because of a lack of family values and genetically induced criminal behavior.[42]

Head Start is another marvel of tokenism. It serves only four-year-olds for one year. The 28-year-old program can claim to have helped more than 13 million poor children prepare for school. Head Start has been used to provide health care services to poor children. It helps families get social services and provides parents with jobs. Head Start has become the favorite anti-poverty program because of the visibility and the "biggest bang for the buck" available. However, once the children start elementary schools the benefits from Head Start wear off quickly and the status quo is restored.[43]

For students from the mostly rentier working class families, the first disadvantage is the disparity in spending among school districts within the same state. In Texas the 10 highest school districts spent $5,243 per student compared to $1,848 per student for the 10 lowest school districts. Such disparities affect class sizes, teacher's salaries and the facilities. Though the need for well-trained and experienced teachers is highest in working class neighborhood schools such schools have the highest percentage of classes taught by ESRP's (Emergency Substitute in Regular Position). To rationalize this neglect of education for working class students studies by Eric Hanushek of the University of Rochester have concluded that neither smaller classes, better facilities, higher teacher pay, nor more teacher training consistently yield educational gains. In fact most of the achievement differences from one district to another could be accounted for by the students' backgrounds.[44]

The tracking method keeps the working class students in their place. In high schools students are methodically sorted into various categories depending on the school's appraisal of their destination in life. As a result students are assigned to one of three typically available curricula such as college-preparatory, general and vocational. Once the working class students are placed in the general or vocational lanes their chances of entering or graduating from college become remote. I.Q. tests which are biased by class are used to categorize the students. The working class students may end up taking courses in stenography, typing, home economics, building trades, retailing and automobile servicing and find difficulty in getting employment after they drop out or graduate from high school. A few gifted students from the working class homes are allowed to pass through the sieve and serve as tokens to show the system works.[45]

Busing also affects working class students. The nature and extent of busing for achieving more equal opportunity is determined by local administrators and courts. The Supreme Court ruled in 1974 that school busing plans may not be imposed across school district lines. This provides a shield for the middle class who are homeowners and can move to the suburbs. But for both black and white working class students busing may involve a waste of time and resources for the students to travel to distant schools to achieve the politically correct makeup. For the class system busing provides a unique opportunity to demonstrate that the system does not discriminate across racial lines while enforcing the division along class lines. In reality the middle and upper classes are protected from busing while educational opportunity for working class and under class students is a matter of numbers and statistics.[46]

Working class families have no savings. They have trouble meeting the basic requirements and unless the family can forego a child's earnings he or she will not be able to take advantage of a "free" high school education. The problems for a working class student grow more acute when he starts high school and he may have to work just to obtain books, supplies and other basic needs. Sometimes the pressure to get an automobile in high school can be so overwhelming that students will work 20 to 40 hours after school to possess one. Their school work suffers and they drop out of it. The odds are stacked against working class students.[47]

Local control of education and funding based on property taxes provides the right mix for privileged educational opportunities for the middle and upper classes. The property taxes are deductible from income along with mortgage interest, allowing indirect public subsidies for the haves. Tiebout explains the system of class segmentation:

> At the real world level, the existence of unequal income has led to the "tax colony". That is, people with high incomes band together in communities which keep low income residents out . . . When you seek good schools for your children, you often find the rents and housing prices are high. This is not to suggest any single direct causality . . . it is simply a suggestion as to how . . . the rich avoid paying taxes for the poor.

New Jersey has been divided into 611 small school districts to facilitate manipulation. The well-to-do citizens of Princeton Township pay a property tax of only 1.59 percent, but spend $8,659 per pupil, compared to working class Trenton, which pays property taxes at a 3.09 percent rate but only spends $6,881 per pupil.[48]

Although civil right laws prohibit racial discrimination the middle and upper classes are protected by de facto segregation, which is seen as an innocent by-product of socioeconomic forces—especially in the housing market. The government encourages this at all levels. Most of the Federal Housing Administration loans and guarantees benefit middle class families. Neighborhoods and school districts are partly determined by decisions as to the number of schools to build, their size and their location. In conjunction with new school construction, gerrymandering by restructuring school attendance zones can be used for segregation. Another tactic to achieve segregation or integration is to use optional zones where students are permitted to choose the schools they will attend. A "breakthrough" concept for promoting equal opportunity are the schools for "gifted" children. But in reality the "gifted child" program is used to direct resources in servicing upper class groups almost exclusively. The system is structured to provide special educational opportunities to the middle and upper class at public expense shared by all the classes.[49]

The upper class have little use for public schools, with more than 130 private schools with a total student body between 60,000 and 70,000 catering to their needs. These serve as training grounds for the children of the rich to enter the Ivy League colleges. The upper class children are groomed to assume leadership roles in society with proper connections. Wealth and the ability to pay are directly used to create an exclusive network while token scholarships provide a semblance of diversity.[50]

The system uses college education as a screening device. Out of every 100 pupils in the fifth grade in the fall of 1967 only 22 were likely to receive a college degree in the fall of 1973. By the 1970s there was a huge reservoir of graduates who were unable to obtain jobs in line with their qualifications and expectations. As a result the employers raised their educational requirements as a sorting threshold whereby upper and middle class youth got preference in jobs. An advertisement for topless dancers in the recession of 1971 said it all: "Topless Dancers. Must have two years college. Prefer English major, language or humanities". Education may influence who gets the available jobs but the demand for labor determines the number of jobs. Although individual incomes may be related to educational attainments, class segmentation cannot be removed by raising educational attainments for most people.[51]

Using college degrees as a screening device fits perfectly with the needs of the class system. The chances of getting a college degree are closely related to economic class. In a 1957 survey of top I.Q. high school graduates who planned to attend college, those who made it had an average of 1.9 children in their family while those who could not go had an average of 2.8. Other research has shown that well-off students with weak academic records are far more likely to attend college than poor students with strong records. Even among college graduates, degrees from Ivy league colleges are used to separate the upper class from the middle class. Non-scholarship students graduating from Harvard came from a family with a median income nearly five times the national average. The scholarship aid goes to children of the professional and managerial members of the middle class and is ineffective in creating interclass mobility. An associate director of admissions at Harvard explained the process:

> The extremely needy student tends to get helped if he can reduce his need by commuting or if he is so able, active, and personable as to stand head and shoulder above competitors. If he is just "very good" we send him an admission certificate, deny him a scholarship, let him go to college locally and become more of a success than his father, and then wait to award a smaller scholarship to his children in the next generation.

College degrees help the weeding out process and provides a framework for allocating positions of leadership by class.[52]

According to the Bureau of Labor Statistics almost 19 percent of the college graduates in 1980 held menial jobs or were unemployed. Forecasts show that nearly one in three college graduates between 1990 and 2005 are expected to take jobs that don't require a sheepskin—like flipping burgers, hawking jeans or faxing memos. While educational opportunity is determined by class origins, the education attained is used to create the impression that rewards in the class system are based on merit.[53]

Ideology and Answers

Equality of opportunity is an illusion in America. The class structure could not exist without careful control of educational opportunity and life chances. The ideology insists America is a classless society with equal opportunity and rewards based on merit. The myth is sustained with Horatio Alger stories, free market and survival of the best tales of Milton Friedman and token examples of mobility between the classes with instant fortunes.[54]

The message of American class system ideology—strive and succeed—was spread with the adventure stories of Horatio Alger, Jr., popularizing the myth of the self-made man. However, a look at some of Alger's novels shows that although the heroes were indeed honest and hard working, they never succeeded on their own. Heroic deeds such as foiling kidnappers or rescuing a drowning child were followed by the timely appearance of a rich stranger who rewarded the hero with cash and a job in his counting house along with a generous dose of advice. In *Ragged Dick*, the story that shot Alger to fame, the wealthy benefactor Mr. Whitney tells the young bootblack Dick: "I hope, my lad, you will prosper and rise in the world. You know in this free country poverty in early life is no bar to a man's advancement . . . Remember that your future position depends mainly on yourself and that it will be high or low as you choose to make it." Such stories do little harm as long as poor boys do not hold their breath hoping to make it just because they made the right choice.[55]

Milton Friedman interpreted equality in the Declaration of Independence as equality before God; equality in the hereafter was guaranteed for all Americans. Though the aberration of slavery was removed after the Civil War and "equality of opportunity" restored, equality of opportunity was not to be interpreted literally. Like every ideal, it is incapable of being fully realized. More important is the rapid strides made by the blacks and the concept of a "melting pot" reflected by the goal of equal opportunity and the expansion of "free" education at elementary, secondary and higher levels. The existence of nonprofit hospitals, privately endowed colleges and universities and a plethora of charitable organizations directed to helping the poor show that the dominant value of society is promotion of equal opportunity. The rapid rise in the economic and social position of various less privileged groups demonstrates that the obstacles to equal opportunity were by no means insurmountable. In short, equal opportunity is on the way and we are moving in the right direction. Those who disagree are really asking for equality of outcome, which is an absurdity. The United States is a free market economy and personal choices determine individual outcomes based on merit. How a class system based on wealth can evolve in a free market economy is not addressed.[56]

A persistent theme of class system ideology is the continuous mobility between the classes. Andrew Carnegie said society in industrial America would not fail to reward a man of talent. If a man is worthy of escaping poverty's terrors, he can do so by escaping into a higher class. If he doesn't have the ability to "make it" what right does he have to complain? The reality is vastly different, with little mobility across class lines. Approximately 40 percent of the male population inherit the class position of their parents. Another 35 percent are upwardly mobile and the remaining 25 percent experience downward mobility. Much of this occurs within the working class and middle class, while access to the upper class is more restricted. Members of the underclass are generally snared in a "vicious circle of poverty" which means the economic deprivation of parents handicaps the educational and vocational attainments of their children, thus condemning subsequent generations to inherited deprivation. On examining the *Forbes* magazine list of the 400 richest people in America in 1987 Lester Thurow, the dean of MIT's Sloan School of Management, discovered that all of the 82 wealthiest families, and 241 of the wealthiest individuals, had inherited all or a major part of their fortunes. Yet class system ideology will stress interclass mobility and rags to riches possibilities by citing the examples of billionaires Ross Perot and Sam Walton.[57]

Before considering ways of restoring investment in human capital it is necessary to understand why opportunity, including education and training, are restricted. Historically the working class was kept at the basic, reproducible level to minimize consumption and maximize output while a permanent, unemployed underclass was necessary to control and motivate the working class. With the globalization of the economy slave labor can be found overseas and domestic slavery becomes redundant. Even the slaves in a high technology economy need to be educated. Equal opportunity in education and vocational training is essential if the working class is to arrest the declining standard of living.

Food is the first priority for young minds. Right now token breakfast and lunch programs cost less than $5 billion and reach a small minority of the students while agricultural subsidies of $30 to $40 billion go to upper class farmers for products which rot in storage bins. If the agricultural subsidies are redirected to schools for nutrition, it would improve the conditions for learning and yet stabilize the market for agricultural commodities.[58]

To ensure that basic necessities are available for students it is necessary to guarantee jobs for the parents at the minimum wage. This has to be true for high school graduates as well. With an effective unemployment rate of more than 10 percent, which is much higher for young adults, there is no incentive for students to finish high school. On the other hand guaranteed jobs, even at the minimum wage, would motivate students to finish high school.

Education is a basic necessity while defense spending needs a system of checks and balances, and the funding for the two could be interchanged. If schools are funded from federal revenues then revenues can be allocated more equally, providing national standards to be met by students and schools. On the other hand defense spending funded by property taxes would force the taxpayers to determine how much defense is really needed. The defense establishment has vast facilities and abilities for training. With a volunteer armed force it could easily operate a chain of military boarding schools to meet their manpower needs. Working class youth would benefit from the training with an assured future.

The U.S. educational system is set up to prepare students for college, though 79 percent of all Americans never get an undergraduate degree. Skilled workers require a four-year apprenticeship instead of four years in college. Yet there is little investment in training. Employers are afraid to invest in the training of employees because they cannot prevent a competitor from attracting the employee after the training is over. An employee does not want to invest in training when there is no guarantee of a job. A program like the German Apprentice System would boost human capital investment. Any apprenticeship training program has to be tied to a job with incentives and protection for the investment by the employer and the trainee. Labor Secretary Robert Reich notes, "There is no way to create a competitive [international] advantage other than through people. Firms are discovering slowly that highly motivated and skilled employees are the key to long-term profitability". But there is no union or legal guarantee to facilitate organized investment in human capital.[59]

The importance of investment in human capital is clear, yet obstacles to equal opportunity in education and training are retained. The shepherds have so successfully held on to their privileges for so long that it will call for a miracle to make the transition to the new global economy.

CHAPTER 12

LIBERTY AND JUSTICE FOR ALL

If a free society cannot save the many who are poor, it cannot save the few who are rich.–**John F. Kennedy**[1]

The political problem of mankind is to combine three things: Economic Efficiency, Social Justice, and Individual Liberty.
                                        –**John Maynard Keynes**[2]

We have always known that heedless self interest was bad morals; we know now that it is bad economics.
                                        –**President Franklin D. Roosevelt**[3]

A good man leaveth an inheritance to his children's children.–**Proverbs, XII:22**[4]

For the first time in world history, we have the abundance and the ability to free every man from hopeless want, and so free every person to find fulfillment in the works of his mind or the labor of his hands.–**Lyndon B. Johnson**[5]

On January 20, 1992, the Japanese House Speaker, Yoshio Sakurauchi, blamed the economic difficulties of the United States on what he termed illiteracy and sloth of the American workers. In a speech to supporters he warned the United States risked becoming nothing more than "Japan's subcontractor" and said "the deterioration in quality of U.S. workers" was the true source of the trade gap between the United States and Japan. Sakurauchi charged that American managers could not give their factory workers written instructions, because one third of Americans "cannot even read".[6]

Diane Ravitch, Assistant Secretary for the U.S. Office for Educational Research and Improvement, defended the American worker by noting that less than five percent of the U.S. population was illiterate. Owen Bieber, president of the United Auto Workers Union, called Sakurauchi's remarks bigoted. Although Sakurauchi apologized, claiming he did not intend to "disparage or slight American workers", his views reflected similar sentiments on the part of many Japanese. A college graduate noted from her data, "laziness and 30 percent illiteracy is a social problem for America". A housewife asked, "Why do you think you can't produce better cars? You must be extremely dumb to do such lousy cars year after year. We are so upset the way the Americans push us around!"[7]

The ultimate answer and vindication for Mr. Sakurauchi came from a Ford assembly plant worker outside a Toyota dealership near Detroit who carried a placard which read: "JAPAN SAID YOUR [SIC] LAZY. NO TO JAPANESE IMPORTS". *Fortune* magazine in an article titled "The Truth About the American Worker" said a deficient workforce would erode the nation's power because new plant and equipment can only go so far in raising competitiveness. The American public was for the first time faced with the stark question: Can it be that decadence and demoralization really have overtaken the American workforce; that the American worker lacks both the knowledge and the character to make late 20th century technology work its full magic in his or her hands? One of the prophets of American "declinism" asks, "It is not emblematic, that the many American prostitutes working in Tokyo—except for the blondest of them—no longer command a premium for their services, so utterly has glamour of American power and specialness faded in the eyes of those who know best?"[8]

The stability of the economic system is determined in the longterm by economic efficiency and productivity. Economic efficiency is ultimately related to inequality and the class structure. In the modern world a class structure based on the work or starve principle will retard economic efficiency. Economist Benjamin Friedman noted, "When production technologies are changing rapidly, investment in training the labor force can be just as important as investment in new factories for advancing the productivity of key industries that are at the forefront of a country's competitiveness".[9]

The American class system is based on extreme inequality consistent with short-term stability. Robert Kuttner, author of *The Economic Illusion*, admits, "When the top 0.8 percent of families own 40 percent of the property wealth and the bottom 25 percent own no wealth, it becomes extremely difficult to defend that outcome as inherently desirable or inherently just". In a global economy where economic inefficiency shows up rapidly the U.S. economy is declining. There is a definite relationship between inequality, decline and the American class system.[10]

A classless society model provides rewards for working hard and working smart but is designed for economic efficiency and productivity of the U.S. economy. To survive in the global economy it may be necessary to liberate the U.S. economy and the workers from the shackles of the American class system. This will also coincide with principles of liberty and justice for all.

The Global Class System

Since the 1950s American investment has been moving overseas. The nation's savings were concentrated in the largest 1,000 corporations and accumulated as retained earnings. Owing to saturated local markets the companies invested their funds overseas creating a need for their products and using their manufacturing and marketing know-how.

Once the American companies decided to expand overseas they had to transfer technology and set up manufacturing facilities to get access to the markets. Initially there was no competition overseas for the American oligopolies and there was no danger of products manufactured abroad being sold in the home market. By the 1970s the transfer of technology overseas was not only complete but the Japanese and the Germans had developed manufacturing techniques for better quality control and were offering strong competition for the corporations domestically. The trends in trade have reversed and despite profits from investments overseas in the 1980s, America had a trade deficit exceeding $150 billion and became a net debtor.

The American companies were caught in a bind. They had become used to operating in a monopoly environment for so long that they did not know how to survive in a free market competitive economy. To protect their investments overseas the American companies could not retreat from their free trade ideology. So they decided to join their overseas competitors instead of fighting them. As a result every U.S. auto company has become partner to the Japanese one way or another. Producers of electronic equipment, computers, even aircraft have developed similar arrangements with the Japanese.

After losing the edge in manufacturing knowhow, quality control and investment, the new competition was based on minimizing labor costs. The idea was to play one country against another to minimize overall labor costs. The American companies went so far as to shut down U.S.-based manufacturing facilities and export the jobs overseas.

Because of the globalization of the U.S. economy and the need for U.S. multinationals to survive competitively, U.S. manufacturing jobs are moved overseas, leaving American workers to fend for themselves. This has put the unions on the defensive, reducing unionized workers to less than 15 percent of the workforce in the 1990s. By closing U.S. factories, investment in plant and equipment and any tax abatements are also wasted. There is a worldwide overcapacity of manufacturing facilities. Automobile factories worldwide have the capacity to produce 45 million cars annually for a market which can absorb in the best years about 35 million cars. A Chrysler executive remarked, "We have too many cars chasing too few drivers". As a result somebody has to close his automobile factory so that supply can meet the demand. In this fierce competition for competitive advantage the factories which pay the highest wages and benefits without increased productivity are going to lose out.[11]

One of the ironies of the global economy is that U.S. multinationals have free access to the domestic market. Therefore products manufactured overseas by subsidiaries of U.S. corporations are sold in the United States without any restrictions. The U.S. corporations are taking the lead in transferring jobs overseas and importing products manufactured abroad for domestic consumption. This vicious cycle has disastrous consequences for the economy because at some point the earnings of the workers will not be enough to pay for the imported products and there is a limit to the trade deficit and the associated borrowing.

When manufacturing jobs are transferred overseas the American workers have to compete for the service jobs. Most of these pay the minimum wage without any health benefits or job security. As a result U.S. wages have been gradually eroded since the 1970s. In constant dollars an average weekly paycheck worth $270 in 1981 declined to $254 by 1991. Middle class jobs are being replaced by working class jobs, and this will continue in the 1990s.[12]

As more workers are shifted from the middle class to the working class they are expected to stay alive at the basic replacement level. If a worker is constantly struggling to meet his basic needs, free education is of limited benefit. Learning or training on an empty stomach or if the worker is feeling sick is not very effective.

Akron-based investor David Brennan, who owned several manufacturing companies, discovered that 30 percent of his workers read below the fifth-grade level, and two-thirds that level in math. There are no standards in American schools to ensure minimum proficiency for math and verbal skills before a high school diploma is awarded. The diploma only vouches that the student had the opportunity to attend 12 years of schooling. The teachers and educators prefer this automatic award of high school diplomas because they can escape any responsibility for actual learning. The teachers cannot be blamed if the students are denied the basic environment at home for learning.

Even the corporations are not interested in educating and training the working class, preferring to blame the educational system for failing to do its job. Most corporate spending on education and training goes to workers with college and graduate degrees. Of the $2.3 billion spent by corporations on education in 1989, only $400 million went to support the public schools, while the rest went to colleges and universities. Most corporate expenditure on training goes to executives for attending conferences and symposia at exotic locales. These are supposed to raise the morale and reward managers for past performance; training is provided to those who need it the least.[13]

It is certain that with investment in education and training the American workers perform at par with foreign workers. Japanese and West German companies emphasize job training, continuous development of new skills and job security with higher wages. The results can be observed by comparing the performance of American workers working for Japanese companies and U.S. corporations in America. According to a recent survey an American worker in a Japanese factory can assemble a car in 19.5 hours compared with 26.5 hours it takes an average American worker to do so in an American auto factory. The effectiveness of human capital investment in education and training is beyond question.[14]

In 1990 American firms planned to boost capital investment abroad by 16 percent compared with 5.4 percent at home. American firms increased their overseas spending on research and development by 35 percent between 1986 and 1988 compared with a 10 percent increase in the United States. With these trends the decline of the U.S. economy is inevitable.[15]

Inequality and Decline

According to the Federal Reserve Study the upper class had 71.8 percent of the wealth while the middle class had less than 28.2 percent, assuming the working class had a negligible amount. With the emergence of a global competitive economy and decline in productivity domestically the upper class could only increase its share of the wealth at the expense of the other classes. Once the pie stops expanding, fights over the shares cannot be stopped.

As a result of the class system and structured inequality, about one in every five children was born in poverty in the United States. In the 1990s the Bureau of Labor Statistics reports that one in three college graduates will be forced to take jobs not requiring a degree. Since 1981 employment in the service sector has grown by 10 million jobs, with the majority of these being created in retail sales (including fast food restaurants) and paying the minimum wage for an overall average of about $200 per week, before taxes, for full-time employment. Most of these jobs did not provide health insurance and are insufficient to start a family. According to Barry Bluestone, a professor of economics at Boston College, with growing inequities and a shrinking middle class, the "American Dream" itself must be called into question, since even the opportunity of becoming middle class is no longer open to everyone.[16]

Another indicator of the declining U.S. economy is the amount of borrowing overseas resulting in it becoming the world's largest debtor. The Department of Commerce reported that by the end of 1991 total foreign investment in the United States exceeded investment abroad by a record $521.33 billion. This reversal of fortunes occurred in the 1980s when Americans maintained their standard of living by buying foreign manufactured goods on credit and America became a net debtor country from a net creditor status. Every American household owes almost $5,000 to foreigners and there will be more pressure on income and savings because of the interest payments in the 1990s. With a net debtor status the U.S. economy exposes itself to a subservient role in the global economy as traditional wisdom proclaims, "The rich ruleth over the poor, and the borrower is servant of the lender".[17]

Even more disastrous for the economy and inequality is the increase in the federal debt. Starting with $1 trillion in 1980 it had grown to more than $4 trillion in 1992. Of this increase about $600 billion was owed to foreigners while the rest was debt owed to the upper class. This appeared to be the result of financial manipulation, where over a 12-year period the upper class transferred to themselves more than $2 trillion from the public treasury and lent it back to the government to earn interest. In the 1990s the sheep in America will be squeezed further because of interest payments to the upper class for debt amounting to $34,000 per household.[18]

Borrowing for human or capital investment to improve productivity makes sense if the returns exceed the interest costs, but borrowing for defense or for consumption is unheard of. It is like eating your seed corn instead of planting it. Creating public debt with transfers from the lower classes to the upper class has disastrous consequences. David Hume writes about the inflation of public debt: "Either the nation must destroy public credit or public credit will destroy the nation". Debt tends to concentrate wealth in the hands of the few as interest payments grow beyond the capabilities of the many. This brings great pain to society and causes instability. Federal deficits are a proven recipe for financial ruin and political disaster.[19]

The upper class raided the public treasury through savings and loan guarantees and health care subsidies. By 1989, the accumulated guarantees encumbered the government with roughly $5.7 trillion in potential liabilities, compared to a GNP of $5.1 trillion that year. Once the vicious circle of interclass money lending and extreme inequality starts it is difficult to reverse the trend without drastic measures.[20]

Homeownership is probably the most important indicator of the polarization in the U.S. economy. Starting with a homeownership rate of 55 percent in 1950 it increased over the years to reach a peak of 65.6 percent in 1980. From 1980 it changed direction and fell to 64 percent in 1990. The change in homeownership ratio during the 1980s was limited because of a standard of living artificially maintained on borrowing. Now the interest to be paid on the debt has grown substantially and the borrowing limits of the middle class are being exceeded. Fewer families will be able to afford houses and homeownership may decline faster.[21]

The growing inequality has resulted in a shrinking middle class, trade imbalances and deindustrialization. An economy managed by the class system has led to unemployment, loss in productivity, growing federal deficits and debt. These outcomes make it necessary to evaluate the classless society for national survival.

The Classless Society

A classless society does not mean equality of capacity or equality of condition for all the people. What it does mean is the absence of enforced wage slavery and an artificially created underclass. Wage slavery by itself is not the result of immutable economic laws but depends on the institutions, and the character of the institutions is determined by the values, preferences, interests and ideals prevalent in society. R.H. Tawny says the objective of a classless society is to plan, "property rights, and the organization of industry, and the system of public health and education as far as possible, to emphasize and strengthen, not the class differences which divide, but the common humanity which unites them". The rules of the game in the U.S. economy have to be changed to provide a bare minimum of opportunity at the starting line in life.[22]

A classless society model (see Table 1) first eliminates the underclass by merging it with the working class. With the elimination of wage slavery the working class is allowed to accumulate some wealth, ensuring economic security. However, to motivate them the working class would have a third the average wealth of the middle class worker. This means the working class would end up with 16.5 percent of the national wealth. Keeping the same incentives for the classes, the middle class would get 40 percent of the wealth and the gatekeepers 27 percent. With these assumptions the trustees would be left with 16.5 percent of the wealth. The net result would be that the top one percent would have the same wealth share as the bottom fifty percent of the population. This would imply an inequality of 50 : 1 between the trustees and the working class.

Table 1   Distribution of wealth : classless society

	Upper Class Trustees	Upper Class Gatekeepers	Middle Class 40%	Working Class 40%	Under Class 10%
Theory %	30%	30%	40%	0%	0%
Per Unit	30%	3.3	1.0	0.0	0.0
Reality %	40.6%	29%	27.2%	3.2%	0%
Per Unit	40.6	3.2	0.68	0.08	0
Classless Soc.%	**16.5%**	**27%**	**40 %**	**13.2%**	**3.3%**
Per Unit	16.5	3.0	1.0	0.33	0.33

Assuming a national wealth pot of $10 trillion and 100 million households in the U.S., a working class household would have a net worth on the average of $33,000. This works out to an average net worth of $100,000 for the middle class, $300,000 for the gatekeepers and $1.6 million for the trustees. The current wealth distribution already approximates this goal for the middle class and the gatekeepers, which together constitute fifty percent of the households. Therefore, the proposed wealth distribution for a classless society only involves a transfer of wealth from the top one percent of the population to the bottom 50 percent. This entails a conceptual change in the American class system from a system of wage slavery to one of equal opportunity.

Once the target wealth distribution is defined, the income distribution, along with the taxation policies and subsidies, can be adjusted to give the best result. Eliminating the underclass calls for the government to provide a job at the minimum wage to all adults who are looking for one and who are willing and able to work. Anyone wanting to improve his economic condition will have to compete in the private job market by acquiring skills or working harder and smarter. If the basic needs are met the person would be in a position to acquire the education and training skills. Many students drop out of high school because they see college graduates who are unemployed. With a guaranteed job every student would have an incentive to complete high school and get his diploma. Polls show that 79 percent of the population supports the concept of a guaranteed job for all.[23]

Guaranteed jobs for everyone brings up the question of how they are to be created and what the workers would do. As long as the United States has a trade deficit exceeding $100 billion, no matter what the workers produce or do would help the economy. With a labor force of more than 100 million and an unemployment rate of 10 percent there would be need for at least 10 million jobs. Once the government is willing to subsidize part of the wages even industry would find it economical to create jobs.

As a last resort the government could provide employment for 10 million by providing subsidized childcare and transportation for the nation. The government could place 10 million taxis in the cities. If the taxis could increase the occupancy rate from one to two persons per car the savings would probably exceed the subsidies required. This will provide the basic public transportation needed by a classless society.

The citizens in a classless society will understand that economic condition is tied to family size; the standard of living depends upon the quality of reproduction rather than the quantity. With equal opportunity the rungs up the economic ladder are within reach. The first step is obtaining high school diploma. Investment in education and training should be continued until enough can be saved for making a down payment on a home. In a classless society the procreation is concentrated in the middle and upper class and not in the working and underclass.[24]

So long as the illusion of a fair distribution of wealth is maintained the short-term security of the upper class is assured, though that might jeopardize the U.S. economy. A plan for liberating the U.S. economy and providing equal opportunity to the American people in pursuit of happiness is available.

Liberation Program

The elimination of the American class system is the goal of the liberation program. If the artificial divisions between the classes are removed, progress up the economic ladder based on work, ability, skills and investment in the future is assured. The liberation program provides a bare minimum floor under every citizen so that the person has a real choice about the future. It is based on existing incentives in the U.S. economy and would not affect the standard of living for the middle class and the gatekeepers.

In principle the program is not revolutionary. It only fulfills the previously implied right to survival and recognizes the fact that liberty for all is possible only with ownership of property, that is, savings. Arrangements which encourage the accumulation of property, even at a basic level, are essential if every citizen is to have a stake in the American dream and responsibility in a true democracy. President Franklin Roosevelt's message to Congress in 1944 declared that:

> true individual freedom cannot exist without economic security and independence . . . People who are hungry and out of a job are the stuff of which dictatorships are made . . . In our day these economic truths have become accepted as self evident. We have accepted, so to speak, a second Bill of Rights, under which a new basis of security and prosperity can be established for all.

Roosevelt then enumerated the economic rights, including:

- The right to a useful and remunerative job in the industries or shops or farms or mines;
- The right to earn enough to provide adequate food and clothing and recreation;
- The right of every farmer to raise and sell his products at a return which will give him and his family a decent living;
- The right of every businessman, large and small, to trade in an atmosphere of freedom from unfair competition and domination by monopolies at home or abroad;
- The right of every family to a decent home;
- The right to adequate medical care and the opportunity to achieve and enjoy good health;
- The right to adequate protection from the economic fears of old age, sickness, accident, and unemployment;
- The right to a good education.[25]

Roosevelt asked Congress to find ways of implementing this economic Bill of Rights for the American people. The American upper class has resisted this program for the last 50 years because it would destroy the class system. A 10-point program to implement the economic bill of rights for the liberation of the U.S. economy follows :

One—Restore Democracy: America is currently governed by the shepherds in a system of mock democracy. Money, not votes, secures electoral victory. In a real democracy votes should take precedence over money and the interests of the middle class, who are the backbone of the country, should determine the outcome of elections.

To restore democracy voting should be made easy and convenient for the lower classes. Registration for elections should be encouraged at the time of obtaining a driver's license. In this way the 50 percent of the population who do not own homes and have to frequently move for work will be registered automatically. The "Motor Voter" Bill signed into law by President Clinton is a move in the right direction. The elections should be held on weekends and on holidays instead of Tuesdays. Even the primaries should be held on weekends. To prevent false-choice elections between two candidates, third party candidates should be placed on the ballot without hindrance.

Campaign contributions and lobbying expenditures are in reality a legalized form of bribery and corruption. As the Supreme Court intends to protect the upper classes by disallowing limits on campaign spending, the deductibility of campaign contributions and lobbying expenses should be eliminated. Instead, public assistance for elections in the form of television access and debates should be guaranteed. Probably the increase in tax receipts from eliminating deductions would be sufficient to finance elections.

The terms of the members of Congress should be limited. This would prevent a lifetime of cozy relationships between money and the incumbents which are contrary to the spirit of democracy. Another way of limiting the power of money is to have a direct election of the President by popular vote instead of an electoral system where the winner takes all. Without a democratic form of government responsible to a majority of the voters the status quo will prevail.

Two—Full Employment: The class system has corrupted the meaning of full employment to a minimum acceptable level of unemployment as defined by the Labor Department. Full employment means that a job at the minimum wage is guaranteed to every adult wanting, willing and able to work. By accepting the responsibility for providing jobs to all in the workforce, export of jobs overseas will be evaluated closely for efficiency.

Assuming that full employment requires 10 million new jobs and each job require an investment of $10,000, this amounts to a total investment of $100 billion. This compares very favorably with an annual trade deficit exceeding $150 billion, or the $100 billion estimate for fraud in the $800 billion annual expenditures for health care, or the $130 billion annual advertising expenditure or the annual defense budget exceeding $300 billion. No economic theory can justify forced unemployment of 10 million workers for the sake of efficiency. Whatever useful output is produced by these jobs is an improvement on the present situation.

Three—Equal Opportunity: Equal opportunity can be provided by meeting the bare minimum needs and ensures that everybody gets a chance to advance at least to the first step on the economic ladder.

Homeownership should be facilitated once a job is guaranteed to a worker. This can be done by allowing a deduction for rent so that the worker is encouraged to save and is not penalized at the starting line. Housing loan guarantees should help the working class. To make a down payment the workers should be allowed to borrow against their social security payments, which should be funded in a trust account. The idea is to put the working class on the same footing as the other classes; for this to happen, mortgage deductions for housing should be limited, if not eliminated, for the upper class.

Universal health care at affordable cost is a necessary condition for equality of opportunity. The health care system is based on reverse subsidies. Not only does this lead to 40 million Americans going without health care, but also the working class pays for misdirected and wasted resources. Every person should pay for the level of health care desired. Health care premiums should be declared as income for each tax payer. Every individual should be able to choose the level of his resources to be utilized for housing, health care or education.

It should be recognized that a minimum of high school education is a basic necessity for the individual and the U.S. economy. For learning to occur the basic needs of food and a secure environment are essential. This means spending for school breakfast and lunch programs should have top priority. Libraries could provide a secure environment where homework could be done and learning could take place. Agricultural subsidies paid to corporations should be directed for school nutritional and hunger abatement programs. School funding should be based on state and federal revenues instead of local taxes.

Four—Progressive Income Tax: Each person should pay in proportion to the wealth which he respectively enjoys under the protection of the state. Over the last few decades most

Americans have been paying a flat tax rate of 25 percent independent of income. The payroll taxes for social security should be eliminated. Payroll and sales taxes have to be restricted so that almost fifty percent of the population who have few assets are not burdened with regressive taxes.

The income tax code has to be simplified so that the hundreds and billions of dollars wasted for accounting and to collect taxes are not necessary. Studies show the same revenue can be collected by simply having a standard deduction of say $20,000 and a flat rate with no loopholes or subsidies. Capital gains, charitable deductions, mortgage interest subsidies, state and local tax deductions can be eliminated. People with high school education should be able to understand and fulfil their obligations under the income tax code. With a properly designed tax system 50 percent of the population would have no need to file income tax returns because there is very little there to tax once the showmanship is eliminated.

Five—Restore Free Markets and Competition: Allocation of capital based on competition is a basic feature of a free market economy and must be enforced in the U.S. economy. This requires that most of the profits earned by the corporations should be distributed to the shareholders. The shareholders will individually decide where the capital investments will be made. Not only will this force companies to compete and justify their use of funds, it will also prevent the automatic diversion of American savings overseas.

To restore free markets the corporate income tax should be replaced by a Value Added Tax (VAT) which eliminates opportunities for loopholes and accounting gimmicks. This will force all multinationals, whether U.S.-based or foreign, to pay their fair share of taxes to the U.S. government which can be used to invest in the national infrastructure. With the elimination of the corporate income tax the double taxation of dividends will end and the managers will have to pay for their mistakes and accept the risks and rewards of a free market economy. The horror stories of corporations with hundreds of millions of dollars in earnings who escape paying taxes and executives earning millions of dollars in salaries and benefits when the corporations are officially losing money will be ended. Globally, the VAT will allow the United States to get in line with the rest of the world, reduce the trade deficit and keep the jobs at home.

Six—Eliminate Waste: The opportunity for waste is rampant in defense spending because the traditional checks and balances of raising taxes for defense have been eliminated. Defense spending should be paid for by the classes whose wealth is to be protected. Defense spending should be tied to the property tax or wealth tax. This will quickly eliminate waste because the upper class will critically evaluate defense requirements and keep away from offensive adventures overseas.

Advertising spending of approximately $130 billion is mostly a waste of the nation's resources. To eliminate wasteful advertising, opportunities, especially on television, should be limited by restricting the minutes of commercials and prohibit interruption of programs. Another method of reducing waste is to eliminate the deduction for advertising. Postal subsidies for junk mail and magazines should be eliminated.

The American public pays more than $100 billion a year as a tort tax, which is a plain and simple waste of national resources. This amounts to a subsidy for the upper class and serves no other purpose. No-fault auto insurance laws are necessary nationwide to curb the menace. There should be laws limiting liability for individuals and corporations and caps on jury awards. It is necessary to rationalize the criminal justice system so that it does not cost millions of dollars in lawyers' fees to execute a single criminal.

Transportation based on automobiles is a colossal wastage of national resources. To reduce this waste a 50 cents per gallon gasoline tax should be collected to provide incentives for the use of public transportation. This will assure that national resources are allocated to public transportation, which requires a large capital commitment.

Health care in the United States is supposed to be a virtually free benefit to be paid for by the employers. To reduce waste the subsidies for health care should be skewed towards the poor instead of the rich and individual responsibility should be established where the person decides on the proportion of resources which are to be allocated for health care.

Seven—Balance Budget and Pay Off Federal Debt: Federal debt grew from less than $1 trillion in 1980 to more than $4 trillion in 1992. Federal debt and interest payments to the upper class generate inequality which will cripple the U.S. economy. As the lower classes have been squeezed to the limit, these interest payments cannot be made without affecting the nation's productivity. The only way of eliminating the federal deficit is to stop the raids on the federal treasury and impose an annual wealth tax. Wealth tax structured to equal the interest payments on the federal debt makes good past transfers by the upper class.

The federal debt should be paid off within 20 years. It took only 12 years for the debt to increase four-fold and it could be retired the same way it was created. An effective inheritance tax should be used to payoff the federal debt in one generation. An effective solution taxes the recipients of inheritances instead of the givers and closes the loopholes such as generation-skipping trusts.

Eight—Human Capital Investment: The only way of winning the competitive game in the global economy is by human capital investment. Full employment must take precedence over free trade or any other goal. A level playing field should be provided in terms of benefits and basic employment policies. A large employer or a small business should be on an equal footing in providing the basic minimum requirements for all employees. This means setting a minimum wage and benefits package which satisfies basic economic rights for the individual and responsibility for providing this minimum floor for the entire workforce.

The workforce has to be represented at the political level. Right now the unions represent a small part of the middle class workers while the rest of the middle class has some leverage because of their skills or professional standing. Most of the working class and the underclass have no political voice. Unions representing the entire workforce could provide a voice for everyone. Sweden serves as a model for a free market society which ensures human capital investment and equal opportunity for every worker.

Nine—Press Freedom: A free press is supposed to provide the checks and balances in a true democracy. The press in America has been co-opted by the class system to reflect its values and policies by making it dependent on advertising revenues.

To restore press freedom the umbilical cord between the press and the class system has to be cut by eliminating the deduction for advertisements for corporations. Once the press comes to depend on the majority of the people for their funding it will have to cater to the needs of its readership. It is necessary to create competition in the media by preventing cross ownership. Making the media responsive to the public also requires adjustment of the subsidies and taxes and control of licenses for television stations.

Ten—Recognize Limits: There are limits in all economic activity such as growth, inequality, population. Awareness of the limits prevents instability. Differences in quantity and quality have to be noted. Blindly following a one dimensional goal without balance can result in disaster.

Continuous economic growth is an impossibility. All economies follow cycles of ups and downs. The United States with five percent of the world's population uses one-third of the world's resources. Only a very small portion of the world's population can ever reach the average standard of living in the USA. Even in this country, limits could arise from environmental hazards or pollution or energy usage. Strategies for conservation, efficiency and avoidance of waste should get precedence over growth.

Overall indexes of the U.S. economy ignore the inequality. In reality there are limits to inequality. It has been recognized that there has to be a balance between investment and consumption. The upper class owns 70 percent of America's wealth while the middle class owns 30 percent and home ownership is falling. A more equal distribution of wealth will be required to avoid political instability and is essential for improved productivity and international competitiveness.

Population control and the human development of the workforce is decisive. For a classless economy the pro-creation should be encouraged in the middle class. In fact one of the methods of rising up the economic ladder is to delay procreation until middle class status is achieved.

Doing It

With permanent unemployment, industrial overcapacity, trade deficits, federal debt, waste and overall decline of the U.S. economy along with extreme inequality the need for change is obvious. In the 1920s when the U.S. economy was going through a similar phase Thorstein Veblen noted:

> So long as no such change of base is made, what is confid-ently to be looked for is a regime of continued and increasing shame and confusion, hardship and dissension, unemployment and privation, waste and insecurity of persons and property such as the rule of Vested Interests in business has already made increasingly familiar to all the civilized peoples.

The question is that when what needs change is the economic class system and when the upper class controls the show, how is change to occur?[26]

The upper class can be counted upon to resist change. Justice Brandeis has pointed out that the greatest domestic danger to the stability of America's government is the failure of free enterprise capitalism to make the adjustments needed to cure real injustice and prevent the emergence of wide-spread, revolutionary dissatisfaction. The basic dilemma of the upper class was noted by Justice William O. Douglas: "When the machine displaces man and does most of the work, who will own the machines and receive the rich dividends?" If the machines sit idle because there is no demand there will be no dividends either. To maximize dividends the wealth has to be shared with the rest of the population in order to create demand which will keep the machines busy.[27]

The shepherds have justified extreme inequality by claiming it necessary for productivity and growth of the economy. Experience shows that until a certain point inequality helps productivity and growth. But beyond it inequality cuts down the total demand resulting in economic stagnation. Inequality in the 1980s extended beyond the optimum point. A comparison with the Japanese model points to this conclusion. Japanese companies pay their workers about a third of their compensation in the form of variable bonuses, which amounts to a profit sharing plan. Pay differentials between managers and workers are low. Overall pay differences within Japanese companies are from one-half to one-third those in American firms. It is difficult to swallow the myth of inequality as a productivity and growth strategy for the U.S. economy.[28]

The simple reality is that there is not enough wealth or natural resources on Earth for every person to be rich, or even affluent, no matter how hard we all work. Even future improvements in technology and increased production of goods is unlikely to improve the standards of living for all Americans. The task is to arrest the decline in the standard of living for our children. By pretending that America is a classless society the shepherds rob the working class of equal opportunity and dignity. Workers are placed in a double bind: They are regarded as inferior if they remain in the working class; but when they try to climb the economic ladder, as the dream encourages them to do, they find the class system has placed barriers in their path.[29]

The class system cannot be simply made to disappear by not collecting data on wealth. The data on wealth can be employed to fine-tune the economy for maximum productivity and growth. Instead of prohibiting the collection and dissemination of wealth data, the Federal Reserve Board and the Internal Revenue Service should be required by law to collect them periodically as part of economic policy planning.

As the American class system was written into the Constitution and has survived for two centuries, no sudden revolutionary change can be expected. But the trends have clearly been reversed in the 1980s. Inequality is going to become increasingly visible and cannot disappear even with the threat of force. Hopefully, the explosive situation will be defused with the emergence of a third party just like Abraham Lincoln's Republican Party before the Civil War. The Civil War resulted in the abolition of black slavery. Elimination of white wage slavery and the class system could result from the new political environment.

The goal of all economic development is to make wealth abundant and men able to use wealth properly. For the first time in American history the public is faced with a declining standard of living. The shepherds have broken faith with the future generations of America. They will pay a heavy price if they forget Thomas Jefferson's axiom: "The earth belongs to the living".[30]

GLOSSARY

AAA: American Automobile Association

ABA: American Bar Association

ABC: American Broadcasting Company

ADM: Archer Daniels Midland Corporation

AFDC: Aid for Families with Dependent Children

AFL: American Federation of Labor

AMA: American Medical Association

AWOL: Absent Without Official Leave

BAC: Business Advisory Council

BOMC: Book Of the Month Club

CBS: Columbia Broadcasting System

CEO: Chief Executive Officer

CIA: Central Intelligence Agency

CIO: Congress of Industrial Organ-izations

DNC: Democratic National Committee

EEOC: Equal Employment Opportunity Commission

EPA: Environmental Protection Agency

ESRP: Emergency Substitute in Regular Position

FBI: Federal Bureau of Investigation

FCC: Federal Communications Commission

FDA: Food and Drug Administration

FDIC: Federal Deposit Insurance Corporation

FDR: Franklin Delano Roosevelt

FHA: Federal Housing Administration

GDP: Gross Domestic Product

GE: General Electric

GI Bill: Government Issue Bill

GM: General Motors

GNP: Gross National Product

GOP: Grand Old Party (Republican)

ICC: Interstate Commerce Commission

IQ: Intelligence Quotient

IRA: Individual Retirement Account

IRS: Internal Revenue Service

JDL: Jewish Defense League

MAD: Mutually Assured Destruction

MGM: Metro Goldwyn Mayer

MIT: Massachusetts Institute of Technology

NAACP: National Association for Advancement of Colored People

NBC: National Broadcasting Company

NLRB: National Labor Relations Board

NRA: National Rifle Association

OFCC: Office of Federal Contract Compliance

PAC: Political Action Committee

R&D: Research and Development

SDI: Strategic Defence Initiative

SEC: Securities and Exchange Commission

UAW: United Automobile Workers

UCLA: University of California at Los Angeles

UPI: United Press International

VA: Veterans Administration

VAT: Value Added Tax

VCR: Video Cassette Recorder

WASP: White Anglo Saxon Protestant

NOTES

Chapter 1.   Is There A Class System?

1. Adam Smith, *Wealth of Nations*, quoted in *Money and Class in America* by Lewis H. Lapham, p. 130.
2. Quoted in *America as a Civilization* by Max Lerner, p. 273.
3. Quoted in *American Class Society in Numbers*, edited by Bob Howard and John Logue, p. 101.
4. Quoted—*Money and Class in America,* by Lewis H. Lapham, p. 10.
5. *Money and Class in America*, by Lewis H. Lapham, p. 88.
6. *Money and Class in America*, by Lewis H. Lapham, p. 85.
7. *The Works and Correspondence of David Ricardo*, ed. by Piero Sraffa, Vol. VIII, p. 278
8. Hugh Brogan, *The Penguin History of the United States of America*, p. 181.
9. J.R. Pole, *The American Constitution For and Against*, p. 152.
10. Edward Pessen, *Riches Class and Power Before the Civil War*, p. 165.
11. Herbert Spencer, *Social Statics*, p. 413 ; William Graham Sumner, *The Challenge of Facts and Other Essays*, edited by Galloway Keller, p. 90; Ibid, p. 57.
12. Veblen, *The Theory of the Leisure Class*, p. 37; Ibid, p. 17.
13. John Kenneth Galbraith, *Economics in Perspective—A Critical History*, p. 124.
14. Max Weber, *Economy and Society*, Vol. 1, edited by Guenther Roth and Claus Wittich.
15. Lenski, *Power and Privilege*, p. 481; pp. 51–52.

16. George Lukacs, *History and Class Consciousness*, p. 73; Ernest Mandel, "Workers and the Permanent Revolution", in George Fisher, ed., *The Revival of American Socialism*, p. 84; C.Wright Mills, *White Collar*, pp. 294–95.

17. Irving Fisher, *Elementary Principles of Economics*; Anthony B. Atkinson, *The Economics of Inequality*; "Theories of Personal Income Distribution: A Survey," Gian Singh Sahota, *Journal of Economics Literature*, March 1978, pp. 1–55.

18. Howard P. Tuckman, *The Economics of the Rich*, p. 6.

19. Paul Samuelson, *Economics from the Heart*, p. 220.

20. Paul Samuelson, *Economics from the Heart*, p. 221.

21. Milton and Rose Friedman, *Free to Choose*, p. 22.

22. Milton and Rose Friedman, *Free to Choose*, p. 22.

23. Ibid., pp. 128–29.

24. Ibid., p. 135.

25. John Kenneth Galbraith, "What happened to the Class Struggle", *Washington Monthly*, Washington D.C.; John Kenneth Galbraith, *The Culture of Contentment*, p. 15; J.K. Galbraith, *The Great Crash*, pp. 182–183.

26. Paul Blumberg, *Inequality in the Age of Decline*, p. 35; Rolf Dahrendorf, *Class and Class Conflict in Industrial Society*, p. 117.

27. Leonard Reissman, *Class in American Society*, p. 204.

Chapter 2.   Class System Theory

1. Thomas Balogh, *The Irrelevance of Conventional Economics*, p. 32.

2. Quoted in *Wall Street Journal*, January 22, 1993.

3. *The Concentration of Wealth in the United States* by the Democratic Staff of the Joint Economic Committee, United States Congress, 1986, p. 10.

4. Louis and Patricia Kelso, *Democracy and Economic Power*, 1986, p. 114.

5. *Business Week*, November 18, 1991, pp. 845–86.

6. *The Christian Science Monitor*, March 30, 1990, p. 1.

7. *The American Profile Poster* by Stephen J. Rose, p. 31

8. WEALTH DISTRIBUTION BY NET WORTH (1983)
Source : (1) Financial Characteristics of High Income Families, *Federal Reserve Bulletin*, March 1986, p. 167.
(2) *The Concentration of Wealth in the United States*, the Democratic Staff of the Joint Economic Committee, U.S. Congress—July 1986., The Congressional committee was able to obtain additional data from the Federal Reserve Survey not disclosed in the *Financial Reserve Bulletin*.

9. *The Concentration of Wealth in the United States,* the Democratic Staff of the Joint Economic Committee, U.S. Congress, July, 1986, p. 15.
10. Ibid., pp. 16–17.
11. Ibid., p. 18.
12. Ibid., p. 13.
13. Ibid., pp. 7 and 16.
14. "Financial Characteristics of High Income Families", *Federal Reserve Bulletin,* March 1986, p. 166.
15. *Wealth and Power in America* by Gabriel Kolko, p. 23.
16. Ibid., p.10
17. Internal Revenue Service, *Statistics of Income 1988, Individual Income Tax Returns,* Washington D.C. 1991, p. 18. These data were used to obtain percentages of total income by income decile; percentage of wealth by income decile was obtained from *The American Profile Poster* by Stephen J. Rose, p. 31.
18. Column A—Survey of Consumer Finances, 1983, *Federal Reserve Bulletin,* September 1984., For upper class approximate split, *Internal Revenue Service, Statistics of Income, 1988,* p. 18. Column B—See Figure 6. Column C, D, E, F—*Concentration of Wealth in the United States,* U.S. Congress, July, 1986, p. 24. For overall confirmation of data see "The Growing Divide: Class Polarization in the 1980's" by Jerry Kloby, *Monthly Review,* September 1987, pp. 1–8.
19. *Wealth and Power in America* by Gabriel Kolko, p. 50.
20. CLASS AND HOMEOWNERSHIP
Source: "Survey of Consumer Finances, 1983, A Second Report," *Federal Reserve Bulletin,* December, 1984, pp. 862, 864.
21. RACE COMPOSITION BY CLASS (1988)
Source: *Household Wealth and Asset Ownership: 1988* Series P-70, No 22, U.S. Dept of Commerce p. 1.
22. CLASS AND EDUCATION (1988)
Source: *Household Wealth and Asset Ownership: 1988* Series P-70, No 22, U.S. Dept. of Commerce p. 19.
23. JOB SECURITY & CLASS
Source: *Household Wealth and Asset Ownership: 1988* Series P-70, No 22, U.S. Dept of Commerce p. 19.
24. MARITAL STATUS AND CLASS (1988)
Source: *Household Wealth and Asset Ownership: 1988* Series P-70, No 22, U.S. Dept of Commerce p. 19
25. LABOR FORCE PARTICIPATION OF WIVES BY CLASS
Source: *The American Profile Poster* by Stephen J. Rose, p. 20.
26A. DISTRIBUTION OF WEALTH BY CLASS 1962–1983
Source: Dorothy Projector and Gertrude Weiss, *Survey of Financial Characteristics of Consumers* (Federal Reserve Board, 1966), Tables A2, A8 and A16.

26B. Source: "Survey of Consumer Finances, 1983: A Second Report," *Federal Reserve Bulletin*, December 1984, p. 862.

27. Letter to James Madison, October 28, 1785, in *The Papers of Thomas Jefferson*, ed., Julian P. Boyd, Vol. VIII, pp. 681–683; John Kenneth Galbraith, *The Great Crash*, pp. 182–183.

28. *Concentration of Wealth in the United States,* U.S. Congress, July 1986, p. 43.

Chapter 3. History

1. Lewis H. Lapham, *Money and Class in America*, p. 32.

2. Adam Smith, *An Inquiry into the Nature and Causes of the Wealth of Nations*, pp. 309 and 311.

3. C. Wright Mills, *Power Elite*, p. 22.

4. Lyndon B. Johnson (June 26, 1964) quoted in *The American Class Structure* by Dennis Gilbert, Joseph A. Kahl, p. 286.

5. Edward Pessen, *Riches Class and Power Before the Civil War*, p. 2.

6. Ibid., p. 3

7. Adolf A. Berle, *Power*, p. 278; Lewis H. Lapham, *Money and Class in America*, p. 33.

8. Sidney H. Aronson, *Status and Kinship in the Higher Civil Service*, pp. 35, 41; Jackson Turner Main, *The Social Structure of Prerevolutionary America*.

9. Michael Parenti, *Democracy for the Few*, p. 55; Herbert Apthekar, *Early Years of the Republic*, p. 41.

10. Edward Pessen, *Riches Class and Power Before the Civil War*, p. 32.

11. Charles A. Beard, *An Economic Interpretation of the Constitution of the United States*, p. 28; Apthekar, *Early Years of the Republic*, p. 137.

12. Apthekar, *Early Years of the Republic*, pp. 144–5; David Szatmary, *Shays' Rebellion: The Making of an Agrarian Insurrection*.

13. Charles A. Beard, *Economic Origins of Jeffersonian Democracy*, p. 316–17.

14. Charles A. Beard, *The Economic Basis of Politics*, p. 39.

15. Charles A. Beard, *An Economic Interpretation of the Constitution of the United States*, p. 199.

16. Max Farrand (ed.), *Records of the Federal Convention*, Vol I.

17. Michael Parenti, *Democracy of the Few*, p. 58;TheFederalist issue No 10. appeared in *The Daily Advertiser*, November 22, 1787.

18. Charles A. Beard, *The Economic Basis of Politics*, p. 142.

19. Mortimer J. Adler, *We hold These Truths*, p. 219.

20. J.R. Pole, *The American Constitution For and Against*, p. 11.

21. Lewis H. Lapham, *Money and Class in America*, p. 34.

22. Michael Parenti, *Democracy of the Few*, p. 60.
23. J.R. Pole, *The American Constitution For and Against*, p. 18.
24. Michael Parenti, *Democracy of the Few*, p. 66.
25. J. Allen Smith, *The Spirit of American Government*, p. vii.
26. Lewis H. Lapham, *Money and Class in America*, p. 35.
27. Peter F. Drucker, *Men Ideas and Politics*, 1971, p. 258.
28. Miller, *The Federalist Era*, p. 32; Pfeffer, *This Honorable Court*, pp. 36, 39, 41.
29. I. Warren, *The Supreme Court*, p. 277.
30. Beard, *Jeffersonian Democracy*, pp. 322–352.
31. Ibid., p. 358.
32. Schlesinger, *The Age of Jackson*, p. 322.
33. Ibid., p. 97.
34. Ibid., p. 171.
35. Ibid., p. 90.
36. Russell Galloway, *The Rich and the Poor in Supreme Court History*, pp. 58, 59.
37. Edward Pessen, *Riches Class and Power Before the Civil War*, pp. 32–38.
38. Ibid., p. 32.
39. Ibid., p. 302.
40. Howard Zinn, *A People's History of the United States*, pp. 213, 216.
41. *The Personal Distribution of Income and Wealth*, James D. Smith, editor, p. 234.
42. Peter J. Parish, *The American Civil War*, p. 633.
43. Ibid., p. 634.
44. Josephson, *The Robber Barons*, p. 395.
45. Russell Galloway, *The Rich and the Poor in Supreme Court History*, p. 70.
46. Matthew Josephson, *The Robber Barons*, p. 365; William Preston, Jr., *Aliens and Dissenters*, p. 24.
47. Magrath, *Morrison R. Waite*, pp. 182–83.
48. Jackson, *The Struggle for Judicial Supremacy*, pp. 39–40.
49. Ibid, pp. 39–40.
50. Boyer and Morais, *Labor's Untold Story*, p. 180; James Weinstein, *The Corporate Ideal in the Liberal State*, 1968, p. 87.
51. Boyer and Morais, *Labor's Untold Story*, p. 181.
52. Kolko, *The Triumph of Conservatism*, pp. 283–84.
53. Robert Murray, *Red Scare*, pp. 95–98.
54. Frank Ackerman and Andrew Zimbalist, *Capitalism and Inequality in the U.S.*, p. 301.
55. Brandeis Mason, *A Free Man's Life*, p. 530; Zinn, *A People's History*, p. 376; Boyer and Morais, *Labor's Untold Story*, p. 237
56. Boyer and Morais, *Labor's Untold Story*, p. 249; Zinn, *A People's History*, p. 378.

57. Bernstein (ed.), *Toward a New Past*, p. 269; Frances Fox Piven and Richard Cloward, *Regulating the Poor*, Chapter 2 and 3.
58. Unger, *Beyond Liberalism*, p. 226.
59. Bernstein, *Toward a New Past*, pp. 264–65.
60. Jackson, *The Struggle for Judicial Supremacy*, pp. xii–xiii.

Chapter 4. The Haves

1. Arthur M. Schlesinger, Jr., *The Coming of the New Deal*, Vol. 2 of The Age of Roosevelt, p. 479.
2. Lewis H. Lapham, *Money and Class in America*.
3. Ibid.
4. Celeste MacLeod, *Horatio Alger Farewell*, p. 16.
5. Benjamin De Mott, *The Imperial Middle*, p. 41.
6. Peter Collier and David Horowitz, *The Rockefellers—An American Dynasty*, p. 59; Robert Heller, *The Age of the Common Millionaire*, p. 3.
7. *U.S. News & World Report*, May 7, 1990; Robert Heller, *The Age of the Common Millionaire*, p. 346.
8. "Harvard Chagrined by Agreement with Donors", *The New York Times*, November 15, 1987, p. 68.
9. "George Bush's Search for the Middle Class," *U.S. News and World Report*, January 27, 1992, p. 13.
10. *Concentration of Wealth in the United States*, U.S. Congress, July 1986, pp. 22–29.
11. Kevin Phillips, *Politics of the Rich and Poor*, p. 157.
12. G. William Domhoff, *Who Rules America*, p. 16.
13. Source: *Economic Report of the President, 1991*, pp. 375–386.
14. G. William Domhoff, *Who Rules America*, p. 10.
15. "Finance Characteristics of High Income Families," *Federal Reserve Bulletin*, March 1986, p. 176; 1992 Green Book, U.S. House of Representatives, p. 1490.
16. Jim Hightower, "You've Got to Spread it Around", *Mother Jones*, May 1988, p. 56; Kevin Phillips, *Politics of Rich and Poor*, p. 24.
17. Thomas Byrne Edsall, *The New Politics of Inequality*, p. 142; Herman P. Miller, *Rich Man Poor Man*, p. 217.
18. Ferdynand Zweig, *The Worker in an Affluent Society*, p. ix; "Did Money Win? Labor's Credibility Gap," *The Nation*, January 1, 1973, pp. 13; "Labor and Nixon: Moving the Hard Hats In," *The Nation*, January 1, 1973, pp. 41–43.
19. "Congress's Reconstruction Theory"*The Washington Monthly*, January 1990, pp. 10–16; Mickey Kaus, *The End of Equality*, p. 97.
20. "Sacked and Looted (Ronald Reagan and the Savings and Loan Scandal)," *The Nation*, May 7, 1990, p. 620.

21. "Health Care with a Difference," *Time*, January 18, 1993, p. 26.
22. Building a Peacetime Economy, John E. Ullmann, August/September, 1991, p. 58.
23. "Prisons Running Out of Cells, Money and Choices," *New York Times*, May 28, 1993.
24. C. Wright Mills, *The Power Elite*, p. 97.
25. *American Society Inc*, (editor) Maurice Zeitlin, p. 364.
26. "The Richest People in America," *Forbes 400*, October 22, 1990; "Follow the Money," Forbes, October 26, 1992.
27. Thorstein Veblen, *The Theory of the Leisure Class*, p. 176.
28. Ibid, p. 87; John Kenneth Galbraith, *The Age of Uncertainty*, p. 61; Lewis H. Lapham, *Money and Class in America*, p. 33.
29. Robert Heller, *The Age of the Common Millionaire*, p. 370.
30. "A very rich dessert, Struggling voters, hungry for a piece of the pie, abandon Bush," *U.S. News & World Report*, May 23, 1992.

Chapter 5.   The Havenots

1. Alexis de Tocqueville, *Democracy in America*, Vol. 2, p. 171.
2. Dennis Gilbert, Joseph A. Kahl, *The American Class Structure*, p. 286.
3. Louis O. Kelso, Patricia Hetter Kelso, *Democracy and Economic Power*, p. 23.
4. *The New York Times*, November 13, 1977.
5. Mortimer J. Adler, *We Hold These Truths*, p. 146.
6. "Food Stamp Users Up Sharply is Sign of Weak Recovery," *New York Times*, March 2, 1993.
7. "Wealth of a Nation," *The Christian Science Monitor*, March 30, 1990.
8. *1992 Green Book*, U.S. House of Representatives, p. 1490.
9. Adam Smith, *Wealth of Nations,* Ch. VIII; Alexander Gray, *The Development of Economic Doctrine*, p. 163.
10. Jared Taylor, *Paved with Good Intentions*, p. 288.
11. Dennis Gilbert, Joseph A. Kahl, *The American Class Structure*, p. 300.
12. Ibid., p. 300.
13. "Food Stamps Users Up Sharply Is Sign of Weak Recovery," *New York Times*, March 2, 1993.
14. Andrew Levison, *The Full Employment Alternative*, p. 34–35; The Labor Picture in May, *The New York Times*, June 5, 1993.
15. Chapter II.
16. Mickey Kaus, *The End of Equality*, p. 106.
17. Thomas Georgean, "Which side are you on?; Don't count labor out," *Utne Reader*, March/April 1992, pp. 78, 84.

18. Gabriel Kolko, *Wealth and Power in America*, p. 78.
19. William Greider, *Who Will Tell the People*, p. 185.
20. Ibid., p. 186.
21. "New Jobs Lack the Old Security in Time of 'Disposable Workers,'" *New York Times*, March 15, 1993.
22. "Workers Are Forced to Take More Jobs with Few Benefits," *Wall Street Journal*, March 11, 1993.
23. "The Temping of America," *Time*, March 29, 1993.
24. "Poverty is Cited as Divorce Factor," Robert Pear, *New York Times*, January 15, 1993.
25. Victor Perlo, *Economics of Racism, USA*, p. 166.
26. Ibid., p. 169.
27. Thomas Dennis, *Political Affairs*, March 1974.
28. Victor Perlo, *Economics of Racism, USA*, p. 173.
29. Philip Green, *The Pursuit of Inequality*, p. 110.
30. Dennis Gilbert, Joseph A. Kahl, *The American Class Structure*, p. 318.
31. Frances Fox Piven and Richard A. Cloward, *Regulating the Poor*, p. 3–4.
32. Robert Kuttner, *The Economic Illusion*, p. 235.
33. Richard A. Long, "Scape Goat Victory: The President's White Mandate", *The Nation*, December 4, 1972, pp. 555–57; Prager, *White Racial Privilege and Social Change*, p. 393–408.
34. Bradley R. Schiller, *The Economics of Poverty and Discrimination*, p. 167.
35. Nick Kotz, *Let Them Eat Promises*, pp. 226–227.
36. "Annual Message to the Congress. January 4, 1935", *The Public Papers and Addresses of Franklin D. Roosevelt*, vol. 4, pp. 19–20.
37. Ibid., pp. 20–23.
38. Frances Fox Piven and Richard A. Cloward, *Regulating the Poor*, p. 82.
39. Celeste MacLeod, *Horatio Alger Farewell*, p. 217.
40. Ibid., p. 217.
41. Ibid., p. 218. 42. Editorial, "Lower The Minimum Wage", *Wall Street Journal*, September 9, 1976, p. 16.
43. William Greider, *Who Will Tell the People*, p. 196.
44. Bernstein, *The Politics of Welfare*, p. 36.
45. Patterson, *American Struggle*, pp. 171, 179.
46. Jared Taylor, *Paved with Good Intentions*, p. 291.
47. Max Lerner, *America as a Civilization*, p. 522; "Philosopher with a Mission," *Time*, June 7, 1993, p. 60.
48. Edward C. Budd, editor, *Inequality and Poverty*, p. 206.
49. Andrew Levison, *The Full Employment Alternative*, p. 31.
50. Jared Taylor, *Paved with Good Intentions*, p. 318; America's Soaring Prison Population, Patrick Langan, *Science*, 29 March, 1991.

51. Prisons Running Out of Cells, Money and Choices, *New York Times*, May 28, 1993; With Prison Costs Rising, Florida Ends Many Mandatory Sentences, *New York Times*, May 29, 1993.

52. "Majority in Poll Back Ban on Handguns," *New York Times*, June 4, 1993; "Short Lives, Bloody Deaths," *Newsweek*, December 17, 1990.

53. Jared Taylor, *Paved with Good Intentions*, pp. 320–321.

54. "Youngsters Finding a Cheap High in Malt Liquor '40s'," *New York Times*, April 16, 1993.

55. Jared Taylor, *Paved with good intentions*, p. 297.

56. "Evolution of Federal Welfare Programs," *Congressional Digest*, February 1988, pp. 35–36.

57. Susan Chira, "Crack Babies Turn 5, and Schools Brace", *The New York Times*, May 25, 1990.

58. "New U.N. Index Measures Wealth as Quality of Life," *New York Times*, May 21, 1993.

59. Thomas Byrne Edsall, *The New Politics of Inequality*, p. 177.

60. William Greider, *Who Will Tell the People*, p. 195; Thomas Byrne Edsell, *The New Politics of Inequality*, p. 146.

61. Andrew Levision, *The Full Employment Alternative*, pp. 192–195.

62. Jonathan H. Turner and Charles E. Starnes, *Inequality Privilege and Poverty in America*, p. 139.

63. *Washington Post*, January 24, 1983; "A Million Jobs with No Takers," *Business Week*, January 19, 1976, p. 16; Robert Lindsey, "Jobs, Skilled and Unskilled, Go Begging in Many Cities", *New York Times*, July 1, 1975, p. 1.

64. *Atlanta Constitution*, June 1, 1976.

65. Adam Walinsky, "Keeping the Poor in Their Place," *New Republic*, July 4, 1964.

66. "Americans Feel Families and Values Are Eroding but they Disagree Over the Causes and Solutions," Gerald F. Seib, *The Wall Street Journal*, June 11, 1993.

67. Frances Fox Piven and Richard A. Cloward, *Regulating the Poor*, p. 25.

68. Mickey Kaus, *The End of Equality*, p. 172.

Chapter 6. Monopoly And Free Markets

1. Adam Smith, *Wealth of Nations*, 1776.

2. Edgar Snow, *Journey to the Beginning*.

3. Arthur M. Okun, *Equality and Efficiency*, p. viii.

4. Lewis H. Lapham, *Money and Class in America*, p. 18.

5. Paul A. Baran and Paul M. Sweezy, *Monopoly Capital*, preface.

6. Chapter 2, Figure 3.
7. "America is Saving More Now, Not Less—if You Count it Right," Robert Kuttner, *Business Week*, April 13, 1992; John K. Galbraith, *The New Industrial State*, p. 39.
8. Harry E. Figgie, *Bankruptcy 1995: The Coming collapse of America and how to stop it*, p. 143
9. John K. Galbraith, *The Affluent Society*, p. 9.
10. Thurow Lester C., *Generating Inequality*, p. 151.
11. John K. Galbraith, *The Affluent Society*, p. 124.
12. John K. Galbraith, *American Capitalism: The Concept of Countervailing Power*, pp. 58, 115, 171.
13. Paul A. Samuelson, *Economics*, 10th ed., p. 532.
14. William Shepherd, *Market Power and Economic Welfare*, pp. 152–53.
15. Anthony Giddens, *The Class Structure of the Advanced Societies*, p. 160.
16. "Flexible Pricing: Industry's New Strategy to Hold Market Share Changes. The Rules for Economic Decision Making," *Business Week*, December 12, 1977, p. 63.
17. Andrew Levison, *The Full Employment Alternative*, p. 95.
18. Ernest Mandel, *Marxist Economic Theory*, pp. 435, 202.
19. A.B. Atkinson, editor, *Wealth Income and Inequality*, p. 387; George H. Hilderbrand, "American Unionism, Social Stratification and Power", *American Journal of Sociology*, Vol. 58, 1952–53, p. 387.
20. R. M. Gable, "NAM: Influential Lobby or Kiss of Death?", *Journal of Politics*, May, 1953, p. 271; Louis O. Kelso and Patricia Hetter Kelso, *Democracy and Economic Power*, p. 141.
21. Andrew Levison, *The Full Employment Alternative*, p. 95.
22. William Seeri, *The Company and the Union*, pp. 161–162.
23. Andrew Levison, *The Full Employment Alternative*, p. 96.
24. G. William Domhoff, *The Higher Circles*, p. 250; Susan Tolchin and Martin Tolchin, *Dismantling America: The Rush to Deregulate.*
25. William Greider, *Who Will Tell the People*, p. 110.
26. Grant McConnell, *Private Power and American Democracy*, p. 284;
27. *Interim Report on the Business Advisory Council*, Antitrust Subcommittee on the Judiciary, U.S. House of Representatives, 84th Cong., 1st Sess. (1955), pp. 3, 4.
28. Ibid., p. 16, 23.
29. Ibid., p. 17.
30. *The New York Times*, January 9, 1964.
31. Paul Baran, *Monopoly Capital*, p. 80.
32. Lester C. Thurow, *Generating Inequality*, p. 146.

33. Robert Kuttner, *Revolt of the Haves*, p. 271.
34. Adolf A. Berle and Gardiner C. Means, *The Modern Corporation and Private Property*, p. xxii.
35. Charles H. Anderson, *The Political Economy of Social Class*, p. 214.
36. Donald L. Barrett and James B. Steele, *American Democracy*, p. 253;
37. John K. Galbraith, *Economics in Perspective*, p. 163; Zeitlin, editor, *American Society Inc*, The Patman Committee, pp. 54–62.
38. Charles H. Anderson, *The Political Economy of Social Class*, p. 213; Leslie Wayne, "The Corporate Raiders", *New York Times Magazine*, July 18, 1982, pp. 18, 47–51;
39. John K. Galbraith, *The Culture of Contentment*, p. 57.
40. The flap over executive pay, *Business Week*, May 6, 1991, p. 90.
41. Adolf A. Berle and Gardiner C. Means, *The Modern Corporation and Private Property*, p. 313.
42. "For New Opportunities: Now, the Word Is 'Go Abroad'," *U.S. New & World Report*, June 1, 1964.
43. "Multinational Companies", *Business Week*, April 20, 1963; *Statistical Abstract of the United States*, 1972, p. 754; *Horatio Alger, Farewell*, Celeste MacLeod, p. 265.
44. *The New York Times*, January 18, 1987.
45. Robert Reich, *The Work of Nations*, quoted in David P. Calleo, *The Bankrupting of America*, p. 169; Celeste MacLeod, *Horatio Alger, Farewell*, p. 267.
46. *Economic Report of the President*, 1990, p. 410;
47. Robert Kuttner, *Revolt of the Haves*, p. 265, 266; Harry E. Figgie, *Bankruptcy 1995*, p. 102, 143.
48. Harry E. Figgie, *Bankruptcy 1995*, p. 143.
49. John E. Ullmann, "Building a Peacetime Economy," *Technology Review*, August/September 1991; Joel Kurtzman, *The Decline and Crash of the American Economy*, p.149.
50. "Foreign Firms Income in U.S. Is Understated," *The Wall Street Journal*, June 4, 1993; Donald L. Barlett and James B. Steele, *America What Went Wrong*, p. 89; *Economic Report of the President*, U.S. Government Printing Office, 1991, p. 256.
51. The Flap over executive pay, *Business Week*, May 6, 1991; Donald L. Barlett and James B. Steele, *America what went Wrong*, p.20
52. "Investigators Say Bid Rigging Is Common in Milk Industry," *New York Times*, May 22, 1993.
53. "Methods of Marketing Infant Formula Land Abbott in Hot Water", *The Wall Street Journal*, May 25, 1993, p. 1.
54. Lewis H. Lapham, *Money and Class in America*, p. 232.
55. Ben H. Bagdikian, *The Media Monopoly*, pp. 50, 51.
56. "Trade and Investment, Weep Not Jeremiah," *The Economist*, July 4th, 1992; Robert Kuttner, *The Economic Illusion*, p. 92.

57. Walter Adams, *Planning, Regulation and Competition in Hearing before Subcommittees of the Select Committee on Small Business*, U.S. Senate, 90th Congress, 1st sess. (Washington D.C.: U.S. Government Printing Office, June 29, 1967), pp. 11–16; Gabriel Kolko, *Wealth and Power in America*, pp. 60, 62.
58. "Executive Pay," *Business Week*, March 30, 1992, p. 57; "Put Them at Risk," *Forbes*, May 25, 1992, p. 159; *Facts on File*, January 16, 1992, p. 18.
59. Lewis H. Lapham, *Money and Class in America*, p. 231.
60. Ross Perot, *United We Stand*, p. 64; Evan G. Galbraith, "What Is the Right Amount of Saving?," *National Review*, June 16, 1989, p. 29.
61. Robert Kuttner, *Revolt of the Haves*, p. 264.
62. "Answer: A Value Added Tax," Lester C. Thurow, *The New York Times*, June 8, 1993.
63. "Clinton Seeks Taxes on Hidden Profits," *The New York Times*, October 24, 92; "Out of Money: Clinton Mulls a Value Added Tax," *The Wall Street Journal*, April 16, 1993.
64. "Not VAT Again," *Wall Street Journal*, April 16, 1993.

Chapter 7.   Taxation And Waste

1. Milton Friedman, *There Is No Such Thing as a Free Lunch*.
2. George Cooper, *A Voluntary Tax?*, p. 2.
3. Howard P. Tuckman, *The Economics of the Rich*, p. 194.
4. *Congressional Quarterly*, June 27, 1981.
5. Phil Kuntz, "Tax Aide's Clothes Line," *Congressional Quarterly*, June 13, 1992, p. 1680.
6. Adam Smith, *Wealth of Nations*, Book 5, Chapter 2, Part 2
7. Joseph A. Pechman, *Federal Tax Policy*, p. 53.
8. Joseph Pechman, *Who Paid the Taxes*.
9. See Table 1;

Table 1 Expenditures on basic necessities as a percentage of net Family income by class (1974)

Expenditure as % of Net Income	Under Class %	Working Class %	Middle Class %	Upper Class %
Food	107.6	32.8	20.9	15.5
Energy	41.7	13.6	8.9	6.1
Shelter	105.2	24.3	13.3	12.2
Medical Care	29.4	9.3	5.0	4.6
All Necessities	284	80.0	48.1	38.4

Source: Leslie Ellen Nulty, *Understanding the New Inflation*. The Importance of the Basic Necessities (Washington D.C.: Exploratory Project for Economic Alternatives, 1977), pp. 55–56.

10. Kevin Philips, *The Politics of Rich and Poor*, p. 80.
11. Kevin Philips, *The Politics of Rich and Poor*, p. 80; Ross Perot, *United We Stand*, p. 47.
12. "Privatize Social Security, Robert Genetski," *Wall Street Journal*, May 21, 1993.
13. "R.I.P.: The Good Corporation," Robert J. Samuelson, *Newsweek*, July 5, 1993; "What Do You All Call U.S. Taking Cut of Payrolls," *The Wall Street Journal*, June 1, 1993.
14. Donald L. Barlett and James B. Steele, *America What Went Wrong*, p. 217.
15. Ibid., p. 197.
16. Ibid., p. 200.
17. Ibid., p. 216; "The Capital Gains of the Well-to-do," *U.S. News and World Report*, October 2, 1989, p. 26.
18. Ross Perot, *United We Stand*, p. 43; "Follow the Money," *Forbes*, October 26, 1992, p. 138.
19. "Follow the Money, *Forbes*," October 26, 1992, p. 138
20. "Where Do Charity Dollars Go," *American Legion Magazine*, December 1988, p. 22.
21. "Politicians in Tax-exempt Activities," *National Journal*, December 9, 1989.
22. Joseph A. Pechman, *Who Paid the Taxes 1966–85*, pp. 1, 4, 17, 48, 80. See Table 2 and Table 3.

Table 2 Federal state and local taxes by source 1980.

	Percent
Personal Income Taxes	41.7
Corporate Profit taxes	8.5
Indirect Sales, Excise and Property Taxes	27.1
Payroll Taxes	22.7
Total	100.00

Table 3 Distribution of tax burden by class

Year	Under Class %	Working Class %	Middle Class %	Upper Class %
1970	25.8	25.1	26.2	27.8
1980	24.7	23.3	25.4	26.1
1985	25.0	23.5	25.0	24.3

24. Colman McCarthy, "The Faulty School Buses", *Saturday Review*, March 11, 1972
25. "Media," *Industries Surveys*, February 13, 1992 p. M16; Ben H. Bagdikian, *The Media Monopoly*, pp. 136, 197.

26. "Media," *Industries Surveys*, February 13, 1992, p. M16; Milton Friedman, *There's No Such Thing as a Free Lunch*, p. 238.
27. "Read This!," *Time*, November 26, 1990; "A Costlier Christmas?," *Time*, July 29, 1991.
28. John Rothschild, "The Screwing of the Average Man", *The Washington Monthly,* October, 1971, p. 39; Ben H. Bagdikian, *The Media Monopoly*, p. 148.
29. John E. Ullmann, Building a Peacetime Economy, *Technology Review*, August/September, 1991, p. 57.
30. Richard C. Edwards, editor, *The Capitalist System*, pp. 392–406.
31. *Washington Post*, February 24, March 30 and July 11, 1985 and August 21, 1983; *New York Times*, November 20, 1983.
32. Charles H. Anderson, *The Political Economy of Social Class*, p. 252.
33. Bernard Winter, M.D., "Health Care: The Problem Is Profits", *Progressive*, October 1977, p. 16.
34. Henry Aaron, *Serious and Unstable Condition*, pp. 66–67.
35. Ibid, p. 93; John Ehrenreich, *The American Health Empire*, p. 136
36. "What Doctors Earn," *Newsweek*, April 5, 1993; "International Price Gap," *The Wall Street Journal*, June 29, 1993; "Let's Really Cure the Health System," *Fortune*, March 23, 1992.
37. "Up in Smoke," *Wall Street Journal*, April 1, 1993; "Tobacco Industry Tax Break Is Threatened," *Wall Street Journal*, March 11, 1993; "Tobacco Aid," *Common Cause Magazine*, March/April, 1991, p. 9; "Two Bucks Will Finance Health Care," Jeffrey E. Harris, *New York Times*, June 4, 1993.
38. "America's Parasite Economy," *The Economist*, October 10th, 1992.
39. "Lawyers Reassess Job Bias Lawsuits," *The Wall Street Journal*, July 6, 1993; "The Tort Tax," *Forbes*, February 17, 1992.
40. "Too Many Lawyers and Too Many Litigations," *Business Week*, April 13, 1992.
41. "Tort Tax, *Forbes*," February 17, 1992; "The Malpractice Mess," *Newsweek*, February 17, 1986.
42. "Too Many Lawyers and Too Many Litigations," *Business Week*, April 13, 1992; "The Tort Tax," *Forbes*, February 17, 1992.
43. "Bars and Stripes Forever," *Time*, January 14, 1991; "Public Safety Poses Danger To Taxpayers," *The Wall Street Journal*, June 22, 1993.
44. "Too Many Lawyers and Too Many Litigations," *Business Week*, April 13, 1992; "Slump Hits Elite Firms," *Wall Street Journal*, June 29, 1993; "Are Contingent Fees Unethical and Illegal," *USA Today*, December 1991; There's Still No Free Lunch, *Newsweek*, April 12, 1993.
45. Empty Seats: "Despite 20 Years of Heavy Spending, Transit Systems Are Failing to Lure Back Riders," *Wall Street Journal*, June 29, 1993.

46. Bradford Snell, *American Ground Transport* (Washington, D.C.: Government Printing Office, 1973); Jonathan Kwitny, "The Great Transportation Conspiracy" in Cargan and Ballantine, editors, *Sociological Footprints*.

47. Bradford Snell, *American Ground Transport* (Washington, D.C.: Government Printing Office, 1973).

48. "Auto Expenses may Drive You Out of Your Car," *Contra Costa Times*, March 6, 1993; "Let Drivers Opt Out of Auto Tort System," *Wall Street Journal*, September 23, 1992.

49. Coping with the Disabilities Act, *Governing*, August, 1992, p. 18.

50. William Greider, *Secrets of the Temple*, p. 401; George F. Will, "What Dukakis Should be Saying", *Washington Post*, September 15, 1988.

51. **Table 4** Percentage of total national savings by class

Year	Under Class %	Working Class %	Middle Class %	Upper Class %	Total %
Savings 1929	−13	0	27	27.8	100
Savings 1935–36	−9	−15	20	105	100
Savings 1941	−4	0	31	73	100
Savings 1945	−2	12	44	46	100
Savings 1950	−16	−2	45	73	100
(Wealth) 1983	−0.4	3.2	27.2	69.6	100

52. Benjamin M. Friedman, *The Day of Reckoning*, p. 262.

53. Robert E. Lipsey and Irving B. Kravis, *Savings and Economic Growth: Is the United States Really Falling Behind?* The Conference Board, 1987.

54. Milton Friedman, *There Is No Such Thing as a Free Lunch*, p. 93; "Try the Flat Tax," *Wall Street Journal*, May 14, 1993.

55. Robert S. McIntyre and Dean C.Tipps, *Inequity and decline*, p. 84

56. "Try the Flat Tax," W. Kurt Hauser, *Wall Street Journal*, May 14, 1993.

57. Edward C. Budd, editor, *Inequality and Poverty*, p. 116.

Chapter 8. Mock Democracy

1. Adam Smith, *Wealth of Nations*, p. 311.

2. Lewis H. Lapham, *Money and Class in America*, p. 33.

3. Louis O. Kelso and Patricia Hetter Kelso, *Democracy and Economic Power*, p. 105.

4. Lewis H. Lapham, *Money and Class in America*, p. 34

5. Michael Parenti, *Democracy for the Few*, p. 4.

6. Larry Gilbert, "Japan Buys a Used President," *New York Times*, November 6, 1989.
7. John Locke, *Treatise of Civil Government*, p. 82.
8. Paul Baran and Paul Sweezy, *Monopoly Capital*, p. 157.
9. Maurice Zeitlin, editor, *American Society Inc.*, p. 346.
10. Donald R. Mathews, *U.S. Senators and their World*, p. 2.
11. C. Wright Mills, *The Power Elite*, p. 248.
12. Gregory A. Fossedal, What Gets Made in Congress, *Harpers*, February, 1985; *Congressional Quarterly*, November 7, 1992, p. 9
13. Elizabeth McCaughey, "Court Deals a Blow to Racial Gerrymandering," *The Wall Street Journal*, June 30, 1993.
14. Jonathan H. Turner and Charles E. Starnes, *Inequality: Privilege and Poverty in America*, p. 79.
15. "The New Limousine Liberals," *Time*, August 3, 1992; "Business Losses and Interest Deductions Help the Wealthy Escape Taxes," *Wall Street Journal*, July 7, 1993.
16. Michael Parenti, *Democracy for the Few*, p. 235.
17. Dennis Gilbert and Joseph A. Kahl, *The American Class Structure*, pp. 227–228.
18. "Clinton's People: President's Team Is an Elite Group," *Wall Street Journal*, January 21, 1993; "Cabinet's Fortunes Hit a 12-year High," *Contra Costa Times*, January 27, 1993.
19. *Seattle Post-Intelligencer,* July 16, 1976; William Shannon, *New York Times*, July 22, 1975.
20. G. William Domhoff, *Who Rules America?*, p. 109; Joel B. Grossman, *Lawyers and Judges: The ABA and the Politics of Judicial Selection*.
21. Dexter Perkins, *Charles Evans Hughes*, p. 16; Felix Frankfurter, *Mr. Justice Holmes and the Supreme Court*, p. 54; Tom Wicker, "Purifying the Courts", *New York Times*, April 19, 1985.
22. Russell Galloway, *The Rich and the Poor in Supreme Court History 1790–1982*, p. 181; *Hammer v. Dagenhart* (1918).
23. Howard Kurtz, "Hostility to 'New Federalism' Is Bipartisan Among Mayors", *Washington Post*, December 10, 1984.
24. Grant McConnell, *Private Power and American Democracy*, p. 189.
25. C. Wright Mills, *The Power Elite*, p. 259.
26. Max Lerner, *America as a Civilization*, p. 368.
27. Frank Sorauf, *Party Politics in America*, 3rd ed., p. 17.
28. "Today It's Advertising Agencies," *New York Times*, October 6, 1986.
29. Ladd, *Where Have All the Voters Gone?* p. 17;
30. Simon Gerson, *Does the U.S. Have Free Elections?*; Richard Walton, "The Two-Party Monopoly", *Nation*, September 8, 1980, pp. 176–78.

31. Walton, *The Two-Party Monopoly*, p. 177; *Progressive*, March 1977, p. 14.
32. Maurice Duverger, *Political Parties*, p. 248.
33. *Washington Post, June 19*, 1981; *Wall Street Journal*, October 2, 1985; *Washington Post*, June 16, 1986.
34. Bob Howard and John Logue, editors, *American Class Society in Numbers*, p. 79; *New York Times*, August 18, 1984.
35. Richard Cloward and Frances Fox Piven, *Trying to Break Down the Barriers*, 1985, p. 436; John Conyers, Jr. and Neil Kotler, "The Blacks", *Progressive*, October 1982, p. 40.
36. Jack Anderson, "U.S. Squelches Some Voter Drives", *Washington Post*, October 5, 1985; *Vote Fraud Trials Threaten Democracy*, Alabama Blackbelt Defense Committee, Gainesville, Ala., February, 1986.
37. "The Campaign Goes on a Furlough," *U.S. News and World Report*, October 3, 1988.
38. Voters Know What They Don't like, *Business Week*, June 11,1984
39. Thomas Byrne Edsall, *The New Politics of Equality*, p. 97.
40. Ibid, p. 91.
41. Douglas Bailey, *The Washington Post*, April 20, 1990; Douglas Bailey Seminar, Progressive Policy Institute, February 26, 1990.
42. William Greider, *Who Will Tell the People*, p. 275.
43. Ibid, p. 273.
44. Michael Parenti, *Democracy for the Few*, p. 207; Steven Stark, "Labor's Kiss of Death", *The New York Times*, May 22, 1983.
45. Thomas Byrne Edsall, *The New Politics of Inequality*, p. 50.
46. Andrew Jaffe, "Democrats at the Crossroads", *Los Angeles Herald Examiner*, November 11, 1984.
47. William Greider, *Who Will Tell the People*, p. 248.
48. Ibid., p. 252.
49. Ibid., p. 258.
50. Robert S. McIntyre and Dean C. Tipps, *Inequality and Decline*, p. 49; Dom Bonafede, "Textbook Candidate" , *PS*, Winter 1983, p. 55.
51. Robert S. McIntyre and Dean C.Tipps, *Inequality and Decline*, p. 50; Herbert Alexander, "Political Parties and the Dollar", *Society*, January/February 1985, pp. 55–57; "Special Interests Give $205 Million to Campaigns," *Wall Street Journal*, October 23, 1992.
52. James B. Steele and Donald L. Barlett, *America What Went Wrong*, p. 194.
53. William Greider, *Who Will Tell the People*, p. 259.
54. "Racial Divide", *Wall Street Journal*, July 14, 1993.
55. "Campaign Reform that Incumbents Love to Hate," *Wall Street Journal*, May 17, 1993; William Greider, *Who Will Tell the People*, p. 51.

56. Heinz Eulau, "The Politics of Happiness", Antioch Review, 16, 1956, pp. 259–64; William Greider, *Who Will Tell the People*, pp. 21, 50.
57. "Campaign Finance Reform," *Congressional Digest*, March 1992, p. 67.
58. "Campaign Finance Reform," *Congressional Digest,* October 1990, p. 226.
59. "Report Discusses 'Soft' Contributions to Parties in 1992," *The Wall Street Journal*, March 4, 1993.
60. Mickey Kaus, *The End of Equality*, p. 89.
61. Ross Perot, *United We Stand*, p. 24.
62. "Peddling Power for Profit," *Time*, March 22, 1993.

Chapter 9.   Press Freedom

1. Daniel J. Boorstin, *Hidden History*, p. 128.
2. Nick Kotz, *Let Them Eat Promises*, p. ix.
3. John Kenneth Galbraith, *The Age of Uncertainty*, p. 90.
4. Ibid, p. 86.
5. Dan Rather, *The Camera Never Blinks*, p. 260.
6. Ibid., pp. 272–276.
7. "News by the Numbers," *Time*, March 16, 1987; "Star Power," *Time*, August 7, 1989; "Corporate America's Most Powerful People," *Forbes*, May 25, 1992.
8. Ben H. Bagdikian, *The Media Monopoly*, p. xix.
9. Ibid., p. xi.
10. Ibid., p. xi.
11. Herbert Schiller, "Behind the Media Merger Movement", *Nation*, June 8, 1985; "A Deal That's Fit to Print," *Newsweek*, June 21, 1993, p. 49; Charles Perlik, address before the Newspaper Guild, *Daily World*, November 7, 1985
12. Gerald Jay Goldberg and Robert Goldberg, *Anchors and the Evening News*, p. 103.
13. James Aronson, "Packaging the News," *New York Times*, February 15, 1977.
14. Ben H. Bagdikian, *The Media Monopoly*, p. 121.
15. Ibid., p. 123.
16. Ibid., p. 127.
17. Ibid., p. 131.
18. Ibid., p. 133.
19. Robert Goldberg and Gerald Jay Goldberg, *Anchors and the Evening* News, p. 31.
20. Radio and T.V. Broadcasting, *Industry Surveys*, February 13, 1992.
21. Edwin Diamond, *The Media Show*, p. 203; "Star Power," *Time*, August 7, 1989.
22. Robert Parry, *Fooling America*, p. 42; Robert Goldberg and Gerald Jay Goldberg, *Anchors and the Evening News*, p. 240.

23. *National Journal*, May 5, 1990; *Washington Post*, January 20, 1989; *The Wall Street Journal*, December 28, 1989.
24. Barry Sussman, *What Americans Really Think*.
25. William Greider, *Who Will Tell the People*, pp. 289, 302.
26. Ben H. Bagdikian, *The Media Monopoly*, p. 56.
27. David Ignatius, "Fishing for a Few Good Ideas", *Washington Post*, March 11, 1990.
28. Ellis Cose, *The Press*, p. 17.
29. William Greider, *Who Will Tell the People*, p. 305.
30. Dan Rather, *The Camera Never Blinks*, p. 252.
31. Ibid., pp. 253, 254.
32. Helen Thomas quoted in *Washington Post*, June 10, 1985.
33. Robert Parry, *Fooling America*, p. 46.
34. Ibid., p. 47
35. "How the Media Blew It", *Newsweek*, November 21, 1988.
36. *New York Times*, October 3, 1986; Mike Zagarell, "News Reporting—the Military Vies for Command", *World Magazine*, November 1, 1984, p. 8.
37. Michael Isikoff, "U.S.'Power'on Abductions Detailed", *The Washington Post*, August 14, 1991, A14; "Objective Journalists or State Propagandists?" *Extra!*, a publication of Fairness and Accuracy in Reporting, January–February, 1990, p. 6.
38. Ben H. Bagdikian, *The Media Monopoly*, p. 37.
39. Ibid., p. 39.
40. Ibid., p. 42.
41. Ibid., p. 155.
42. Ibid., p. 156.
43. Ibid., p. 157.
44. Ibid., p. 158.
45. Ibid., p. 160.
46. Ibid., p. 162.
47. Ibid., p. 163.
48. Ibid., p. 163.
49. Ibid., p. 166.
50. Ibid., p. 167.
51. Ibid., p. 170.
52. Benjamin De Mott, *The Imperial Middle*, p. 114.
53. Ibid., p. 121.
54. Ibid., p. 122.
55. Ben H. Bagdikian, *The Media Monopoly*, pp. 58, 217.
56. Robert Goldberg and Gerald Goldberg, *Anchors and the Evening News*, pp. 213–218.
57. Ben H. Bagdikian, *The Media Monopoly*, pp. 182, 186.
58. Dan Balz, "Report Finds Americans Angry at Political System", *The Washington Post*, June 5, 1991; Robert Parry, *Fooling America*, p. 12.

59. Robert Parry, *Fooling America*, p. 12.
60. "ABC Agrees to a Cable Deal," *New York Times*, July 15, 1993.
61. Ben H. Bagdikian, *The Media Monopoly*, pp. 230.
62. "Advertising Girds for Biggest Tax Battle Ever," *Advertising Age*, March 15, 1993.

Chapter 10.   War And Peace

1. Adam Smith, *Wealth of Nations*, 1776.
2. Eliot Janeway, *The Economics of Chaos*, p. 375.
3. John Kenneth Galbraith, *The Age of Uncertainty*, p. 227.
4. "Quayle Hunt," *The Economist*, August 27, 1988.
5. "Anatomy of a Smear," *Time*, October 19, 1992.
6. James M. McPherson, *Battle Cry of Freedom*.
7. Charles Moskos, *A Call to Civil Service*, pp. 23, 40.
8. Lewis H. Lapham, *Money and Class in America*, p. 230.
9. Benjamin DeMott, *The Imperial Middle*, p. 175.
10. William Broyles, *Brothers in Arms*, pp. 135, 137.
11. *America's Vietnam Experience*, (Berlin: Conelsen Verlog, 1991), p. 13.
12. Benjamin DeMott, *The Imperial Middle*, p. 177.
13. Ibid., p. 177.
14. "Dan Quayle, One of Us", *The New Republic*, September 12 & 19, 1988, p. 16.
15. Benjamin DeMott, *The Imperial Middle*, p. 179.
16. "Greetings, You Have Been Selected", *Time*, August 29, 1988.
17. "The American Class System," *Newsweek*, 29th, June 1970 p.88; Albert J. Mayer and Thomas F. Hoult, "Social Stratification and Combat Survival", *Social Forces* 34 (December, 1955): 155–159.
18. National Advisory Commission on Selective Service, *In Pursuit of Equality: Who Serves When Not All Serve?* (Washington, D.C: Government Printing Office, 1967) pp. 75, 79.
19. Milton Friedman, *There's no such thing as a free lunch*, p. 192.
20. *Congressional Record*, February 3, 1987, S 1615.
21. *Social Representation in the U.S. Military*, Congressional Budget Office, Washington D.C.: Suptd. of Documents, p. 25.
22. Ibid., Table 3, "Percentage of Females Among Recruits," p. 28.
23. "Pentagon Plans to Allow Combat Flights by Women", *The New York Times*, April 28, 1993.
24. "What's Fair in Love and War", Randy Shilts, *Newsweek*, February 1, 1993, p. 58.
25. Ibid., p. 59.
26. Robert I. Vexler, ed., *Dwight D. Eisenhower, 1890–1969*, p. 143; "Spendthrifts for Defense" *The Nation*, August 25, 1962, p. 63.

27. Oliver C. Cox, *Capitalism and American Leadership*, New York, p. 118.
28. H.L. Nieburg, *In the Name of Science*, pp. 188–189.
29. John K. Galbraith, *The Culture of Contentment*, p. 137.
30. Gerard Piel, "Can Our Economy Stand Disarmament?" *The Atlantic*, September 1962, p. 40.
31. Michael Parenti, *The Sword and the Dollar*, p. 153.
32. Fred J. Cook, "Juggernaut: The Welfare State", *The Nation*, October 20, 1961, p. 300.
33. Fred Halliday, *The Making of the Second Cold War*, p. 48; *Washington Post*, February 20, 1987.
34. Daniel Patrick Moynihan, *On the Law of Nations*.
35. "U.S. Imperialism Today", *Political Affairs* 45 (June 1970), p. 26.
36. *Washington Post*, February 2, 1984; *New York Times*, February 20, 1984; James Petras, *Critical Perspective on Imperialism and Social Class in the Third World*.
37. Richard Barnet and Peter Kornbluh, "Contradictions in Nicaragua", *Sojourners*, May 8, 1984, p. 10.
38. Marrin Gettleman et al, *Vietnam and America*, p. 461; *Indochina Newsletter*, Dorchester, Mass. issue # 18, November–December, 1982.
39. William Hoffman, "Vietnam: The Bloody Get-Rich-Quick Business of War", *Gallery*, November 1978, p. 42.
40. Robert Parry, *Fooling America*, p. 133.
41. Ibid., p. 145.
42. Pierre Salinger and Eric Laurent, *Secret Dossier: The Hidden Agenda Behind the Gulf War*, p. 67.
43. Rick Atkinson and Ann Devroy, "Bush: Iraq Won't Decide Timing of Ground War", *The Washington Post*, February 2, 1991,A1
44. Robert Parry, *Fooling America*, p. 161.
45. Thomas C. Hayes, "Oil Prices Fall on Speculation About Iraqi Exports", *New York Times*, July 3, 1993.
46. Michael Parenti, *The Sword and the Dollar*, p. 110; Robert Parry, *Fooling America*, p. 150; Michael Parenti, *Democracy for the Few*, p. 96
47. Joel Kurtzman, *The Decline & Crash of the American Economy*, p. 94
48. George Soros, "A Great Light in the East?", *Geopolitique*, No. 26, 1989.
49. William Greider, *Who Will Tell the People*, p. 368.

Chapter 11.   Education And Equal Opportunity

1. Thomas Byrne Edsall, *The New Politics of Inequality*, p. 18.
2. Daniel J. Boorstin, *Hidden History*, p. 207.

3. Charles H. Anderson, *The Political Economy of Social Class*, p.8
4. Ed Clayton, *Martin Luther King*, p. 110.
5. Andrew Levison, *The Full Employment Alternative*, p. 53.
6. Lewis H. Lapham, "Justice Horatio Alger," *Harper's Magazine*, September 1991, pp. 8–10; "Notebook," *The New Republic*, July 29, 1991.
7. "A Man with a Minority Viewpoint," *Time*, July 15, 1991; "The Case of the Missing Black Judges," A. Leon Higginbotham, *New York Times*, July 29, 1992.
8. "A Man with a Minority Viewpoint," *Time*, July 15, 1991.
9. Ibid.
10. "Bush May Have Won More than a New Justice," *Business Week*, October 28, 1991.
11. *Plessey v. Ferguson*, 163 U.S. 537 (1896).
12. *Time* magazine, November 9, 1959, p. 17.
13. Jacob K. Javits, *Discrimination USA*, p. 10.
14. Paul Sweezy and Paul Baran, *Monopoly Capital*, p. 275.
15. Chapter 2, Table 6B.
16. Bradley R. Schiller, *The Economics of Poverty and Discrimination*, p. 207.
17. Ibid., p. 208
18. Edward Snow, "The Grove City Horror Show", *Chronicles*, p. 51.
19. Bradley R. Schiller, *The Economics of Poverty and Discrimination*, p. 208.
20. Ibid., 208.
21. "Justices Increase Workers Burden in Job-bias Case," *New York Times*, June 26, 1993.
22. Stephen Wermiel, "Justices Affirm Interpretation of Rights Law", *The Wall Street Journal*, June 16, 1989; "Coyly, the Court Turns 180 Degrees", *The New York Times*, June 12, 1989; "Affirm-ative Action Ain't Broke, so . . . " *Business Week*, June 26, 1989, p. 170.
23. Paul Barrett, "President Vetoes Job Bias Legislation: Democratic Proponents Assail the Move", *The Wall Street Journal*, October 23, 1990; Timothy Noah and Albert Karr, "What New Civil Rights Law Will Mean", *The Wall Street Journal*, November 4, 1991, p. B1.
24. "Rich-Poor Gulf Widens Among Blacks," *New York Times*, September 25, 1992.
25. Thernstrom, "Permaffirm Action", p. 18; Kathleen Teltsch, "Grant Seeks to Attract Minorites to Teaching," *The New York Times*, September 23, 1990.
26. "The NAACP Faces a Struggle Over the Future," *New York Times*, March 31, 1993; "NAACP Faces Charge it has Lost its Edge," *The Wall Street Journal*, Friday, April 9, 1993.

27. Chapter 2 Table 6B.
28. "Public Ideology and the Class Composition of Women's Liberation", *Berkeley Journal of Sociology* 16 (1971–72): 154–56.
29. Frank Parkin, *Class Inequality and Political Order*, p. 15.
30. "As Holocaust Memory Fades, Israel Faces a Difficult Transition," *Wall Street Journal*, March 31, 1993; "Dead End for the Mainline?" *Newsweek*, August 9, 1993; "How to End the Impasse," Cornel West, *New York Times*, April 14, 1993.
31. Blacks Rejecting Gay Rights As Equal With Their Fight, *New York Times*, June 29, 1993.
32. Herbert Mitgang, "The Battle by the Disabled for their Civil Rights," *New York Times*, June 2, 1993.
33. Kenneth S. Tollett, "For Mandela, South Africa Comes First", *The New York Times*, July 25, 1990; "Newspaper Editors to Name a Black as President," *The New York Times*, March 29, 1993.
34. Thomas Sowell, "Affirmative Action Reconsidered" in Barry R. Gross, ed., *Reverse Discrimination*, p. 129; Shelby Steele, "A Negative Vote on Affirmative Action", *The New York Times Magazine* (May 13, 1990), p. 49; "Civil Rights and Wrongs," *The Wall Street Journal*, July 19, 1990.
35. Dennis Gilbert, Joseph A. Kahl, *The American Class Structure*, p. 108.
36. Ivan Jankovic, *Crime and Social Justice*, (Fall-Winter, 1977).
37. "Wide Health Gap, Linked to Income, Is Reported in U.S.", Robert Pear, *The New York Times*, July 8, 1993.
38. "Soviet Commitment to Education," *U.S. Department of Health, Education and Welfare Bulletin 1959* No. 16, Washington, 1959, p. 116.
39. Dennis Gilbert, Joseph A. Kahl, *The American Class Structure*, p. 170.
40. "A Nation Still at Risk," *Newsweek*, April 19, 1993; Chapter 7, Taxation and Waste.
41. Nick Kotz, *Let Them Eat Promises*, p. 45; Sexton, *Education and Income*, pp. 134–135; *1992 Green Book*, Committee on Ways and Means, p. 1683; "In Stevens Point," Wisconsin, *NEA Today*, May/June, 1990.
42. Felicia R. Lee, "Newark Students Struggle to Make Do," *The New York Times*, May 15, 1993.
43. Edward Zigler, "Head Start, the Whole Story," *The New York Times*, July 24, 1993; Michael Kramer, "Getting Smart About Head Start," *Time*, March 8, 1993.
44. "The Money Questions That Have Schools Stumped," *Business Week*, June 4, 1990.
45. Sexton, *Education and Income*, p. 152.
46. Bradley R. Schiller, *The Economics of Poverty and Discrimination*, p. 217.

47. Ibid., p. 142.
48. Charles Tiebout, "An Economic Theory of Fiscal Decentralization" in James Buchanan (ed), *Public Finances: Needs, Sources and Utilization*, p. 94; John R. Logan and Reid M. Golden, "Suburbs and Satellites: Two Decades of Change", *American Sociological Review 51* (June 1986): 436.
49. Sexton, *Education and Income*, p. 60; Bradley R. Schiller, *The Economics of Poverty and Discrimination*, pp. 210–214.
50. Christopher Jencks, *Inequality: A Reassessment of the Effects of Family and Schooling in America*, p. 27.
51. Office of Education, *Digest of Educational Statistics*, 1972, p. 8; *Playboy*, December 1971, p. 26.
52. Gabriel Kolko, *Wealth and Power in America*, pp. 115–117.
53. Christina Duff, "Poor Prospects", *The Wall Street Journal*, July 28, 1993.
54. Richard Parker, *The Myth of the Middle Class*, p. 205.
55. Alger, *Strive and Succeed*, p. 52.
56. Milton and Rose Friedman, *Free to Choose*, pp. 128–134.
57. Jonathan Cobb, *The Hidden Injuries of Class*, p. 72; E.F. Tully, Elton F. Jackson, and R.F. Curtis, "Trends in Occupational Mobility in Indianapolis", *Social Forces*, 49 (December 1970), pp. 186–200; Lewis H. Lapham, *Money and Class in America*, p. 22.
58. "Farm Subsidies Soar," *Fortune*, August 18, 1986, p. 8.
59. Kevin G. Salwen, "German-Owned Maker of Power Tools Finds Job Trainng Pays Off," *The Wall Street Journal*, April 19, 1993; "Firms Need Prodding to Improve Workplaces, Labor Secretary Reich Says," *The Wall Street Journal*, July 6, 1993.

Chapter 12.   Liberty And Justice For All

1. Bob Howard and John Logue, editors, *American Class Society in Numbers*, p. 50.
2. Robert Kuttner, *The Economic Illusion*, p. 5.
3. Franklin D. Roosevelt, Second Inaugural Address, 1937.
4. Benjamin Friedman, *Day of Reckoning*, p. 5.
5. Dennis Gilbert and Joseph A. Kahl, *The American Class Structure*, p. 286.
6. Japan, *Facts on File*, January 23, 1992, p. 46.
7. *National Review*, February 17, 1992, p. 25.
8. "The Sick Society," *National Review*, March 2, 1992, p. 64; "The Truth About the American Worker," *Fortune*, May 4, 1992.
9. Benjamin M. Friedman, *The Day of Reckoning*, p. 29.
10. Robert Kuttner, *The Economic Illusion*, p. 7.
11. William Greider, *Who Will Tell the People*, p. 399.

12. *Economic Indications*, Joint Economics Committee, May 1991.
13. "Metamorphosis of the American Worker", by Robert B. Reich, *Business Month*, November 1990, p. 59.
14. Ibid., p. 61.
15. Ibid., p. 60.
16. John Kenneth Galbraith, *The Culture of Contentment*, p. 107; "Poor Prospects," Christina Duff, *The Wall Street Journal*, July 28, 1993; Joel Kurtzman, *The Decline and Crash of the American Economy*, p. 100.
17. "Net Debtor Position of U.S. in 1992 Was a Record," *The Wall Street Journal*, July 1, 1993; Benjamin E. Friedman, *The Day of Reckoning*, p. 51.
18. Benjamin E. Friedman, *The Day of Reckoning*, p. 91.
19. David P. Calleo, *The Bankrupting of America*, p. 40; Joel Kurtzman, *The Decline and Crash of the American Economy*, p. 76.
20. David P. Calleo, *The Bankrupting of America*, p. 28.
21. "Home Ownership Declines in Census Report," *The New York Times*, June 16, 1991.
22. A.B. Atkinson, ed., *Wealth Income and Inequality*, pp. 12–14.
23. Bradley R. Schiller, *The Economics of Poverty and Discrimination*, p. 235.
24. Gabriel Kolko, *Wealth and Power in America*, p. 92.
25. Mortimer J. Adler, *We Hold These Truths*, p. 148.
26. Thorstein Veblen, *The Engineers and the Price System*, p. 147.
27. Russel Galloway, *The Rich and the Poor in Supreme Court History*, p. 184; Louis and Patricia Kelso, *Democracy and Economic Power*, p. 75.
28. David I. Levine and Laura d'Andrea Tyson, "Participation, Productivity and the Firms Environment" in *Paying for Productivity*, p. 224.
29. Celeste Macleod, *Horatio Alger, Farewell*, pp. 281–282.
30. Daniel J. Boorstin, *Hidden History*, p. 209.

BIBLIOGRAPHY

1. Aaron Henry, *Serious and Unstable Condition: Financing America's Health Care*, Washington, D.C., Brookings, 1991.
2. Adler Mortimer J., *We Hold These Truths—Understanding the Ideas and Ideals of the Constitution*, Collier Books, Macmillan Publishing Co., 1987.
3. Anderson Charles H., *The Political Economy of Social Class*, Englewood, New Jersey: Prentice Hall, 1974.
4. Apthekar Herbert, *Early Years of the Republic*, International Publishers, 1990.
5. Atkinson Anthony B., *The Economics of Inequality*, London: Oxford University Press, 1975.
6. Atkinson Anthony B., *Wealth Income and Inequality*, Oxford University Press, 1980.
7. Bagdikian Ben H., *The Media Monopoly*, Boston: Beacon Press, 1990.
8. Balogh Thomas, *The Irrelevance of Conventional Economics*, London: Weidenfeld and Nicolson, 1982.
9. Baran Paul A. and Sweezy Paul M., *Monopoly Capital: an essay*, Monthly Review Press, 1966.
10. Baran Paul A., *Political Economy of Growth*, Monthly Review Press, 1957.
11. Barlett Donald L. and Steel James B., *America—What Went Wrong*, Universal Press Syndicate Co., 1992.
12. Beard Charles A., *An Economic Interpretation of the Constitution of the United States*, New York: Macmillan, 1936.
13. Beard Charles A., *The Economic Basis of Politics*, New York: Vintage Books, 1957.
14. Beard Charles A., *Economic Origins of Jeffersonian Democracy*, New York: The Free Press, 1915.

15. Bendix R. and Lipset S.M., *Class Status and Power*, The Free Press, 1966.
16. Berle Adolf A. and Means G., *Modern Corporation and Private Property*, Harcourt Brace & World, 1968.
17. Berle Adolf A., *Power*, Harcourt, Brace & World, 1967.
18. Bernstein (ed.), *Toward a New Past*, New York: Pantheon, 1963.
19. Bloom Alan, *Closing of the American Mind*, Simon & Schuster, 1987.
20. Blumberg Paul, *Inequality in the Age of Decline*, Oxford University Press, 1980.
21. Boorstin Daniel J., *Hidden History–Exploring our Secret Past*, Harper & Row, 1987.
22. Boudon Raymond, *Education Opportunity and Social Inequality—Changing Prospects in Western Society*, John Wiley & Sons, 1973.
23. Boyd Julian P. ed., *The Papers of Thomas Jefferson* Vol. VIII, Princeton: Princeton University Press, 1953.
24. Brittain John A., *The Inheritance of Economic Status*, The Brookings Institution, 1977.
25. Brogan Hugh, *The Penguin History of the United States of America*, 1985.
26. Broyles William, *Brothers in Arms*, New York: Knopf, 1986.
27. Buchanan James, *Public Finances: Needs, Sources and Utilization*, Princeton, N.J.: Princeton University Press, 1961.
28. Budd Edward C. (editor), *Inequality and Poverty*, W.W. Norton & Co., 1967.
29. Calleo David P., *The Bankrupting of America*, William Morrow & Co., 1992.
30. Cargan and Ballantine (editors), *Sociological Footprints*, Belmont, California: Wadsworth, 1982.
31. Clayton Ed., *Martin Luther King*, New York: Pocket Books, 1968.
32. Cobb Jonathan, *The Hidden Injuries of Class*, New York: Alfred A. Knopf, 1972.
33. Collier Peter and Horowitz David, *The Rockefellers, An American Dynasty*, New York: Holt, Rinehart and Winston, 1976.
34. Congressional Budget Office, *Social Representation in the U.S. Military*, Washington, D.C., U.S. Government Printing Office, 1989.
35. Cooper George, *A Voluntary Tax? New Perspectives on Sophisticated Estate Tax Avoidance*, Washington, D.C., The Brookings Institution, 1979.
36. Cornwall John, *Modern Capitalism—Its Growth and Transformation*, St. Martin's Press, 1977.
37. Cose Ellis, *The Press—Inside America's Most Powerful Newspaper Empires*, New York: William Morrow & Co., 1989.

38. Cox Oliver C., *Capitalism and American Leadership*, New York, 1962.

39. Dahl Robert A., *Who Governs? Democracy and Power in an Amer-ican City*, Yale University Press, 1961.

40. Dahrendorf Rolf, *Class and Class Conflict in Industrial Society*, Stanford University Press, 1965.

41. Democratic Staff of the Joint Economic Committee, *The Concentration of Wealth in the United States*, United States Congress, 1986.

42. De Mott Benjamin, *The Imperial Middle: Why Americans Can't Think Straight about Class*, New York: William Morrow, 1990.

43. Diamond Edwin, *The Media Show—Changing Face of News, 1985–90*, Massachusetts Institute of Technology, 1991.

44. Domhoff G. William, *The Higher Circles—Governing Class in America*, Random house, 1970.

45. Domhoff G. William, *Who Rules America*, Prentice Hall, 1967.

46. Downs Anthony, *An Economic Theory of Democracy*, Harper & Row Publishers, 1957.

47. Drucker Peter F., *Men Ideas and Politics*, Harper & Row, 1971.

48. Duverger Maurice, *Political Parties*, New York: Wiley & Sons, 1955.

49. Edsall Thomas Byrne, *The New Politics of Inequality*, New York: W.W. Norton & Co., 1984.

50. Edwards Richard C. (editor), *The Capitalist System*, 1986.

51. Ehrenreich John, *The American Health Empire: Power, Profits and Politics*, New York: Vintage Books, 1971.

52. Farrand Max, (editor), *Records of the Federal Convention*, New Haven: Yale University Press, 1927.

53. *Federal Reserve Bulletin*, Financial Characteristics of High Income Families, March 1986.

54. *Federal Reserve Bulletin*, Survey of Consumer Finances, January, 1992.

55. Figgie Harry E., *Bankruptcy 1995: The Coming collapse of America and how to stop it*, Little Brown & Co., 1992.

56. Fisher George, editor., *The Revival of American Socialism*, New York: Oxford University Press, 1971.

57. Fisher Irving, *Elementary Principles of Economics*, New York: Macmillan, 1912.

58. Frankfurter Felix, *Mr. Justice Holmes and the Supreme Court*, New York: Atheneum, 1965.

59. Friedman Benjamin M., *The Day of Reckoning—Consequences of American Economic Policy under Reagan and After*, New York: Random House, 1968.

60. Friedman Milton and Rose, *Free to Choose*, Harcourt Brace Jovanovich, 1980.

61. Friedman Milton, *There's No Such Thing as a Free Lunch*, Glenridge, New Jersey: Thomas Horton, 1976.
62. Friedman Milton and Rose, *Tyranny of the Status Quo*, Harcourt Brace Jovanovich, 1984.
63. Galbraith John Kenneth, *The Affluent Society*, Boston: Houghton Mifflin Co., 1969.
64. Galbraith John Kenneth, *The Age of Uncertainty*, Boston: Houghton Mifflin Co., 1977.
65. Galbraith John Kenneth, *American Capitalism: The Concepts of Countervailing Power*, Boston: Houghton Mifflin Co, 1952.
66. Galbraith John Kenneth, *The Culture of Contentment*, Houghton Mifflin Co., 1992.
67. Galbraith John Kenneth, *Economics in Perspective—A critical history*, Houghton Mifflin Co., 1987.
68. Galbraith John Kenneth, *The Great Crash*, Boston: Houghton Mifflin Co., 1972.
69. Galbraith John Kenneth, *The New Industrial State*, Boston: Houghton Mifflin Co., 1967.
70. Galbraith John Kenneth, "What happened to the Class Struggle," *Washington Monthly*, Washington, D.C.
71. Galloway Russell, *The Rich and the Poor in Supreme Court History*, Greenbrace, California, Paradigm Press, 1982.
72. Gettleman Marvin E., et al, *(editors), Vietnam and America*, New York: Grove Press, 1985.
73. Georgean Thomas, *Which Side Are You On?* Farrar, Strauss Giroux, 1991.
74. Gerson Simon, *Does the U.S. Have Free Elections?* New York: International Publishers, 1994.
75. Giddens Anthony, *The Class Structure of the Advanced Societies*, London: Hutchinson & Co., 1973.
76. Gilbert Dennis and Kahl Joseph A., *The American Class Structure*, Chicago: The Dorsey Press, 1987.
77. Gilder George, *Wealth and Poverty*, Basic Books, 1981.
78. Goldberg Robert and Gerald Jay, *Anchors and the Evening News*, Birch Lane Press, Carol Publishing Group, 1990.
79. Gray Alexander, *The Development of Economic Doctrine*, 1931.
80. Green Philip, *The Pursuit of Inequality*, New York: Pantheon Books, 1981.
81. Greider William, *Secrets of the Temple*, New York: Simon & Schuster, 1987.
82. Greider William, *Who Will Tell the People—The Betrayal of Amer-ican Democracy*, Simon & Schuster, 1992.
83. Gross Barry R., *Reverse Discrimination*, Buffalo: Prometheus Books, 1977.

84. Grossman Joel B., *Lawyers and Judges: The ABA and the Politics of Judicial Selection*, New York: Wiley, 1965.
85. Halliday Fred, *The Making of the Second Cold War*, London: Verso, 1983.
86. Harrington Michael, *Poverty in the United States*, Macmillan,1962
87. Harris Donald J., *Capital Accumulation and Income Distribution*, Stanford University Press, 1978.
88. Heilbroner Robert, *Between Capitalism and Socialism*, Random House, 1970.
89. Heilbroner Robert L., *Quest for Wealth—Study of Acquisitive Man*, Simon & Schuster, 1956.
90. Heller Robert, *The Age of the Common Millionaire*, E.P. Dutton, 1988.
91. Howard Bob and Logue John (editors), *American Class Society in Numbers*, Kent Popular Press, 1981.
92. Janeway Eliot, *The Economics of Chaos—On Revitalizing the American Economy*, New York: E.P. Dutton, 1989.
93. Javits Jacob K., *Discrimination USA*, Washington Square Press, 1962.
94. Jencks Christopher, *Inequality: A Reassessment of the Effects of Family and Schooling in America*, New York: Basic Books Inc, 1972.
95. Josephson Matthew, *The Robber Barons*, New York: Harcourt Brace, 1934.
96. Kaus Mickey, *The End of Equality*, Basic Books, Harper Collins Publishers, 1992.
97. Keller Galloway, ed., *William Graham Sumner, The Challenge of Facts and Other Essays*. New Haven: Yale University Press, 1914.
98. Kelso Louis O., and Patricia Hetter, *Democracy and Economic Power*, Ballinger Publishing Co., Harper Collins, 1986.
99. Kolko Gabriel, *The Triumph of Conservatism: A Reinterpretation of American History*, The Free Press, 1977.
100. Kolko Gabriel, *Wealth and Power in America—An Analysis of Social Class and Income Distribution*, Praeger Publishers Inc, 1962.
101. Kotz Nick, *Let Them Eat Promises—Politics of Hunger*, Prentice Hall, 1969.
102. Kozol Jonathan, *Savage Inequalities—Children in America's Schools*, Crown Publishers Inc., 1991.
103. Kurtzman Joel, *The Decline and Crash of the American Economy*, W.W. Norton & Co, 1988.
104. Kuttner Robert, *The Economic Illusion—False Choices between Prosperity and Social Justice*, Boston: Houghton Mifflin Co., 1984.

105. Kuttner Robert, *Revolt of the Haves—Tax Rebellions and Hard Times*, New York: Simon & Schuster, 1980.
106. Kuznets Simon, *Shares of Upper Income Groups in Income and Savings*, National Bureau of Economic Research, 1953.
107. Lampman Robert J., *Share of Top Wealth Holders in National Wealth*, Princeton University Press, 1962.
108. Lapham Lewis H., *Money and Class in America*, New York: Weidenfeld & Nicholson, 1988.
109. Lebergott Stanley, *Wealth and Want*, Princeton University Press, 1975.
110. Lenski Gerhard E., *Power and Privilege: A Theory of Social Stratification*, University of North Carolina Press, 1984.
111. Lerner Max, *America as a Civilization*, Simon & Schuster, 1957.
112. Levison Andrew, *The Full Employment Alternative*, Coward, McCann & Geoghegan, 1980
113. Locke John, *Treatise of Civil Government*, New York: Appleton-Century-Croft, 1937.
114. Lukacs George, *History and Class Consciousness*, Cambridge: MIT Press, 1971.
115. MacLeod Celeste, *Horatio Alger Farewell—The End of the American Dream*, New York: Sea View Books, 1980.
116. Mandel Ernest, *Europe Vs. America: Contradictions of Imperialism*, Monthly Review Press, 1970.
117. Mandel Ernest, *Marxist Economic Theory*, Monthly Review Press, 1968.
118. Matthews Donald R., *U.S. Senators and Their World*, The University of North Carolina Press, 1960.
119. McConnell Grant, *Private Power and American Democracy*, New York: Alfred A. Knopf, 1966.
120. McIntyre Robert S. and Tipps Dean C., *Inequality and Decline*, Center on Budget and Policy Priorities, 1983.
121. McKibben Bill, *The Age of Missing Information*, Random House, 1992.
122. McPherson James M., *Battle Cry of Freedom*, New York, Oxford University Press, 1988.
123. Meade J.E., *Efficiency, Equality and the Ownership of Property*, George Allen & Unwin Ltd., 1964.
124. Miller Herman P., *Rich Man Poor Man*, Thomas Cromwell Co., 1971.
125. Mills C. Wright, *Power Elite*, Oxford University Press, 1956.
126. Mills C. Wright, *Power Politics and People*, Oxford University Press, 1963.
127. Mintz Beth and Schwartz Michael, *The Power Structure of American Business*, The University of Chicago Press, 1985.

128. Moore David W., *The Super Pollsters—How they Measure and Manipulate Public Opinion in America*, New York: Four Walls Eight Windows, 1992.
129. Moskos Charles, *A Call to Civil Service*, New York: Free Press, 1988.
130. Moynihan Daniel Patrick, *On the Law of Nations*, Harvard University Press, 1990.
131. Murray Robert, *Red Scare*, New York: McGraw Hill, 1955.
132. National Advisory Commission on Selective Service, *In Pursuit of Equality: Who Serves When Not All Serve?*, Washington, D.C., Government Printing Office, 1967.
133. Nieburg H.L., *In the Name of Science*, Chicago: Quadrangle Books, 1964.
134. Okun Arthur M., *Equality and Efficiency*, The Brookings Institution, 1975.
135. Okun Arthur M., *The Political Economy of Prosperity*, The Brookings Institution, 1970.
136. Osberg Lars, *Economic Equality in the U.S.*, M.E. Sharpe Inc., 1984.
137. Parenti Michael, *Democracy of the Few*, New York: St. Martin's Press, 1988.
138. *Make Believe Media—The Politics of Entertainment*, St. Martin's Press, 1992.
139. Parenti Michael, *The Sword and the Dollar*, New York: St. Martin's Press, 1989.
140. Parish Peter J., *The American Civil War*, Holmes and Meier Publishers, 1975.
141. Parker Richard, *The Myth of the Middle Class*, New York: Liveright, 1972.
142. Parkin Frank, *Class Inequality and Political Order*, New York: Frederick A. Praeger, 1971.
143. Parry Robert, *Fooling America—How Washington Insiders Twist the Truth and Manufacture Conventional Wisdom*, New York: William Morrow & Co., 1992.
144. Pechman Joseph A., *Federal Tax Policy*, New York: W.W. Norton & Co., 1971.
145. Pechman Joseph A., *Who Paid the Taxes 1966–85*, Washington, D.C., Brookings Institution, 1985.
146. Pen Jan, *Income Distribution*, Allen Lane, The Penguin Press, 1971.
147. Perkins Dexter, *Charles Evans Hughes*, Boston: Little Brown, 1956
148. Perlo Victor, *Economics of Racism, USA*, International Publishers, 1974.
149. Perot Ross, *United We Stand—How We Can Take Back our Country*, New York: Hyperion, 1992.

150. Pessen Edward, *Riches Class and Power Before the Civil War*, D.C. Health & Co., 1973.
151. Petras James, *Critical Perspective on Imperialism and Social Class in the Third World*, New York : Monthly Review, 1978.
152. Pfeffer Leo, *This Honorable Court*, Hippocrene Books, 1978.
153. Phillips Kevin, *Politics of the Rich and Poor*, Random House, 1990.
154. Piven Frances Fox and Cloward Richard A., *Regulating the Poor: The Functions of Public Welfare*, New York: Pantheon Books, 1971.
155. Pole J.R., *The American Constitution For and Against*, 1987.
156. Preston William Jr., *Aliens and Dissenters*, Harvard University Press, 1989.
157. Projector Dorothy and Weiss Gertrude, *Survey of Financial Characteristics of Consumers*, Federal Reserve Board, 1966.
158. Rather Dan, *The Camera Never Blinks—Adventures of a TV Journalist*, New York: William Morrow & Co., 1977.
159. Reich Robert B., *The Next American Frontier*, Times Books,1983
160. Reissman Leonard, *Class in American Society*, Free Press, 1959.
161. Rose Stephen J., *The American Profile Poster*, Pantheon Books, 1986.
162. Roth Guenther and Wittich Claus, (editors), Max Weber, *Economy and Society*, University of California Press, 1979.
163. Rothman Robert A., *Inequality and Stratification in the United States*, Prentice Hall, 1978.
164. Sahota Gian Singh, "Theories of Personal Income Distribution a Survey," *Journal of Economic Literature*, March, 1978.
165. Salinger Pierre and Laurent Eric, *Secret Dossier: The Hidden Agenda Behind the Gulf War*, New York: Penguin, 1991.
166. Samuelson Paul, *Economics from the Heart*, Harcourt, Brace, Jovanvoich, 1983.
167. Schiller Bradley R., *The Economics of Poverty and Discrimination*, Prentice Hall, 1976.
168. Schlesinger Arthur M. Jr., *The Coming of the New Deal*, Boston: Houghton Mifflin, 1958.
169. Schlesinger Arthur M. Jr., *The Age of Jackson*, Little, 1988.
170. Schlesinger Arthur M. Jr., *The Disuniting of America*, Reflections on a Multicultural Society, W.W. Norton & Co., 1992.
171. Seeri William, *The Company and the Union*, New York: Vintage Books, 1974.
172. Seligman Edwin R.A., *The Economic Interpretation of History*, New York: Gordian Press, 1967.
173. Sennett Richard & Cobb Jonathan, *Hidden Injuries of Class*, Alfred A. Knopf Inc., 1972.

174. Shepherd William, *Market Power and Economic Welfare*, New York: Random House, 1970.
175. Smith Adam, *The Wealth of Nations*, Random House, 1993.
176. Smith J. Allen, *The Spirit of American Government*, New York: Macmillan, 1907
177. Smith James D. (editor), *The Personal Distribution of Income and Wealth*, Columbia Univ. Press, 1975.
178. Snow Edgar, *Journey to the Beginning*, New York: Random House, 1956.
179. Sorauf Frank, *Party Politics in America*, Boston: Little Brown, 1976.
180. Sowell Thomas, *Economics and Politics of Race*, William Morrow & Co., 1983.
181. Sowell Thomas, *Race and Economics*, New York: Longman Inc., 1975.
182. Spencer Herbert, *Social Statics*, New York: D. Appleton, 1878.
183. Sraffa Piero, (editor), *The Works and Correspondence of David Ricardo*, Cambridge University Press, 1981.
184. Sussman Barry, *What Americans Really Think*, New York: Pantheon, 1988.
185. Sweezy Paul and Magdoff H., *Deepening Crisis of U.S. Capitalism*, Monthly Review Press, 1981.
186. Taylor Jared, *Paved with Good Intentions: The Failure of Race Relations in Contemporary America*, Carroll & Graf, 1992.
187. Thurow Lester C., *Generating Inequality*, Basic Books, 1975.
188. Tocqueville Alexis de, *Democracy in America*, New York: Vintage, 1945.
189. Tolchin Susan and Martin, *Dismantling America: The Rush to Deregulate*, New York: Houghton Mifflin, 1983.
190. Tuckman Howard P., *The Economics of the Rich*, Random House, 1973.
191. Turner Jonathan H. and Starnes Charles E., *Inequality: Privilege and Poverty in America*, Goodyear Publishing Co., 1976.
192. U.S. Government, *Economic Report of the President*, U.S. Govt. Printing Office, 1991.
193. Valenti Jack, *A Very Human President*, W.W. Norton Inc., 1975.
194. Veblen Thorstein, *The Engineers and the Price System*, New York: Harcourt Brace and World, 1963.
195. Veblen Thorstein, *The Theory of the Leisure Class*, Boston: Houghton Mifflin Co., 1973.
196. Vexler Robert I (editor), *Dwight D. Eisenhower, 1890–1969*, Dobbs Ferry, New York: Oceana Publications, 1970.
197. Wedderburn Dorothy, editor, *Poverty, Inequality and Class Structure*, Cambridge University Press, 1974.

198. Weinstein James, *The Corporate Ideal in the Liberal State*, Boston, Beacon Press, 1968.
199. Williamson Jeffrey G. and Lidert Peter H., *American Inequality—A Macroeconomic History*, Academic Press Inc., 1980.
200. Zeitlin Maurice (editor), *American Society Inc.—Studies of the Social Structure and Political Economy of U.S.*, Rand McNally College Publishing Co., 1977.
201. Zinn Howard, *A Peoples History of the United States*, New York: Harper and Row, 1980.
202. Zweig Ferdynand, *The Worker in an Affluent Society*, London: Heinemann, 1961.

INDEX

ORDER FORM

**Telephone orders**: Call Toll Free: 1(800) 9-MIDDLE.
Have your Visa, MasterCard or AMEX card ready.

✆   **Fax orders:** (510) 687-6747

✉   **Postal Orders:** Antenna Publishing Co., P.O. Box 23826-101, Pleasant Hill, CA 94523-0826, USA.

❑   Please send _____ copies of *The American Class System.*

Company name: _____

Name: _____

Address: _____

City: _____ State: _____ Zip: _____

Sales tax:
Please add 8.25% for books shipped to California addresses

Shipping:
Book Rate: $2.00 for the first book and 75 cents for each additional book (Surface shipping may take three to four weeks)
Air Mail: $3.50 per book

Payment:
❑ Check
❑ Credit card: ❑ Visa, ❑ MasterCard, ❑ AMEX

Card number: _____

Name on card: _____ Exp. date: ___ / __

Call toll free **1-800-9-MIDDLE** and order now